Explore the

NELLES

CANARY ISLANDS

Author:
Bernd F. Gruschwitz

*An Up-to-date travel guide with 145 color photos
and 11 maps*

**First edition
1999**

Dear Reader: Being up-to-date is the main goal of the Nelles series. Our correspondents help keep us abreast of the latest developments in the travel scene, while our cartographers see to it that maps are also kept completely current. However, as the travel world is constantly changing, we cannot guarantee that all the information contained in our books is always valid. Should you come across a discrepancy, please contact us at: Nelles Verlag, Schleissheimer Str. 371 b, 80935 Munich, Germany, tel. (089) 3571940, fax. (089) 35719430, e-mail: Nelles.Verlag@t-online.de

Note: Distances and measurements, including temperatures, used in this guide are metric. For conversion information, please see the *Guidelines* section of this book.

LEGEND

★★ ★★	Main Attraction *(on map)* *(in text)*	Santa Cruz *(Town)* Iglesia *(Sight)*	Places Highlighted in Yellow Appear in Text		Expressway
★ ★	Worth Seeing *(on map)* *(in text*	◀ ◀	International/National Airport		Principal Highway
		🌳	Nature Reserve		Main Road
❽	Orientation Number in Text and on Map	Teide (3717)	Mountain (altitude in meters)		Provincial Road
■	Public or Significant Building	\ 13 /	Distance in Kilometers		Secondary Road
■	Hotel	☀	Beach		Pedestrian Zone
■	Shopping Center	∴	Ancient Site	⚓	Car Ferry
✝	Church	∩	Cave	⑤⑤⑤ ⑤⑤ ⑤	Luxury Hotel Category Moderate Hotel Category Budget Hotel Category *(for price information see "Accomodation" in Guidelines section)*
☀	View Point	ⓘ	Tourist Information		

CANARY ISLANDS
© Nelles Verlag GmbH, 80935 München
All rights reserved

First Edition 1999
ISBN 3-88618-087-5
Printed in Slovenia

Publisher:	Günter Nelles	**Translator:**	David Ingram
Managing Editor:	Berthold Schwarz	**Cartography:**	Nelles Verlag GmbH
Project Editor:	Bernd F. Gruschwitz	**Picture Editor:**	K. Bärmann-Thümmel
English Edition		**Lithos:**	Priegnitz, Munich
Editor:	Chase Stewart	**Printing:**	Gorenjski Tisk

TABLE OF CONTENTS

FEATURES

GUIDELINES

ISLAS

OCÉANO

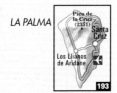

LA PALMA

TENERIFE

LA GOMERA

EL HIERRO

OCÉANO

ATLÁNTICO

CANARY ISLANDS

0   500 km

14°

CANARIAS

ATLÁNTICO

GRAN CANARIA

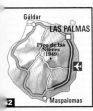

AFRICA

14°

28°—

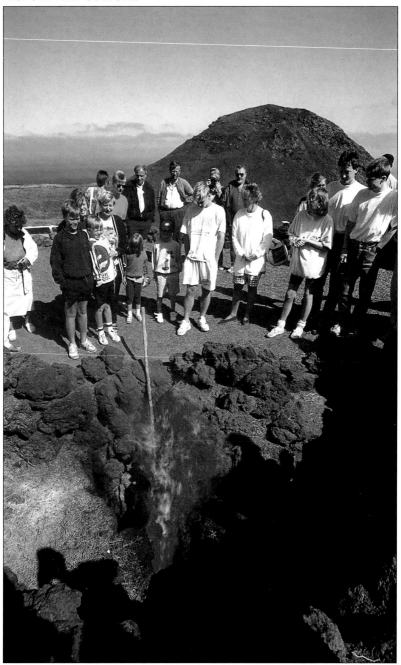

HISTORY
AND CULTURE

GEOGRAPHY

Spanish Islands off Africa

The Canary Islands lie in the tropics, north of the Tropic of Cancer, between the 13th and 19th degrees of longitude north and the 27th and 30th degrees of latitude west. Right beside them, on the continent of Africa to the east, stretches the largest of the world's deserts, the Sahara. Even though geographically the Canary Islands are a part of Africa, they have belonged politically to Spain ever since they were conquered in the 15th century. Located off the southwest coast of Morocco, they are cooled by the Canary Current, which passes the islands in a southwesterly direction. The shortest distance to Africa is roughly 100 kilometers (from the east coast of Fuerteventura to Cape Yuby), and the farthest around 520 kilometers (from the west coast of La Palma to Cape Yuby).

From east to west, the Canarian archipelago consists of seven main islands (*islas* in Spanish), these are: Lanzarote, Fuerteventura, Gran Canaria, Tenerife, La Gomera, La Palma and El Hierro. Four smaller islands (*islotes*), now declared national parks, are also included: Alegranza, Montaña Clara, Graciosa and Los Lobos. There are also numerous uninhabited rocky islets (*roques*), most of them quite close to the large islands, which are home either to vast flocks of birds or – like the Roques de Salmor off El Hierro – a final refuge for a species of giant lizard which very nearly died out a

Previous Pages: La Gería on Lanzarote – farming landscape as a work of art. Folklore in Pueblo Canario, Las Palmas, Gran Canaria. Left: The heat of the Earth sets brushwood aflame at Islote de Hilario, Lanzarote.

few decades ago but is now carefully protected.

Climate

The influence of the Canary Current and its accompanying trade winds ensures that the Canaries have a far more moderate climate than their proximity to the Sahara Desert would suggest. For most of the year – from spring to fall – there is a steady northeast trade wind (Spanish: *alisio*). It creates clouds on the windward sides (*barlovento*) of the mountainous islands at altitudes ranging between 500 and 1,500 meters; those clouds then remain there and cause fog, light rainfall and cooler temperatures high up in the mountains. On the leeward (*sotavento*) sides of the islands the clouds generally tend to break up, so that the sun shines there almost all the time.

In winter the islands are sometimes influenced by west wind drift. This makes the mild weather somewhat changeable. Most of the rain falls between the months of November and February, mainly on the windward side and usually only at higher elevations. Lanzarote and Fuerteventura, with their comparatively low terrain, are the driest islands.

On the island of Tenerife, which has the highest mountain in Spain – and indeed of any of the Atlantic islands – the Pico del Teide (3,717 meters), there is actually snow at elevations above 1,800 meters during the winter, as there also is on the Roque de los Muchachos (2,426 meters) on La Palma and the Pico de las Nieves (1,949 meters) in the center of Gran Canaria.

In the tourist areas near the coast, the weather is generally mild throughout the year. As a rule, the leeward sides of the islands are warmer and drier than the windward sides. The windward sides enjoy pleasant temperatures even in summer, because of the steady breeze. In high summer, however, if the hot wind from

13

the Sahara (*levante*) finds its way to the islands, even the locals complain about the high temperatures.

The water temperatures, on the other hand, are reasonably constant all year round at 20°C (plus or minus two degrees), so that the beaches are always in season; helping to explain the ever growing popularity of this island group as a tourist destination.

How the Archipelago was Formed

When you are on a volcanic island, you are very close to the origin of the universe as a whole. At locations where the earth broke open only recently and volcanoes spilled their lava, the traces of the process on the surface of the landscape can be read like a book of natural history. Whether it's black sandy beaches, multi-

Above: The trade wind clouds on the crater rim at the Caldera de Taburiente, La Palma. Right: Fascinating lava streams that solidified while flowing.

colored layers of lava at the roadside, fields strewn with pumice-stone, rocky walls of basalt resembling organ pipes, cones or craters, vulcanization is everywhere in evidence on this archipelago.

Ever since the (re-)discovery of the Canary Islands by Europeans at the beginning of the 14th century, only Lanzarote, Tenerife and La Palma have shown any volcanic activity. The two worst volcanic eruptions to have occurred on the islands in recent centuries destroyed parts of the wealthy trading city of Garachico on Tenerife in 1706, and buried 10 towns and one quarter of the entire land-mass on Lanzarote between the years 1730 and 1736. Volcanic activity has not diminished on these islands by any means either: the last major eruption took place on La Palma in 1971, and experts are assuming that more may follow.

Geologically speaking, the islands are still relatively young. It's assumed that our solar system – and therefore the planet earth as well, of course – is a little over four and a half billion years old.

"Only" two hundred million years ago the two continents of Africa and America started to drift apart, creating the Atlantic Ocean in the process. This development, caused by volcanism beneath the two edges of the plates which have long since been covered by oceans, is known to geologists as "sea floor spreading," and is still in progress.

Between 30 and 35 million years ago, the first volcanic vent began to form on the sea bed. How this volcanic development to the northwest of the African Plate first originated is uncertain. According to one theory, the mountain-building process of the Moroccan Atlas continued westwards and caused tears in the earth's crust, letting the magma burst through from the core. In the course of the process – which still hasn't finished – the first Canary Islands appeared out of the ocean around 20 million years ago. The oldest islands are the two eastern ones, Lanzarote and Fuerteventura, each between 16 and 20 million years old; the youngest are La Palma and El Hierro, both probably around three million years old, if not less. When they rose from the ocean, Fuerteventura, Gran Canaria, La Palma and La Gomera brought up sediment from 2,000 meters below the sea to the surface.

Several phases of volcanism are in evidence on the largest island in the archipelago, Tenerife. The mountains along its edges – the Teno in the west and the Anaga range in the east – consist of stone that is almost twice as ancient as that of the central Cumbre Dorsal. This was formed between two and three million years ago when a chain of volcanoes erupted at the center of the island. This development ended around five hundred million years ago when a massive volcano erupted, the crater of which, the Cañadas, is the largest in the Canary Islands. It owes its present form to the collapse of the magma chambers inside and to subsequent erosion. Mount Teide rose

up between two and three hundred million years ago from the crater floor of this original *caldera*.

The geographical term "caldera," applied to sunken craters, was first used by the geologist Christian Leopold von Buch, who came to the Canary Islands in 1815 to study volcanism. He took the word from the 1,800-meter-deep Caldera de Taburiente on La Palma, which today is suspected of not being a sunken crater at all.

The Canaries are largely cones of volcanic ejection, formed by eruptions that took place both during and after the Tertiary Period. The lavas on the islands consist mainly of basalts and trachytes. They are geologically related to Madeira, and also the Azores.

It was long thought that a land bridge had once existed between the coast of Africa and the two islands to the east, Lanzarote and Fuerteventura. The theory was supported by the discovery of six-million-year-old fossilized ostrich eggs on Lanzarote. Since ostriches cannot fly, this seemed to prove the theory – but closer examination revealed that the eggs had actually been laid by a species of long-extinct bird, which had a wingspan of six meters and flew very well.

According to another theory, which was popular during the Enlightenment and even later, the Canary Islands were all that remained of the legendary continent of Atlantis. It is true that Plato spoke of an island out beyond the "Pillars of Hercules" (i.e., the Straits of Gibraltar), that was supposed to have been destroyed in a terrible flood – but modern research has now proven that it cannot have been the Canary Islands.

HISTORY OF THE CANARIES

The Origins of Human Settlement on the Islands

Early human settlement of the Canary Islands long provided archeologists and historians with much conflicting evidence, and the mystery has not been solved even today. Ever since the relics of the aboriginal population – mostly discovered in caves – were subjected to radiocarbon dating, it has been assumed that the islands were first settled between the fifth and first centuries B.C. If, like German archeologist Heinrich Schliemann, you base your case on the classic tales of antiquity, this dating will be unsatisfactory, because various authors, including Homer (circa 800 B.C.), kept writing about the "happy islands" out in the mid-Atlantic.

In around 700 B.C., the Greek poet Hesiod took up the legend of the Hesperides, where golden apples were guarded by dragons at the end of the world. These golden apples are thought by some to have been the fruit of the

Right: The dragon tree – a member of the lily family – was worshiped as a sacred tree during the Guanche period.

Canarian strawberry tree or arbutus (*madroño*), and the reference to dragons could have meant the volcanoes – or indeed the famous dragon tree (*Dracaena Draco*), the colorless resin of which becomes dark red when exposed to the air, and which is therefore called dragon's blood.

The Phoenicians probably knew of the existence of the Canary Islands, because after they founded Cádiz in around 1100 B.C., they often made trips into the Atlantic. Two of their voyages of discovery along the west coast of Africa, in the sixth and fifth century B.C., have been proven, and it seems scarcely possible that they could have overlooked the Canaries.

The Phoenicians manufactured vast quantities of cloth, including very expensive purple cloth – and they could easily have used the dyer's lichen (*Roccella tinctoria*; in Spanish, *orchilla*), which grows in profusion on the islands, to dye their wares. According to a report by Pliny the Elder, King Juba II of Numidia and Mauretania, who was set up as king by the Romans, apparently explored the Canary Islands in 25 B.C. and set up purple dye centers on Lanzarote and Fuerteventura. In addition, Pliny mentions that the Mauretanian expedition found no people, but did discover traces of buildings that were ascribed to the Phoenicians.

Nevertheless, the geographer Ptolemy (circa 150 A.D.) knew enough about the location of the Canary Islands to draw the zero meridian through Hierro – the last known island at the "end of the world." The coordinate system in the sea and land maps of numerous European countries was based for many centuries on the "Ferro Meridian." It was only in 1911, after a lot of squabbling, that Greenwich in England was finally decided on as the new zero meridian.

From the Middle Ages until the rediscovery of the Canaries by European seafarers in the 14th century, the (rather

sparse) reports about them largely took the form of over-imaginative additions to ancient texts. A new legend appeared according to which the Irish saint Brendan (Spanish: San Borondón) went on a missionary expedition across the Atlantic some time around 400 A.D., and is supposed to have visited the Canarian archipelago.

A strange reflective phenomenon in the atmosphere above the sea which occurs every now and then, and makes it look as if an "eighth" Canary Island exists, is named after the saint: the "Isla de San Borondón." A number of expeditions were sent out in search of this island until as late as the 18th century, all of them unsuccessful of course.

It seems to be a very strange thing that hardly any reports about the islands came out of the Arab world. When the "Report of Edrisi," written in the year 1124, became known in the West, it mentioned several Arab adventurers setting sail from Lisbon and visiting various islands in the Atlantic Ocean, including an uninhabited

one with sheep, and also another island where they managed to communicate with the natives through an interpreter. The Arabs mention that the islanders had boats and knowledge of the sea, although later reports by Europeans disagree with this – with only one exception – saying that this was hardly likely.

The Origins of the Guanches

No one knows whether the Guanches were stranded on the Canaries after a shipwreck, or sent there as a punishment after incurring the displeasure of the Romans or the Carthaginians. Their origin has not been securely established either. It seems highly probable, however, that they came from North Africa – and anthropological similarities as well as linguistic evidence point to their having been members of a Berber tribe. Some researchers claim that they were a Stone Age people; others say they arrived on the islands with no knowledge of stone tools because they had already passed that

phase of evolution, and that since the islands contained only stone and no metal, they were forced to relearn how to use stone effectively. This is supposed to explain the small number of tools and weapons made of stone which were discovered on the islands.

The Guanches generally lived in caves or under rocky outcrops. Their most civilized product was clay vessels, which they created without the use of a potter's wheel. No one knows how advanced they were in agriculture, terracing and dry farming. Detailed knowledge of the Guanches comes from reports by mariners, priests and visitors, who often knew the various customs only by hearsay, so that legend and reality are rather hard to tell apart.

About Fuerteventura, for instance, we learn that it was divided up into two king-

Above: Private Guanche museum (El Pueblo Guanche) in Orotava, Tenerife. Right: Los Letreros (El Hierro) – just one of numerous, as yet undeciphered, Guanche inscriptions.

doms that were separated by a land wall between the Jandía Peninsula and the rest of the island (*Maxorata*). On Gran Canaria there were two rulers (*Guarnatemes*), one in Gáldar and the other in Telde. In order to defend themselves against the Spanish, they combined forces and took up arms together. On Tenerife, the nine royal descendants of the legendary "Mencey" Gran Tinerfe – who is said to have had complete control of the island – fell into fierce disagreement with each other. This led to the "peace-loving" Guanches in the south collaborating with the Spaniards, and helping to overthrow their enemy brothers in the north.

All the islanders believed in life after death. This is clear from the custom they had of mummifying the corpses of important members of their society and preserving them. Unlike the ancient Egyptians, however, the did not remove the brains from the bodies; nor did they bandage the corpses, wrapping them in goatskin instead.

If European reports are to be believed, women in Guanche society were highly respected. On some islands, men who looked at women too invitingly could be punished by death. Women were asked for their agreement to weddings just as much as men were. One partner only had to express a desire for separation and a marriage would be promptly dissolved. Jointly-owned property was inherited by the mother's line. Guanche women versed in herbal medicine were also respected as healers.

Rediscovery and Conquest of the Canary Islands

The conquest of the Canaries began with their rediscovery in 1312 by Lanzarote Malocello, a Genoese of Provençal descent. He spent two decades on the island that was named after him. After he returned, the first Canary Islands to appear on the Mallorcan map of the cartographer Dulcert (1339) were Lanzarote, Fuerteventura and the Isla de los Lobos, and were shown with the Genoese coat of arms. The "Manuscript of Boccaccio" (1341) makes first mention of the islands being plundered. The Genoese steersman Niccoloso da Recco mentions four Canarian slaves, goatskins, tallow, red earth and red dyewood as booty. In the following years the islands were sacked on numerous occasions by Genoese, Catalonian, Mallorcan and Basque mariners.

Pope Clement VI, who considered himself to be the ideal owner of all undiscovered countries, loaned the Canary Islands to Luís de la Cerda, a great-grandson of Alphonse X of Castile, in return for an annual payment of 400 guilders, and crowned him king of "Fortunia" in 1344.

The new king died, however, before ever setting his eyes on his "property." Eventually a nobleman named Roberto de Bracamonte was generously presented

with the still-independent Canary Islands by Henry III of Castile. Bracamonte handed them on to his Norman cousin, Jean de Béthencourt. From 1402 to 1406 the latter – together with Gadifer de la Salle – conquered Lanzarote, Fuerteventura, Hierro and probably Gomera too, in the name of Castile. Attempts to set foot on the other islands failed as a result of fierce and often ingenious resistance put up by the Guanches. Efforts by the rulers of Lanzarote – Diego de Herrera and Inés Peraza – to take possession of Tenerife in 1464 with a phony contract were foiled by the Guanches just as effectively as a later attempt by Herrera's son-in-law Diego de Silva to subjugate Gran Canaria.

In 1477, dissatisfied with the progress of the conquest of the islands, King Ferdinand of Aragon and Queen Isabella of Castile forced the unsuccessful Diego de Herrera and Inés Peraza to sell the Canary Islands to the Spanish crown.

Despite another attempt one year later to subjugate the islands, the Guanches

pelago's most important function in the years that followed: a center of trade between the continents of Europe, Africa and the Americas.

Alonso Fernández de Lugo began his conquest of La Palma in the same year America was discovered. Within just a few weeks, his 900-man army had subdued all the tribal princes there apart from one, Tanausu, who had holed up with his men inside the Caldera de Taburiente. Lugo's attempt to storm this natural fortress failed, so he resorted to a trick: he pretended he was ready to negotiate, and lured the last king of La Palma into an ambush. In May 1493, the island was conquered. Tanausu died on the ship that was taking him triumphantly back to the Spanish court, after going on hunger strike.

During the year that followed, De Lugo attacked the last independent bastion of Tenerife with an army of 1,200 men. The Mencey of Taoro, his main opponent, lured the soldiers into the region of the Acentejo, where he ambushed them and annihilated three quarters of the Spanish army. When De Lugo returned the following year, the Guanche king abandoned his guerilla tactics and bravely faced the Spaniards on the high plateau of La Laguna, to do open battle. Despite incurring heavy losses, the Guanches managed to withstand the Spanish onslaught – but unfortunately a fatal disease broke out among the Guanches, from which they never recovered. Further battles ensured that the last defenders of the island had subjugated themselves to De Lugo by the end of 1496.

were only finally subdued in 1483 by Pedro de Vera. One of de Vera's colleagues, Alonso Fernández de Lugo, was awarded the right by the Spanish crown to conquer the remaining, still-independent islands.

Portugal, which since the time of Henry the Navigator (1394-1460) had explored the coast of Africa and had also occupied Gomera briefly in 1420, now gave up its claim to the Canary Islands once and for all in the treaties of Alcaçovas (1479) and Toledo (1480).

In 1492, Columbus discovered a new continent which he believed to be India, and claimed it in the name of Spain. On this expedition – as on all the later ones – he stopped over in the Canary Islands to get his ships repaired and to stock up on provisions. This would become the archi-

The Canary Islands Under Spanish Rule

The victorious Spaniards and their men were promised rewards of land, water rights and administrative posts. All Guanches who had survived the battles were captured and sold into slavery. The

Above: Jean de Béthencourt, the Norman conqueror in the service of the Spanish Crown. Right: The first ever monoculture on Canarian soil – sugar cane (tile picture in Ingenio, Gran Canaria).

History and Culture

collaborators and vassals hurriedly forgot their origins in order to rise from being second-class citizens to inhabitants of equal standing with the Spanish; they had themselves baptized, married into Spanish families and changed their names. Within just a few decades, their entire culture, and their language, had been extinguished for ever, apart from a few museum relics.

The islands' new Spanish owners faced a threat, however, from the warring maritime nations of Holland, France and England. Spanish galleons full of gold and silver on their way back from America passed via the Canaries, attracting pirates and freebooters who had been given royal permission to attack them. The eastern islands suffered from attacks by Algerian corsairs; indeed, there were even several attempts to conquer them entirely. The last and most famous of them was Lord Nelson's attack on Santa Cruz de Tenerife in 1797; the engagement at which he lost his right arm and suffered the only defeat of his career.

Ever since the Enlightenment an increasing number of scholars traveled to the Canarian archipelago to study it. One such was the universal scholar Alexander von Humboldt, who arrived on Tenerife in 1799 with the botanist Aimé Bonpland and climbed Mount Teide; another was the natural scientist Vincent de Saint-Bory; the numerous others included the geologist Leopold von Buch, the natural scientist Philip Barker Webb, and the scientifically interested diplomat Sabin Berthelot. They all helped to increase knowledge of the islands.

As a result of this new scientific interest, the first university of the archipelago was founded in 1817 in La Laguna – and this remained the only one until the University of Las Palmas de Gran Canaria was built in 1989.

All the travel reports of those times make mention of the misery endured by the majority of the Canarian population. After long periods of drought, famine was common on the eastern islands. Madrid was a long way away, and little help was expected. For many Canarios, emigration to Latin America was the only solution – and things stayed that way right into the 1950s. Venezuela and Cuba were the most popular destinations; though many also made their ways to Argentina, the countries of Central America, and to the United States as well.

To make the islands more attractive, Isabella II declared the impoverished Canary Islands a free trade zone in 1852. In 1912, Island Councils (*Cabildos Insulares*) were set up. In 1927, competition for precedence between the two main islands led to the division of the Canary Islands into two separate provinces. Santa Cruz de Tenerife became the capital of the western province, and Las Palmas de Gran Canaria that of the eastern one.

It was only accidentally that the islands became a focus of national politics in 1936. General Francisco Franco, who had been exiled to Tenerife by the Republican government of Spain for lack of loyalty, announced the start of the putsch against the Republic over the radio from Tenerife while he was on his way to Gando Airport to join his rebel troops in the Spanish protectorate of Northern Morocco. His victory in the Spanish Civil War in 1939 heralded the establishment of a conservative, religiously-inclined military dictatorship which only came to an end with his death in 1975.

SOCIETY AND CULTURE
The Canary Islands in Democratic Spain

A new era began in Spain after Franco's death. In accordance with the dictator's wishes, the Bourbon Juan Carlos was made king. Two years after Franco's death, the country was given a

Right: Looking for a niche in the world market (banana packing in the region around San Andrés y Los Sauces, La Palma).

democratic constitution with the monarch at its head as representative of the state. In 1982, the Canary Islands were accorded the status of an autonomous region (*Comunidad Autónoma de Canarias*). When Spain entered the European Union in 1986, it negotiated a special status for the Canary Islands until 1996, which temporarily allowed them to remain a free trade zone.

Ever since that deadline passed, various suggestions have been made in Brussels as to how the Canaries can be sheltered from competition in the world market without turning them into a permanently subsidized territory. The Canarian government has suggested the formation of a special economic zone, called the ZEC (*Zona Especial Canaria*), which could turn the islands into a tax haven similar to the Bahamas.

Meanwhile the neighboring country of Morocco continues to lay claim to the Canary Islands, especially since Spain has continually refused to relinquish Ceuta and Melilla – its enclaves on Moroccan soil.

Administration and Politics

The autonomous region of the Canary Islands is divided into two administrative areas (*provincias*): the three eastern islands with Las Palmas de Gran Canaria; and the four western islands with Santa Cruz de Tenerife as their respective capitals. Both cities share the role of capital of the islands as a whole, and the government holds legislative elections every four years.

The parliament with its 60 members always meets in Santa Cruz de Tenerife. The main parties are the right-wing regional Canaries Coalition (CC), the conservative People's Party (PP), and the Social Democratic Workers Party (PSOE). The Canarian Separatists Party (FREPIC), whose graffiti can be admired all over the walls of the islands, has so far

failed to win a mandate in any of the elections. The *Comunidad Autónoma de Canarias* is represented in the Spanish Parliament with 14 out of a total of 350 seats, and in the Senate with 11 from a total of 255 seats.

The highest self-administrating body of each island is the Island Council (*Cabildo Insular*). The islands are divided up into municipalities (*Municipios*), each of which is led by a mayor (*Alcalde*) in his respective town hall (*Ayuntamiento*). There are 77 Municipios all together; Tenerife, the largest island, has 31, while Hierro, the smallest, has just two.

The Economy – Then and Now

For a long time the Canary Islands served as a stopover on the triangle of trade routes between Europe, Africa and the Americas. Sugar cane cultivation began shortly after the *Conquista* and continued until the mid-16th century; it was kept going on a smaller scale for rum pro-

duction until the mid-20th century. Wine cultivation reached its peak in the 16th century and dwindled after 1800; the vine pest phylloxera finished the industry off once and for all in the early 19th century. The islands' wine production only received new impetus after the tourism boom began, especially on Tenerife, where vineyards now take up 56 percent of cultivable land overall.

The production of red dye from the cochineal insect started a cochineal boom from 1830 to 1870. It also seemed to promise the poor a reasonable income, because the fig cactus – the host plant for the insects – even grew in the *malpaís* (badlands). Development of chemical dyes, however, put an end to the dream. Today there is only one small area of cultivation on Lanzarote, which produces cochineal extract for the cosmetic and food industry.

From 1850 on, cultivation of the dwarf banana assumed an important role. The plantations are still a striking feature of many valleys, but they seem to be powerless against competition from Central America. The decision by the European Union in 1993 to introduce a quota on bananas from Latin America gave the Canaries some respite, but those able to diversify since that time have done so: tomatoes, potatoes, cut flowers and exotic fruit are all selling well, too.

Since the 1960s, however, the magic word has been tourism. The service sector already accounts for 80 percent of GDP. Around nine million tourists come to the islands each year, and their numbers keep on increasing all the time. Tourism accounts for much of the 16 percent of GDP, half of which is used in the construction sector: despite the tourism boom, the unemployment rate in 1997 stoos at 20 percent, because the rest of the islands' industry hardly plays a role at all. Alongside the petrochemical industry, energy production, fish processing and cigar production, there are also several smaller chemical, beverage and foodstuff manufacturers.

The People

The Canarian archipelago, with its overall surface area of 7,447 square kilometers, has approximately 1.65 million inhabitants, including around 50,000 immigrants. Most of the inhabitants of the Canary Islands are descended from the Spanish conquerors and colonizers, and from hispanicized Guanches. From the very start members of other nations, especially merchant families and mariners, settled on the islands, as can be seen from names such as Salazar, Monteverde (Gruenenberg), O'Daly, Blanco (White), Wildpret and Schwartz. No one would ever question the "genuineness" of these families as Canarios; and yet there are still discussions about the long-term resi-

Right: Bicycle tourism – a new and popular aspect to the steadily booming tourist industry on the Canary Islands.

dents from Europe who come to spend their last years here, or who have built up an existence around tourism.

Mainland Spaniards (who are rudely termed *godos*) are often accused of taking away qualified jobs from Canarios. Minorities from Africa, the Middle East and India have now settled in the big cities on the large islands as well as in the tourist centers, and most are merchants and small traders.

The average population density of 465 people per square kilometer on Gran Canaria is not only the highest on the archipelago, but is also the highest anywhere in Europe. The lowest population densities are on Fuerteventura, with 26, and on Hierro, with 30 people per square kilometer.

The Roman Catholic Church was the official state church under Franco. Now that state and church have separated under the terms of the constitution, over 96 percent of the population still belong to the religion. Some high religious holidays, such as Easter Week (*Semana Santa*) and Corpus Christi, are staged with much tradition and pomp.

Culture

The Canary Islands impress visitors primarily for their scenic beauty, and for the relaxed and pleasantly withdrawn way of life of the local population. The cultural treasures of the Guanches are generally well displayed in the islands' museums. In the open countryside the caves where they lived and where they buried their dead, their granaries, their places of assembly (*tagoror*), cultic sites and petroglyphs can still be found, although often these remains are rather meager.

Many of the well-preserved town centers still date from the colonial era, with buildings formerly occupied by the colonial administration, the nobility and merchants. Details of traditional Canarian

architecture are often clearly influenced by Andalusian or Portuguese models; these include barred windows, carved wooden balconies and lofts, flowery inner courtyards and artistically rendered church ceilings. Pine heartwood has been used to create staircases, verandas and choir stalls.

The religious structures testify to popular taste, and the formerly very modest standard of living in the municipalities. Exceptions here are the churches in the capitals, especially the Cathedral of Las Palmas de Gran Canaria. In the village churches, baroque retables reach a peak of perfection. Many churches contain highly expressive statues of saints by Luján Pérez (1756-1815), universally regarded as the most important sculptor of the Canary Islands.

There are still a few Art Nouveau structures that survive from the early part of the 20th century, mostly in the large towns. The Lanzarote of César Manrique (1919-1992) is a chapter to itself, and is probably best summed up by the German term *Gesamtkunstwerk*, or "synthesis of the arts."

Twentieth-century Canarian art has more to offer than just this master, however – take the works of the highly versatile Gran Canarian artist Néstor de la Torre (1887-1938), for instance. Since quite a few creative artists have settled throughout the islands over recent years, lovers of modern art will find a great deal of fascinating material in the various galleries and studios.

In the realm of popular music – aside from the cultivation and preservation of traditional Canarian music – Latin American rhythms tend to predominate, mostly in the form of *salsa*. Classical music is celebrated in a festival at the beginning of each year, when world-famous conductors, singers and orchestras perform in both capitals. Indeed, the islands have a very full and active classical music life, in which the excellent Tenerife Symphony Orchestra and the Gran Canarian tenor Alfredo Kraus both play considerable roles.

25

LANZAROTE
Isle of Volcanoes

Lanzarote

Where Man and Nature Meet

All the Canary Islands are volcanic in origin, but each has its own distinctive character. For esthetes with a penchant for the slightly eccentric, Lanzarote is the island par excellence. Quite unlike any of the other Canary Islands, the buildings, towns, fields and landscape in general are all parts of one harmonious synthesis of the arts. The brilliant creations and stylistic influences of the Lanzarote architect and artist César Manrique (1919-1992) are everywhere in evidence. His works, together with the breathtaking volcanic landscape of Timanfaya, and the wine-growing region La Gería with its bizarre landscape, attract visitors here from all corners of the globe.

Lanzarote has a well-tended "stylish" look to it – with its elegant towns such as Haría, Teguise and Yaiza. César Manrique, that never-to-be-forgotten creator of his own homeland, set a standard that has influenced the entire island. Don't bother to look for any billboards on the country roads of this island – you won't find a single one. Houses out in the countryside are all whitewashed as a rule, with

Previous pages: The mountains of fire on Lanzarote – sulfurous, volcanic and eerie. Left: Dromedary rides through the landscape.

green or blue doorways and window frames. In the volcanic region they contrast sharply with the black, pink, purple, ochre and brown tones of the lava. With the exception of the church towers and the shell of the Gran Hotel Arrecife, no building on the island is taller than a Canary Island palm tree.

The tourist centers, located on the east coast where most of the beach fans and sun worshipers tend to congregate, jar slightly with the harmony everywhere else. The holiday village of Costa Teguise, partly designed by César Manrique, Puerto del Carmen, and the quieter Playa Blanca with the magnificent sandy beaches of El Papagayo are popular with package tourists. People traveling on their own without prior reservations can sometimes find it difficult to get accommodation there.

With its excellent climate, small amount of rural traffic and numerous flat regions, Lanzarote is very popular with sports cyclists. Professionals prepare for the forthcoming season during the winter months, and numerous amateurs follow their example. The rather "wilder" west of the island, with its sports center at La Santa, is a real paradise for international sports enthusiasts. Windsurfers are completely in their element in the areas around La Santa and La Caleta.

Arrival

Lanzarote can be reached by either plane or ship. A car ferry runs from Corralejo (Fuerteventura) to Playa Blanca in the south of Lanzarote (four times daily; around half an hour's journey), and another ferry connects Puerto del Rosario (Fuerteventura) with Arrecife on Lanzarote three times every week.

Most vacationers arrive at **Guasimeta** airport, known internationally as the **Aeropuerto de Arrecife**, located seven kilometers to the west of Arrecife. Car rental companies have offices in the arrivals hall, and taxis stand at the ready here. Buses run from the airport to Arrecife and Puerto del Carmen every half hour or hour. A metal wind mobile at the exit road to the airport makes it clear that you have just entered the artistic territory of César Manrique.

ARRECIFE – LANZAROTE'S CAPITAL

On the way into the capital, Arrecife, you'll pass through a small industrial area. A road branches off to the right to the **Playa Honda**. This peaceful little resort, with its sandy beach, promenade, and handful of bars and restaurants, is a favorite with the local population. The jets flying overhead can be somewhat disturbing, however.

Arrecife ❶ (pop. 35,000) is not all that remarkable a place, but is still worth visiting. Take the first exit road and head for the beach end of the town. In an urban wasteland along the western end of Arrecife you'll see the new building housing the island's council, **Cabildo Insular**. The best thing to do is park your car down at the municipal beach of **Playa del Reducto** and follow the coastal promenade. The beach, with its blue flag signifying that the waters here are safe to bathe in, is dominated by the burned-out ruin of the Gran Hotel Arrecife. No one is quite

to Roque del Oeste, La Alegranza
ISLA MONTAÑA CLARA
Punta Gorda
Montaña Bérmeja (157)
Playa Lambra
Playa de las Conchas
Pedro Barba
Parque Nacional de los Islotes del Norte
Las Agujas (266)
ISLA GRACIOSA
Montaña del Mojon (188)
Caleta del Sebo ❽
Playa La Punta
Salinas del Rio
Playa de la Canteria
Playa de la Cocina
Mirador del Rio ❾
Playa Francesa
Órzola ❼
Playa El Arco
MALPAIS DE LA CORONA
El Rio
Guináte ❿
Ye
Los Molinos
Monte Corona (609)
Cueva de los Verdes
Máguez ⓫
Haria
Los Jameos del Agua ❻
Playa de San Juan
Playa de Famara
Monte Corona
Punta Usaje
RISCO DE FAMARA
Los Picachos
Punta Guerra
Arrieta ❺
Punta Prieta
LA ISLETA
Playa de la Garita
La Santa ⓴
La Costa
La Caleta ⓰
Peñas del Cache (671)
VALLE DE TEMISA
Vista Graciosa
aya Teneza
Sóo ⓱
Ermita de las Nieves ⓭
Mala
El Cuchilo
Teneza (368)
Muñique
Los Valles ⓮
EL JABLE
Guatiza ❹
era ca (149)
Tinajo ⓳
Tiagua ⓲
Teguise ⓯
Los Cocoteros
La Vegueta
El Mojón
ico tido 17)
Mancha Blanca ㉑
Tao
Guanapay (425)
Playa de la Tia Vicenta
Mozaga ㉘
Tahiche
Punta de Tierra Negra
Masdache
San Bartolomé ㉙
Fundación César Manrique ❸
Montaña Blanca
Masdache ㉗
Las Salinas
Costa Teguise ❷
Playa de las Cucheras
LA GERIA
Tías
Güime
Castillo de San José
La Asomada
Aeropuerto de Arrecife
ARRECIFE ❶
Mácher
Playa Honda
Playa del Reducto
Puerto Calero
Puerto del Carmen ㉜
San Antonio
Playa de Guasimeta
Los Pocillos
Playa de los Pocillos
Playa de la Arena
Playa Blanca
Puerto del Rosario

LANZAROTE
0   2,5   5 km

sure what will happen to this blot on the landscape; its fate is still being discussed by local politicians. The **Parque Islas Canarias** across to the east isn't all that inviting-looking either: drug users and dealers meet up there, and a monument to mariners, ascribed to César Manrique, can be seen rusting away.

Next you'll see some well-frequented cafés, ice cream parlors and *tapa* bars; this is the place to take a seat beneath a shady tree and enjoy a good snack. If you turn off to the left towards the center of the town, you'll reach the trendy heart of Arrecife after crossing two or three intersections. The music pounds away after midnight on Saturdays in the **Bar Picasso**, in the **El Almacén** cultural center (both of them on Calle José Béthencourt), and in several other establishments nearby. In the Almacén during the daytime there are exhibitions by local artists, workshops, films and lectures. Back by the sea again you'll see the unpretentious and exclusive **Club Náutico**. Further along the coast, Avenida Generalísimo Franco is bordered by the **Parque Municipal**, with a kiosk housing the **Tourist Information Office**.

On the other side of the 16th-century drawbridge, the **Puente de las Bolas** ("Bridge of the Globes"), a footpath leads to the small island of **Islote de San Gabriel**, just off the coast, with its **Castillo de San Gabriel**. The mighty fort here was erected as a defense against pirate attacks and received its present appearance in 1588. Two cannons flank the entrance to the **Museo Arqueológico** housed here. The tiny museum inside the casemates has various funerary gifts, ceramics, idols and petroglyphs on display. The most important exhibit is a basalt monolith covered with undeciphered petroglyphs which was found in the Zonzomas excavation area near San Bartolomé. There's a great view of the sea and the town from the top floor of the fort.

The **Calle León y Castillo** – the main shopping street which has been partly pedestrianized – begins opposite the island, further into the town. Alongside boutiques and tourist shops here you'll find traditional stores full of household goods, textiles, books, tobacco, etc. Fairly near the beginning of this street, on the right-hand side, is the old building of the Cabildo Insular, a glass structure with a tower clock. At the end of the pedestrian precinct on the right is a square, with the seawater lagoon known as ***El Charco de San Ginés** beyond it. This highly attractive corner of the town bears the creative stamp of César Manrique. A newly laid out sea promenade with restored houses, small bridges, cafés and restaurants surrounds the Charco. Fishing boats bob about in shallow water, roller-bladers can be seen racing up and down, and in the evenings the young people of the town meet up at the enormous **Teatro Atlantido** cineplex. On Saturday mornings a colorful market is held on the promenade here.

Narrow streets lead to the peaceful square in front of the church. The tower of the 18th-century **Parroquia San Ginés** parish church dominates the roofs of the Old Town. Highlights inside the church include two late Baroque statues from Cuba, and a ceiling in the *mudéjar* style. From August 25 a fiesta is held in honor of San Ginés, the town's patron saint. In the simple **Market Hall** (Calle Libre, beside the church), fruit, vegetables and spices are on sale (Monday-Saturday, 7 a.m. to noon), and opposite is the hall containing the **Fish Market**.

In the northeastern part of the town, go past the harbor of **Puerto de Naos** and you'll arrive at the **Castillo de San José**, commissioned by the Spanish king Carlos III in 1779. Today it houses the **Museo Internacional de Arte Contemporáneo**, which came into being un-

Right: The Puente de las Bolas in Arrecife connects fort and city.

der the auspices of César Manrique. The painters and sculptors represented here, most of them from Spain and the Canary Islands, were active between the 1950s and 1970s, and include Manrique, Millares, Miró and Mompó. A meal in the stylish restaurant in the castle, with its view of the **Puerto de los Marmoles**, is a good way to round off this excursion.

COSTA TEGUISE AND THE EAST

The road leads northeastwards past typical harbor scenery with a refinery, seawater desalination plant and warehouses to the five-kilometer-distant holiday resort of **Costa Teguise ②**, built under the sponsorship of César Manrique. Originally, the master wanted the place to be an impressive example of how attractive tourism can be. He created the parks and patios of the luxury hotel **Meliá Salinas**, and also the "fishing village" of **Pueblo Marinero**, a holiday resort in the Canary style, and both are impressive examples of the early phase of his work.

The plan to make the entire coastal landscape artistically pleasing and ecologically sound simultaneously was thwarted in the 1980s by the construction firm's decision to change their concept. From that time onwards, plots of land along the coast were built up for the sake of profit, and real estate further inland was used in different ways. This was when the **Ocean Park** amusement center with its many waterslides, the golf course and the Beatriz luxury hotel were built. Costa Teguise has still not been alienated entirely from its original concept however, and is still a good place for a quiet and relaxing vacation.

Surfing and diving centers are available for sports enthusiasts. The largest of the five white sandy beaches here is the centrally-located **Playa de las Cucheras** with its two windsurfing centers. Even if you don't feel like spending a fortune on hotel accommodations here, you can still pay a visit to one of the hotel lobbies, with their plants and fountains, for a cup of coffee or a cocktail.

Pass Ocean Park and the golf course now, and head inland in the direction of Tahiche. In the southern suburb of **Taro de Tahiche**, at an intersection with Manrique wind chimes, the road branches off in the direction of the ****Fundación César Manrique ❸**. For lovers of modern art, architects, and fans of stylish living, a visit here is a must. With this house, located in the middle of a lava field inside five subterranean volcanic bubbles, César Manrique succeeded in showing the whole world how to convert an inhospitable envirnoment into a luxury residence with unmistakable character. The rooms above ground are in the conventional style of the island, but the lava becomes an increasingly noticeable feature of the decor. Modern art from the César Manrique collection is on display in the Fundación, and there is a cafeteria as well as a souvenir shop.

Above: Subterranean living à la César Manrique. Right: Manrique's wind chimes near Arrieta.

Below ground, the outer and inner rooms merge with each other. In one room, for instance, a palm tree grows straight through the roof and into the open. This residence, with its elegant integration of the natural world, was considered so sensational that the artist very soon had no peace and quiet at all here. Reporters spread the word about the eccentric artist's magnificent residence, and from then on the whole world wanted to come and inspect it for themselves. In 1987, Manrique moved to a renovated country house in Haría, and included the architectural jewel of Taro in his foundation. In 1992, the artist died in a traffic accident just 50 meters away from his masterpiece. The site of the tragedy is adorned with fresh flowers daily.

In **Tahiche**, where several houses are built in the Manrique style, take the right fork northeastwards in the direction of Arrieta, and you'll arrive in the town of **Guatiza ❹**, surrounded by fields of cacti. This is one of the last cochineal insect farms on the Canary Islands. The scarlet natural dye extracted from the bodily fluids of the cochineal insect is still used in the production of cosmetics, foodstuffs and textiles. The insects are placed on fig cacti, which thrive here in the shade of small semicircular walls. Since the trade in this dyestuff is now in decline, grape vines can also be seen within the walls.

At the end of Guatiza is César Manrique's last landscape work, the **Jardín de Cactus**. Inside a former quarry for volcanic earth he created an arena-shaped, terraced cactus garden with 16,000 plants from 1,400 species. Between the succulents are large lava sculptures, many of them phallic. Wrought iron gates, door handles and even lavatory doors bear the stamp of Manrique here. The whole area – including the cafeteria and the souvenir shop – is dominated by a renovated *gofio* mill, which affords a fine view of the surrounding land as far as **Mala**.

LOS JAMEOS DEL AGUA AND THE NORTH

North of Mala the road starts getting closer to the sea again. On the section leading into **Arrieta** ❺ a bright red wind chime by Manrique can be seen glinting in the sun. The light sand beach of **Playa de la Garita**, on the southern edge of the town, is very popular with young locals. The most striking building on the side of Arrieta facing the sea is the **Musco de África**, built in 1920 and also referred to as the "Blue House." With its bright colors and high narrow windows, it contrasts sharply with the homogeneous architecture elsewhere on the island. A small African collection has been housed here since 1995, but renovation work started in 1998, and the future of the museum is now rather uncertain. There are some good seafood restaurants in the fishing village of Arrieta.

In the middle of the rough volcanic landscape of Lanzarote, César Manrique

left his stamp on a system of lava caves which have now become the island's tourist attraction *par excellence*. If you continue northeastwards from Arrieta, the main attraction can be seen on the right-hand side of the road in the direction of the sea: **★★Los Jameos del Agua** ❻, considered by many to be the "Eighth Wonder of the World" (in the words of actress Rita Hayworth).

Visitors walk down into a cave (*jameo*) which has been transformed into an open-air bar; one story further down is a broad cave tunnel with a seawater pool glistening inside it. The pool is connected to the sea by a series of fine rivulets, so that the tides can also be experienced here. Throwing coins into the pool is forbidden because the blind albino crabs living inside it die on exposure to corroded metal. At the end of the tunnel is another bar-restaurant, and a picture-postcard swimming pool complete with palm trees.

Spectacular performances of music and ballet are held inside a subterranean auditorium seating around 500 visitors,

and there is also an audiovisual show about Lanzarote by the Canary Islands artist Ildefonso Aguilar. The neighboring section, called **Casa de los Volcanes**, provides a good introduction to the mysteries of vulcanism.

The ***Cueva de los Verdes**, off to the west, is full of weird music and is impressively illuminated. Like Los Jameos del Agua, it belongs to a cave system that begins on the 609-meter-high volcano of **Monte Corona** and ends seven kilometers later, around 50 meters beneath the sea. The subterranean tube alone has a length of 1.5 kilometers.

The guided tour leads one kilometer into the labyrinth of caves and then back again. At the halfway point is an auditorium that is only used for concerts once or twice a year – rather a shame, because the porous stone down here provides brilliant acoustics.

Above: Fresh fish daily in Arrieta. Right: Amazingly remote – Isla Graciosa. In the foreground, the disused Salinas del Río salterns.

On the way along the coast to Órzola and the northernmost point of the island you'll travel through the **Malpaís de la Corona**, bordered to the west by the 609-meter-high Monte Corona. On the coast the dark basalt contrasts sharply with the light sand in the small bays here, and the sparkling greenish-blue of the sea. This is an ideal place for families with children to go bathing. There are several parking spaces beside the bays, too.

Although the fishing village of **Órzola** ❼ has adjusted to tourism and there are several restaurants catering to visitors, the pace of life here is still very slow and relaxed. Even the ferry traffic across to the island of Graciosa hardly disturbs anyone. This is just the place to sit back and enjoy the sunset over a delicious seafood dinner.

If you feel like combining appreciation of César Manrique's architecture (described on the previous pages) with a bicycle tour, it's best to allow a whole day for it. The relatively flat route goes via Arrecife, Tahiche, Guatiza, Arrieta,

Jameos del Agua, Cueva de los Verdes and then along the coast bordering Malpaís de la Corona until Órzola.

Isla Graciosa

The **Isla Graciosa** – which can be reached by ferry from Órzola in around 40 minutes – forms part of the **Parque Nacional de los Islotes del Norte** nature reserve. The "gracious island" is actually an even sleepier continuation of Órzola. There are no surfaced roads, only sandy tracks – but the island still has motor traffic. Any of the 50 or so inhabitants with enough money invest in four-wheel-drive jeeps, and jeep safaris are also offered here – much to the dismay of environmentalists.

If you don't feel like plodding your way through the wasteland here, you can hire a mountain bike at the harbor. The main town of **Caleta del Sebo ❽** actually has a tiny infrastructure consisting of boarding houses, restaurants and a bar. Why do people come here? The lonely

beaches, perhaps – or the chance to rediscover an extremely slow pace of life. The ferries bring visitors here two or three times a day, and hikers enjoy the 90-minute walk to the finest beach on the island, the 500-meter-long **Playa de las Conchas**, located beyond the sand dunes in the northwest (be careful when swimming: the surf here can be extremely dangerous!). A safer place to swim is the fine **Playa de la Cocina** in the south, or the **Playa Francesca**. Don't forget to bring along sun protection!

From Mirador del Río to Los Valles

Most vacationers here also come to enjoy the magnificent bird's-eye view of the island from the steep northern coast of **El Risco**. In 1973, César Manrique built the restaurant **★Mirador del Río ❾** into the rocks of the cliff, and visitors have come to this very impressive location 497 meters above the sea ever since. Through a picture window you can see the wind-swept salterns down in the **Salinas del**

Río, and beyond the Isla Graciosa the uninhabited and protected islands of Montaña Clara, Roque del Oeste and La Alegranza; the tiny island out on its own towards the east is the Roqua del Este.

If you feel the admission fee to the Mirador is too high, you can get a reasonably good view by going a few hundred meters farther up the road to the village of Haría. There are places to park across to the left. A second observation point is located a little farther on along this walled road, and can be reached on foot. A steep path leads down from it to the lonely beach of **La Punta** and to the salterns. You might also see hang-gliders around here; they take off from the panoramic road at the top.

Farther south there's a turnoff to the right in the direction of **Guinate ⑩**, with its British-run **Parque Tropical Guinate**. The gardens and ponds here are

Above: The Mirador del Río – an amazing view. Right: Los Valles – esthetic agricultural landscape.

magnificent, and the aviaries and compounds here contain around 1,300 species of exotic birds, as well as numerous small apes. Trained cockatoos and parrots show off their talents in the celebrated shows in the tropical park. At the end of the road there's a good view from the **Mirador del Guinate**.

Back on the main road, head down into the valley in the direction of **Máguez** and **Haría**. Both of these villages are centers of art and handicraft; **Máguez ⑪**, for instance, is home to the painter Carlos Parra, whose small studio shows how his talents developed over the years. Paintings by several other artists provide a good insight into the post-Manrique art scene.

★Haría ⑫ is located in a high valley amidst a fine forest of Canary palms, now rather exaggeratedly referred to by the tourist industry as the "Valley of Ten Thousand Palms."

Alberto Vázquez Figueroa, a novelist from Tenerife, referred to Haría in his Lanzarote novel *Oceano* as "certainly the

finest village on the island, if not the finest in the world." This is where César Manrique finally retired to, and he was buried in the cemetery here in 1992. He managed to have a ruined church rebuilt in the original traditional style in Máguez, but the church here in Haría that replaced the earlier one, which was destroyed in a storm, is rather unattractive. Incidentally, anyone interested in miniatures should definitely visit the **Museo Internacional de Miniaturas**: it contains the smallest Bible in the world, as well as a picture of a soccer game painted on a grain of rice.

If you leave Haría in a southerly direction, you'll get several fine views of its palm-filled valley, the last of which is from the **Mirador de Haría** (where there is also a restaurant), where the **Valle de Temisa** begins, with its partly cultivated and partly abandoned terraces.

On the road towards Los Valles it is worth taking a detour westwards to the snow-white chapel of **Ermita de las Nieves ⓭**. Located 643 meters above the sea, it provides a fantastic view of the Riscos de Famara cliffs, the plain of El Jable to the southwest, and also of the **Peñas del Chache** which, at 671 meters, is the island's highest mountain. On the left-hand side of the road just before you reach the village of Los Valles, you'll see the largest wind energy station on Lanzarote, the **Parque Eólico de Lanzarote**, where 48 windmills generate five megawatts of energy every hour for the local electricity company UNELCO. The site is closed to public access.

The valley of **Los Valles ⓮** is a beautiful combination of earth-colored natural surfaces and cultivated fields containing lapilli (pumice stone; Spanish: *picón*). The view can best be enjoyed from the edge of the **Guanapay** crater (425 meters) which borders the valley to the southwest and is crowned by the **Castillo de Santa Barbara**. The foundations of this twin-towered castle probably date from the 14th century. Two extensions were made in the 16th century, including one in 1596 by an Italian master builder,

recorded for posterity by Leonardo Torriani, the great chronicler of Canary Islands' history. Inside the castle, the **Museo del Emigrante Canario** documents the emigration of many of the islanders to Latin America. Models of the ships that took them there, photographs and letters all tell the story of that harsh time, when the inhabitants were forced to choose between famine at home or an uncertain fate overseas. A path leads up along the edge of the crater, where you can enjoy a good view of Teguise, the island's former capital.

★Teguise and La Caleta

Teguise **⑮**, founded in 1418 as *Villa Real* ("Royal City"), is one of the oldest towns on the island. Lanzarote's capital until 1852, it is referred to even today by many islanders as *La Villa*. Much of its

Above: Teguise, the capital until 1852, has attractive narrow streets and a colorful Sunday market.

original substance has survived: idyllic narrow streets, traditional houses with carved doorways and wooden balconies, impressive churches and large townhouses can all be admired in this relaxing town with its numerous crafts shops.

At the center of the town is the **Plaza de la Constitución** (also known as Plaza San Miguel), with its large parish church, the **Iglesia de Nuestra Señora de Guadalupe**. The large, reddish-brown bell tower is very striking with its balcony and its octagonal white dome. Damaged on several occasions by pirates who set fire to the town and the church, the church was also seriously damaged by fire in the early 20th century due to a verger's negligence, and had to be rebuilt yet again. The street called **Callejon de la Sangre** ("Blood Alley") just beyond the church is named after the bloodbath that took place here during a raid by Algerian pirates in the year 1586.

Opposite the church is one of the finest and also one of the largest townhouses on Lanzarote, the **Palacio de Spinola**, built in the 18th century and purchased from the Genoese merchant Spinola in 1895. The building, which Manrique helped to restore, contains a **museum** documenting Canarian interior design through the centuries, plus several works of modern art. The President of the Canary Islands resides here when visiting Lanzarote.

On the south side of the plaza, the renovated 17th-century tithe building known as **La Cilla** is a reminder of Lanzarote's feudal history. This was where the tithes from the island's impoverished farmers arrived for the Bishop of Gran Canaria. Instead of the usual tithe the church levied one thirtieth of the harvest – a painful amount, especially since droughts frequently ruined the crops. Today the building is occupied by a branch of the omnipresent bank Caja Canarias.

At the end of the 15th century all of the Canary Islands were subject to Spanish rule. During the 16th century, missionaries from the Franciscan Order built the **Convento de San Francisco** on the southern edge of Teguise. Today's main building, with its baroque ornamentation and attractive wooden portal, had to be rebuilt after a Moorish pirate raid took place in 1618. A museum is being set up inside the convent of the Dominicans (**Convento de Santo Domingo**) to the southwest of the town, which dates from 1726. The extension work has been delayed since 1988, when around a hundred partly mummified human skeletons were discovered on the site. Sunday mornings there's a popular market held in the central square, and the whole place comes alive. In fact, it's hard to move with all the booths that get set up. Visitors are entertained with local music and dancing in a big tent behind the church; snacks are on sale, and you can buy everything you'd normally expect from a flea market – and more besides. The whole place suddenly closes down again at around 2 p.m.

The small traditional stringed instruments known as *timples* are manufac-

tured here in Teguise, and some workshops can be visited – such as the one belonging to Antonio Lemes Hernández at Calle Flores 8. A *timple* can cost anything from about 80 dollars on up.

Teguise is an ideal starting point for a bicycle tour of the coast, through the sandy desert of El Jable and further southwestwards, then up and down a lot of hills via Mancha Blanca and along the Montañas de Fuego (see page 42). There's also a rewarding tour northwards from Teguise with rather steeper hills, which goes via Haría to the Mirador del Río and then downhill as far as Órzola.

A good place to wind down near here is at the beach of the pretty little fishing village of **La Caleta** ⑯ on the coast north of Teguise. Approach the sea across the sand-strewn plain of **El Jable**, and on your right you'll see a collection of neat bungalows known as Famara. The long white and sandy **Playa de Famara** extends from the foot of the steep **Riscos de Famara** cliffs as far as La Caleta, where the remains of a wrecked ship can still be seen above the surface of the water offshore. If you swim here, mind the often powerful currents. La Caleta has only one surfaced road – all the rest are dusty tracks – but there are several good restaurants despite the incredibly remote location. The Casa García on the square in the center is popular with surfers and artists, while more conservative visitors tend to dine in the Casa Ramón.

Teguise is an ideal starting point for a bicycle tour northwards along the coast, through the sandy plain of El Jable and then up and down several mountains and valleys via Mancha Blanca and along to Yaiza. There's a good tour for the very fit from Teguise northwards, via Haría, the Mirador del Río and then down to Órzola.

THE WEST

The road leads from La Caleta along the northern edge of the Jabla plain and past **Sóo** ⑰, which is reminiscent of a desert village with its white houses. Watermelons, vegetables and pumpkins are grown in the sandy soil here. Since Sóo is very windy the houses here had no windows formerly to keep the sand of El Jable outside – instead, the windows were painted on! Modern windows have now ensured that sand stays out.

Further south, beyond the village of Muñique, lies **Tiagua** ⑱. On the left a restored windmill marks a lovingly renovated open-air museum called the **★Museo Agrícola El Patio**, the best of its type on the island. Everyday rural life in the four seasons is displayed in the grounds of the 200-year-old manor house, and the collection documents everything from cheese making to salt production. Wine from the estate can be tasted in the bodega, while a dromedary provides more than enough distraction for the kids.

The village of **Tinajo** ⑲ to the west is famed for its wrestlers, who take part in the local version of the sport, the *lucha canaria*. This is a form of wrestling in which two teams of 12 members compete against each other with just one man from each team wrestling at any one time. If a wrestler remains undefeated, he can take on several more opponents in a row. Each encounter consists of a maximum of three rounds, and the winner is the one who fells his opponent twice within the designated circle, receiving a point for his team. Felling here means forcing him to touch the ground with any part of his body other than his feet.

The imposing wrestling arena is on the main road to Mancha Blanca, and the highlight of the village is its award-winning square, almost submerged in a sea of flowers. The **Paroquia San Roque** parish church has a sundial on its roof, and inside are a statue of Christ by Luján

Right: El Jable – areas of blown sand in the semi-arid west of Lanzarote.

Pérez, a *Madonna* by his pupil Fernando Estevez, and a fine *mudéjar*-style ceiling.

On the coast beyond a lagoon is the **La Santa** ⑳ sports center, providing accommodation and training facilities for 64 Olympic sports – which got it into the *Guinness Book of Records*. No sport hotel anywhere in the world has such a huge infrastructure for whatever sport you care to choose, whether you're a professional or an amateur. The guest list reads like a "Who's Who" of international top sportsmen. In winter the European sporting elite come here to train, and there's even an Olympic pool and a light athletics stadium. The island beside it, **La Isleta**, is connected to the coast by bridges and is popular with joggers. The windy coastline with its high waves here is also very popular with surfers.

If you keep heading west from Tinagua, you'll pass the **Ermita de los Dolores**, containing the black Madonna statue known as *Nuestra Señora de los Volcanes*, on the outskirts of **Mancha Blanca** ㉑. The statue is believed to have protected the village from lava during the last severe volcanic eruption here in 1824. A good way of preparing for the volcanic side of the island is to take a jeep tour and a stroll through the rough *malpais* to the west of Mancha Blanca. A trail crosses the dark, inhospitable landscape, passing the volcanic cone of Teneza (368 meters) and leading down to the steep coast and wild sea further on. The former fishing village of **Playa Teneza** contains numerous empty houses, and only livens up in the summertime. A footpath takes you further along the coast in a south-westerly direction.

★★Parque Nacional de Timanfaya

The true highlight of the Lanzarotean landscape is, without a doubt, the **Parque Nacional de Timanfaya** ㉒, a massive, multicolored and grandiose volcanic plain covering more than 50 square kilo-

meters, containing the **Montañas de Fuego**. To the south of Mancha Blanca, the modern **Centro de Visitantes** informs visitors about the national park. Noticeboards, computer programs and audiovisual presentations provide an introduction to the "mountains of fire."

The road leading into the park is barred by a gate where an entrance fee has to be paid. At the other end of a two-kilometer-long paved road visitors then arrive at an observation hill called the Islote de Hilario, with its El Diablo Restaurant, which is the starting point for the 45 minute bus trip through the park. Various presentations provide a foretaste of the volcanic landscape to come.

Historical sources tell of several dramatic eruptions in this region between 1730 and 1736. On September 1, 1730, the fertile plains and white villages were destroyed by a mighty natural catastrophe. Over 30 volcanoes spewed out fire and smoke, and enormous masses of lava buried entire villages beneath them. Fortunately, the local population was able to escape in time. A quarter of the entire island was transformed into a lava landscape. The earth is still bubbling away quietly under the land today; there's a strong smell of sulfur in the air at several locations, and the temperature below ground very quickly reaches between 100 and 400°C. You can see proof of this for yourself: up at the **Islote de Hilario**, parking attendants stick brushwood into holes in the ground, and it catches fire brightly just a few moments later. The contents of a bucket of water poured down a hole in the ground cause a mighty geyser of steam to hiss high into the sky shortly afterwards.

The **El Diablo Restaurant**, designed by César Manrique, utilizes the heat from underground to cook its meat and seafood over a large grill. The cooks don't mind visitors examining their source of free energy, but don't bend over the deep hole beneath the barbecue section – the air that comes up is unbelievably hot.

This building is just one more example of how Manrique mixed the esthetic with

the practical so successfully. It's very pleasant to sit inside the round restaurant and observe the delighted crowds of tourists through the glass as they stand around the holes in the ground waiting for the next sheet of flame or tower of steam.

The fire mountains of Lanzarote are a protected area. The breathtaking 14-kilometer-long round trip along the ***Ruta de los Volcanes** delights passengers, amazing them whenever the bus drives above the steep drops through the lunar-like, multicolored landscapes. The bus stops for people to take photos, and there are audio commentaries in English, German and Spanish. Two guided hikes across the region are even more exciting – which explains why they're always booked out immediately. If you feel lucky, contact the visitor center in Mancha Blanca, ideally just after you arrive on the island.

Above: Delicious food cooked over hellish heat (El Diablo Restaurant). Right: Seawater lagoon green with algae near El Golfo.

On the way southwards in the direction of Yaiza you'll pass the dromedary station of **Echadero de los Camellos**. A half-hour-long trip on camelback leads through the outer regions of the national park, and the highlight here is more the unusual means of transportation than the view. Tucked away near Echadero is the small **Museo de Rocas** geological museum, with its fascinating documentation of the local rock formations.

*Yaiza – Idyll in Green and White

After such close contact with the molten contents of the earth's core, the idyllic little green and white village of **Yaiza** ㉓ comes as quite a contrast. It was voted the most beautiful village in Spain on two occasions, and its houses are clustered around a tree-filled square beside the church of **Nuestra Señora de los Remedios** (18th-century), which contains a fine wooden ceiling. At the western end of the square, a farmhouse with a large patio houses the **Benito Pérez**

Armas Cultural Center, in memory of the local writer and politician (1871-1937). The best food to be had around here is at the La Era Restaurant, set up inside two former farmhouses by César Manrique and Luis Ibañez Magalef, which serves Canary Islands specialties. The rooms are traditionally decorated, and there's a bodega for wine tasting. The **Galeria Yaiza**, run by German artist Veno and his wife, is located on the road towards the west, in the direction of Playa Blanca. It shows works by him and several other painters, sculptors, photographers, etc. The new and elegant **Hotel Rural Finca de las Salinas**, inside an 18th-century country house, is decorated in the Andalusian style.

*El Golfo and Los Hervideros

To the west of Yaiza a country road leads away to the coast and *El Golfo ㉔. Set against the magnificent backdrop of a reddish-black semi-crater, here is the greenish seawater lagoon of **Lago Verde** (the green comes from the algae), separated from the sea by a black sand beach. It can be reached from the village along a path which provides a good view of it from a rocky ridge above. The contrast of colors is highly unusual and not easily forgotten. The quiet little village of El Golfo is a popular destination for tourists and locals who enjoy good seafood.

Along the road leading south from here, the mixture of lava and seawater has produced a bizarre and fascinating stretch of coastline. In the small bays the sea often seems to be boiling. Near the two caves of **Los Hervideros** there are parking lots and footpaths. To the south, the sea-salt center of **Salinas de Janubio**, laid out like a chessboard, dates from times when freshly-caught fish was salted to preserve it. Ever since modern freezing methods were introduced these salterns have been increasingly neglected. They have been kept as a tourist attraction, and also to preserve the local ecology. The long black volcanic sandy beach of **Playa de Janubio** extends along the coast here

– and if you want to enjoy the finest view of the Salinas de Janubio, go to the observation point south of **Las Hoyas** at sunset, when they glow an intense red color.

The Balcon de Femés and the Wine Region of ★★La Gería

A well-paved road leads off to the right near Las Breñas, and 450 meters higher up to the village of **Femés** ㉕, located on the slopes beneath the 608-meter-high **Atalaya de Femés**. Anyone arriving at the southwestern tip of the island in a four-wheel-drive vehicle can travel up to Femes along a broad dirt track. At the quiet little village square stands the white **Ermita de San Marcial de Rubicón** church (1733). It contains an interesting collection of model ships. The plaza is also known as the **Balcón de Femés**, with its commanding view of the broad plain of **El Rubicón** down below. In clear

Above: Siesta in Uga. Right: Weird geometry in the vineyards of La Gería.

weather you can see the silhouette of Fuerteventura on the horizon, with the dunes of Corralejo. A flight of steps leads from the little church to the cemetery higher up, and there's also a hiking route to the summit of Atalaya.

Femes lies at the end of a fertile valley, with the massif of **Los Ajaches** at its southeastern end. Tomatoes, potatoes, onions, pumpkins and wine are all grown in this region, through which a road runs via Las Casitas de Femés to the main Playa Blanca-Arrecife-Yaiza highway and on to **Uga** ㉖. The latter, known locally as "Yaiza's little sister" and similarly neat and tidy, is the starting point and also the terminus of the daily camel caravan trips through the volcanic landscape.

From Uga a road leads northwestwards through one of the most unique landscapes on the island: the wine growing area of ★★**La Gería**. This is where grapes are grown for the delicious *malvasía* white wines. Lanzarote's famous Malvasía wine is actually slightly honey-

colored and has a faint aroma of almonds. There are several types, and it's worth trying out different wines at the many vineyards along the road here. This region was the most fertile on the island before the big volcanic eruption took place, and after the destruction of the cornfields a different kind of agriculture was introduced known as *enarenado*, whereby the porous volcanic material with its water-storage properties was used as a ground cover. Small holes are dug into the ground even today and filled with earth for the plants before being covered with a layer of moisture-storing pumice. The plants are then protected from the wind by tiny semicircular walls. This has created a very successful wine industry as well as a fascinating landscape: the tiny green plants surrounded by their walls contrast markedly with the black, geometrical volcanic landscape. There really is nothing like this anywhere else in the world – take time to stop at the side of the road and soak in the fantastic scenery before visiting the numerous bodegas

selling their delicious wine along the road through La Geria. The most famous vineyard, and also the oldest, is **El Grifo** in **Masdache ㉗**. The small **Museo del Vino** here mainly documents the development of machinery in wine production. The wines have won several awards, and can be sampled in a special tasting room.

At the end of the wine route, roughly at the geographical center of the island, lies **Mozaga ㉘**, with its monument in honor of the island's farmers. This white abstract **Monumento al Campesino** was created by César Manrique in 1968, using water canisters from ships. If you look at this controversial sculpture through half-closed eyes you can also make out the peasant's helpers: a donkey and a camel. The sculpture was the first created by Manrique on his return to his native island, and marked the beginning of an unparalleled phase of creativity, the evidence of which is now everywhere on the island. The small **Museo Casa del Campesino** beneath the monument contains various everyday farming items,

such as wooden dromedary saddles and plows, and potters and basket-weavers can also be observed at work here. The Campesino Restaurant in the historic country inn serves filling Canary Islands fare.

Like Tinajo, **Tao**, the next village to the north, is a center of *lucha canaria*, the Canary Islands' special form of wrestling. The arena was named after one of its most famous past exponents, who was nicknamed *Pollo de Tao* ("Chicken of Tao"). When wrestlers receive special honors these days they are referred to as *Pollo de ...*

Further south is **San Bartolomé** ㉙, its buildings grouped around a large central square on several levels. On the highest terrace are the Town Hall with its clock tower, the theater and the church. The **Ajei Cultural Center** is housed inside a former farmhouse to the southeast. The

Above: Where Puerto del Carmen gets its fresh fish. Right: El Papagayo – beautiful bays and inlets.

interior courtyard contains a water-filled cistern. To the south of the village there's a go-cart track which is definitely worth a visit – especially if you have kids with you – before continuing on to Arrecife.

RESORTS IN THE SOUTH

On the south coast of the island the ferry harbor and fishing village of **Playa Blanca** ㉚ has developed into a peaceful, attractive little resort, with a promenade, restaurants, shops and a small sand beach. The street beyond the promenade, with its motor traffic and stores, is a little more hectic. The apartment buildings here are all built in the traditional Canary Island style, and also have various kinds of chimney pot. Luxury hotels such as the Timanfaya Palace blend very well architecturally into the scene. The fishing harbor, and the docks where the ferries leave for Fuerteventura, are located to the west of the town center.

*El Papagayo ㉛, the stretch of coastline to the east of Playa Blanca, has sev-

eral attractive bays and excellent sandy beaches. These include the **Playa de las Coloradas**, near the renovated 17th-century bastion of Castillo de las Coloradas, the busier **Playa Mujeres**, with its tents and mobile homes, and the broad beach of **Playa de las Abogaderas**. Environmentalists are pressing for closure of the area and want an organized, national-park-style entrance to it. At present anyone can drive where they like, usually in four-wheel-drive vehicles. There are several vans parked around here offering expensive snacks, so it's best to bring your own food (and water) along yourself.

If you'd like a change from beach life, try traveling westwards and exploring the coast. A track leads to the lighthouse at **Punta de Pechiguera**, from which a path leads along the lonely Costa del Rubicón, with its numerous small bays and inlets.

Bicycles can be hired in Playa Blanca, and the minor road in the direction of Salinas de Janubio which runs parallel to the main highway is ideal because it's mainly flat. After a break at the black sand beach of Playa de Janubio you can cycle off to the left near Las Hoyas along the wild coastline to El Golfo, and then around the Montaña de la Vieja Gabriela (226 meters) and inland to Yaiza. Those feeling extremely fit and eager for more exertion can take a rather more arduous route, which goes back via the mountains to Playa Blanca from Las Hoyas or Uga via Femés.

The biggest tourist center on the island is **Puerto del Carmen** ❷ on the south coast. Once a picturesque little fishing village on a long sand beach, it now has enough beds to accommodate 30,000 tourists. Some of the hotels are quite attractive, with luxuriant subtropical gardens, but many are also uninspiring concrete blocks. Puerto del Carmen jars with the architectural harmony elsewhere on the island. This is what almost every seaside resort on Lanzarote could have ended up looking like if César Manrique had not made his brilliant contribution to shaping the island's modern esthetic image. The region down by the harbor is the most attractive, but even here much of the place's original substance has disappeared. Colorful fishing boats lie anchored beside excursion vessels down by the quayside, and there's a Venetian-style restaurant here providing a good view of busy harbor life.

The long line of pubs, bars and restaurants to the east has virtually nothing in common with Lanzarote apart from the climate. Bars, cafés, ice-cream parlors, amusement arcades and discos extend as far as the eye can see. It really is astonishing that many of the people here seem perfectly happy with the place and never venture away to see the rest of the island. A place like this usually goes unnoticed on a normal tourist island, but the brilliant efforts of Manrique have successfully underlined the grim contrast between what is and what might have been. The whole area gets far quieter after midnight, when most of the action centers on just a few bars, such as the **Centro Comercial Atlantico**. The discos are at their busiest on weekends, when the young Canary Islanders join in the festivities.

During the daytime the beaches of **Playa Blanca** and **Playa de los Pocillos** are where the action is. Long lines of sunshades and chaise longues can be found on both beaches, and swimming here is usually quite safe. Not enough sea and wind for surfers, however. The yacht harbor of **Puerto Calero** to the west, with its water sports center and restaurants, is a lot more elegant.

If you feel like getting away from all the thumping music, amusement arcades, and tired-looking restaurants with ancient, tattered photographs of their wares that have gone blue in the sunshine, try going one bay further to the pebble beach at **Playa Quemada**, where you can eat good Canarian food while enjoying a fine view of Fuerteventura in the distance. As with many other places, extremes are often not very far apart.

LANZAROTE

GETTING THERE: By Plane: Guasimeta Airport (Aeropuerto de Arrecife) is 7 kilometers to the west of Arrecife, tel. 928-811450. There are buses into the capital and to Puerto del Carmen (every 30 or 60 minutes).
By Ship: Naviera Armas shipping company, Arrecife, Calle José Antonio 90, tel. 928-811019, 928-811188. Car ferries: Corralejo (Fuerteventura) – Playa Blanca (4 times a day; 30 minutes). Ferry Puerto del Rosario (Fuerteventura) – Arrecife (3 hours)

THE EAST

ARRECIFE

🏨 😊😊 **Hotel Lancelot**, Avda. Mancomunidad 9, tel. 928-805099, fax. 928-805039. New, near the Playa del Reducto, comfortable, functional rooms, restaurant, pool, garden; **Hotel Miramar**, Avda. Coll 2, tel. 928-810438, fax. 928-801533. Opposite Castillo de San Gabriel. Modern rooms with bath and TV.
😊 **Hostal Cardona**, Calle 18 de Julio 11, tel. 928-811008. Near the nightlife of Arrecife.
🍴 **Bar Restaurante Castillo de San José**, Carretera de Puerto Naos, tel./fax. 928-812321. Designed by Manrique, great local food plus a bar; open daily 11 am to 1 pm, restaurant 1 to 4 and 8 to 11:30 pm; **San Francisco**, Calle Léon y Castillo 10. Atmospheric restaurant / tapas bar, closed Sundays; **Café Pastelería Lolita**, Avda. González Negrín 4, tel. 928-800710. Breakfast coffee, good cakes, ice cream.
🏛 **Museo Arqueológico**, Castillo San Gabriel; Mon-Fri 10 am to 1 pm and 4 to 7 pm, Sat 10 am to 1 pm; **Museo Internacional de Arte Contemporáneo**, Castillo de San José, at the harbor, tel. 928-800616. Contemporary (Spanish) art; Mon-Sat 11 am to 9 pm, admission free.
🎭 **El Almacén** cultural center, Calle José Béthencourt 18, lots of bars all around.
🎵 **Bar Picasso**, Calle José Béthencourt. Fri-Sun live music, tapas bar. DISCOS: Calle José Antonio Primo de Rivera, Sat, Sun until after midnight.
➕ **Hospital General**, Carretera Arrecife – San Bartolomé, tel. 928-801636; **Red Cross (Cruz Roja)**, tel. 928-812222; **Emergency Doctor:** 928-803060; **Police:** Avda. de Coll 5, tel. 928-812350.
📮 POST OFFICE: Avda. General Franco 8, tel. 928-800673, Mon-Fri 9:30 am to 8:30 pm, Sat 9:30 am to 1 pm.
🚌 BUS: Stop for Haría, Órzola and Tinajo: Calle de Velacho; other parts of the island: Playa del Reducto.
TAXI: Tel. 928-803104 and 928-812710.

COSTA TEGUISE

🛏 ❸❸❸ **Hotel Beatriz**, Calle Atalaya 3, tel. 928-591777, fax. 928-591785. Inland from Costa Teguise, seawater pools, tennis, squash, fitness center; **Hotel Meliá Salinas**, Playa de las Cucharas, tel. 928-590040, fax. 928-590390. Subtropical park, sports facilities, entertainment, excellent restaurant; **Hotel Occidental Teguise Playa**, Avda. del Jabillo, tel. 928-590654/658, fax. 928-590979. By the sea, two seawater pools, tennis, squash, fitness.

❌ **Restaurante La Graciosa**, Playa de las Cucharas, tel. 928-590040. In the Hotel Meliá Salinas, elegant, tropical atmosphere, good but not exactly cheap cuisine. Tue-Sat from 7 pm; **Restaurante El Pescador**, Avda. Islas Canarias, in the Pueblo Marinero, tel. 928-590874. Artistically designed establishment – we recommend the fish stew and mushroom omelette – Mon-Sat 12:30 to 3:30 pm and 7:30 pm to midnight.

▶ **Pubs** with Irish-English merriment; **Shows** and animation in the big hotels; **Discos** on the Avda. Islas Canarias, Pueblo Marinero, **Casino** in the Hotel Oasis, Avda. del Mar, tel. 928-592525, daily 9 pm to 5 am.

🏌 *GOLF:* Carretera Costa Teguise – Tahiche, tel. 928-590512, fax. 928-590490. Inland from Costa Teguise, 18 holes, driving range, lessons available.

WATER PARK: **Ocean Park**, inland, tel. 928-592128. Amusement pool, bus connection from Puerto del Carmen, daily 10 am to 5 or 6 pm.

WINDSURFING: **Windsurfing Club**, Centro Comercial Tahiche, Local 18, Playa de las Cucharas, tel./fax. 928-590731. Courses, equipment, tours to Timanfaya National Park, to go surfing in Órzola and Famara, bike tours; **F2 Windsurfing Center,** Playa de las Cucharas, tel. 928-591974. Courses, equipment.

➕ **Clinica Costa Teguise,** Calle de la Rosa, 8, tel. 928-811014; **24-Hour Medical Service**: Apts. Lanzarote Gardens, tel. 928-592026.

☎ *POST OFFICE:* Centro Comercial Las Maretas, mornings.

📞 *TAXI:* Tel. 928-590863.

GUATIZA

🌵 **Jardín de Cactus**: Near Guatiza, tel./fax. 928-529397; daily 10 am to 6 pm, Cafetería 11 am to 4 pm, with souvenir shop.

TAHICHE

🏛 **Fundación César Manrique**, Taro de Tahiche, tel. 928-843138 and 928-843070, fax. 928-843463. With gallery, souvenir shop, cafeteria.
Daily in summer 10 am to 7 pm, in winter Mon-Sat 10 am to 6 pm, Sun 10 am to 3 pm. Evenings there are often book presentations, poetry readings and lectures.

CUEVA DE LOS VERDES

🏛 **Cave system**, tel. 928-173220. Guided tours (around 50 minutes long), daily 10 am to 5 pm.

GUINATE

🏛 **Parque Tropical Guinate**, tel. 928-835500, daily 10 am to 5 pm.

HARÍA

❌ **Restaurante Papa Loca**, Plaza de León y Castillo 5, tel. 928-835670. Canarian cuisine, Tue-Sun 11 am to 8 pm; **Restaurante Los Cascajos**, Calle Ferrer 9, Haría-Máguez road, tel. 928-835471. Substantial cooking, wine, cheese, mojo, souvenirs; **Restaurante Mirador del Valle**, tel. 928-528036, Haría-Máguez road. Canarian grill specialties, daily until 10 pm.

🏛 **Museo Internacional de Miniaturas**: Calle El Palmeral 4, tel. 928-835760, daily 10 am to 6 pm.

☎ *POST OFFICE:* Calle Sol, weekday mornings.

ISLA GRACIOSA

🛏 ❸ **Pensión Enriqueta**, Calle de la Mar de Barlovento 6, at the harbor, tel. 928-420051; **Pensión Girasol**, right at the harbor mole, tel. 928-842101. Some rooms have balconies. Both boarding houses have restaurants.

☎ *POST OFFICE:* Caleta del Sebo, mornings.

🚢 *FERRY:* **Lineas Marítimas Romero**, between Órzola and La Graciosa. Info: Calle García Escámez 11, Isla Graciosa, tel. 928-842055/070. Summer: Órzola – La Graciosa 10 am, 12, 5 and 6:30 pm, La Graciosa – Órzola 8 and 11 am, 4 and 6 pm. Winter: Órzola – La Graciosa 10 am, 12 and 5 pm, La Graciosa – Órzola 8 and 11 am and 4 pm. Tickets available in each harbor.

TAXI: Tel. 928-835031.

LOS JAMEOS DEL AGUA

🏛 **Cave system** designed by Manrique with bar, restaurant and shop, tel. 928-848020, fax. 928-848123. Tue, Fri, Sat folklore, daily 9:30 am to 7 pm, sometimes until 3 am, restaurant 1 to 4 and 8 to 11:30 pm.

MÁGUEZ

🏛 **Paintings**: Carlos Parra's studio, Cuatro Esquinas 5, tel. 928-835844, Tue-Sat 11 am to 5 pm.

ÓRZOLA

❌ **Restaurante Punta Fariones,** Calle La Quemadita 8, tel. 928-842558. At ferry harbor, fresh seafood; **Mirador del Río**, tel./fax. 908-644318. Restaurant with view to the west of Órzola, daily 10 am to 6 pm.

Lanzarote

TEGUISE

Isla Viva, Plaza Clavijo y Fajardo 4, tel. 928-845723, fax. 928-845761, e-mail: islaviva@infolanz.es. Agency for modern and renovated country homes (from Los Valles to La Gería), for 1 to 5 people. Prices depend on size, season, etc. Internet: www.teguise.com.

Bar Cafetería La Tahona, Calle Santo Domingo, tel. 928-845349. Traditional bar, craft store, Fri live music; closed Sat; **Bar Restaurante Acatife**, on market square, Calle San Miguel 4, tel. 928-845037. Building full of nooks and crannies (18th century). International cuisine with a Canaries edge to it, inexpensive, good island wines, closed Sun after the market; **Casa Cristóbal**, road to Arrecife, tel. 928-845295. One of the best restaurants on the island, closed Tue.

Casa Museo Palacio Spinola, Mon-Fri 9 am to 3 pm, Sat-Sun 9:30 am to 2 pm; **Churches and Convents**: Nuestra Señora de Guadalupe, and monasteries of Santo Domingo and San Francisco, Mon-Fri 10 am to 4:30 pm, Sat and Sun 10 am to 2 pm; **Museo del Emigrante Canario**, Castillo de Santa Bárbara, Mon-Fri 10 am to 4 pm, Sat, Sun 10 am to 3 pm.

Market Sun until 2 pm; German, English, Spansh **books**, also second-hand: **Leo**, Plaza Clavijo y Fajardo 4, tel. 928-845663, Tue-Fri 10:30 am to 1:30 pm and 5 to 7:30 pm, Sun 10 am to 2 pm; **Galería La Villa**, Plaza Clavijo y Fajardo 4, fax. 928-845711. Modern art, also for sale, Tue-Fri 10:30 am to 1:30 pm and 5 to 7:30 pm, Sun 10 am to 2 pm; Individual **fashions** for women: **Talia**, Plaza Clavijo y Fajardo 4, tel. 928-845657, Tue-Fri 10:30 am to 1:30 pm and 5 to 7:30 pm, Sun 10 am to 2 pm; **Timples** at Antonio Lemes Hernández, Calle Flores 8; **Jewelry**, Plaza Clavijo y Fajardo 4, modern designs, Tue-Fri 10:30 am to 1:30 pm and 5 to 7:30 pm, Sun 10 am to 2 pm.

POST OFFICE: Calle Flores, weekday mornings.
TAXI: Tel. 928-845533.

THE WEST

LA SANTA

Club La Santa, tel. 928-840100, fax. 928-840050. Club for recreation, training and fitness. Sports, equipment, no extra charge for places (apart from diving, individual lessons and inline skating). Child care facilities. See also **Isla Viva** agency in Teguise.

Bar Zumosport, main street at entrance to town. Fresh juices, ice cream, milkshakes, health food, closed Wed.

SURFING: **La Santa Surf** surfing school, at entrance to town, tel. 928-840279.

PARQUE NACIONAL DE TIMANFAYA

Admission includes bus tour through the "Mountains of Fire" (45 minutes from Islote de Hilario), daily 9 am to 4:45 pm.

Restaurante El Diablo, Islote de Hilario, tel. 928-840056/057. Meat and fish dishes grilled above a volcanic shaft; daily 9 am to 3:30 pm.

Museo de Rocas, Echadero de los Camellos, Carretera Yaiza-Tinajo. Pictures and rock samples from the national park, Mon-Sat 9 am to 2 pm, free.

CAMEL RIDES: Echadero de los Camellos, Carretera Yaiza – Tinajo, daily 9 am to 2 pm

Centro de Visitantes e Interpretación de Mancha Blanca, visitor center, Carretera Yaiza – Tinajo, tel./fax. 928-840839, daily 9 am to 5 pm, admission free; **Oficinas del Parque Nacional de Timanfaya**, Tinajo, Calle Laguneta 85, tel. 928-840238/240, fax. 928-840251, Mon-Fri 9 am to 2 pm.

TIAGUA

Museo Agrícola El Patio, Calle Echeyde 18, tel./fax. 928-529134, Mon-Fri 10 am to 5:30 pm, Sat 10 am to 2:30 pm.

YAIZA

⊕⊕⊕ **Hotel Rural Finca de las Salinas**, Calle La Cuesta 17, tel. 928-830325/6, fax. 928-830329. New, in an 18th-century country house with a pool and a vegetable garden.

⊕⊕ **Vacation house Casa Friedel**, Friedel Leitz, tel./fax. 928-830199. Central, renovated country house, two bedrooms, living room, kitchen, luxury bath.

Restaurante La Era, tel. 928-830016, signposted. 300-year-old estate, excellent Canary cuisine, local wine, sometimes live music, daily 1 to 11 pm.

Galería Yaiza, belongs to German artist named Veno. Carretera to Playa Blanca, Mon-Sat 5 to 7 pm.

Fashion and Handicrafts: Tasteful souvenirs can be bought at **El Pajarito**, Santa Catalina 3, tel. 928-830094, Mon-Fri 10 am to 1:30 and 4:30 to 7:30 pm, Sat 10 am to 1:30 pm.

TAXI: Tel. 928-830163.

THE CENTER

MASDACHE

Museo del Vino, El Grifo Winery, Carretera Masdache 121, tel. 928-520500, Mon-Sat 10 am to 6 pm, admission free, **wine also sold**, tel. 928-800586.

MOZAGA

Casa Museo del Campesino, tel. 928-520136. Rustic museum restaurant, substantial Canarian cuisine, fish, rabbit, island wine, daily 12 to 4:30 pm.

🏛 **Casa Museo del Campesino**, daily 10 am to 6 pm.

SAN BARTOLOMÉ

🚗 *GO-CARTS:* South of San Bartolomé at the traffic circle, tel. 928-520022, open daily.

THE SOUTH

MACHER

🚗 *HORSEBACK RIDING:* **Lanzarote ¡a Caballo!**, Uga – Macher road, tel. 928-830314, daily 10 am to 2 pm, 5 to 8 pm (summer), 4 to 7 pm (winter).

PLAYA BLANCA

🏨 ⑨⑨⑨ **Hotel Timanfaya Palace**, tel. 928-517676, fax. 928-517035. By the sea, Andalusian-Arabic style, lagoon-like pools, modern rooms, no pets; **Playa Dorada**, Avda. Papagayo, tel. 928-517120, fax. 928-517431. Near Playa Dorada, children welcome.

⑨⑨ **Lanzarote Park**, tel. 928-517040, fax. 928-517348. Slightly out of town, nicely-located hotel with apartments.

🚗 *BOAT TRIPS:* With the two-mast schooner **Marea Errota**, tel. 928-517633, fax. 928-517514.

MINIGOLF: In the Calle Los Calamares.

DIVING: **Las Toninas**, in the Hotel Playa Flamingo, tel. 928-517300, fax. 928-517642, daily 10 am to 6 pm.

➕ **24-Hour Medical Service**: In the Centro Comercial Lanzarote Park 17, tel. 928-517643.

📮 *POST OFFICE:* Calle G, Mon-Sat 9 to 11:30 am.

📠 *FERRIES:* **Naviera Armas**, tel. 928-517912/13; **Líneas Fred Olsen**, tel. 928-517301/03, fax. 517214. Both ferry companies do four crossings daily from Playa Blanca to Fuerteventura: the *Volcán de Tindaya* at 9 and 11 am, 5 and 7 pm, and the *Buganvilla* at 8 and 10 am, 2 and 6 pm.

TAXI: Tel. 928-517542.

PLAYA QUEMADA

❌ **Restaurante 7 Islas**, tel. 928173249. Terrace, sea view, inexpensive, good seafood, daily 9 am to 10 pm.

PUERTO CALERO

❌ **El Bar del Club**, tel. 928-510015. Quiet restaurant with terrace by the harbor, Canarian cuisine, Tue-Sun noon to midnight.

🚗 *WATER SPORTS:* Deep sea fishing with the **Lanzamarlin**, departure beween 9 am and 4 pm, night fishing also available. Info at the harbor, tel. 908-022 771, 908-354549 (cell phones); **Catlanza** offers windsurfing, diving and waterskiing, fishing and snorkeling at the beaches of El Papagayo, tel. 928-513022.

SUBMARINE: **Sub Fun 3** goes down as far as 30 meters, from Puerto Calero. Local 2, tel. 928-512898, fax. 928-512906; daily 9 am to 7 pm.

DIVING: **La Ballena Blanca**, Módulo C, Local 4, tel. 928-515264, fax. 928-515312, Mon-Sat., e-mail: white-whale@intercom.es

PUERTO DEL CARMEN

🏨 ⑨⑨⑨ **Los Fariones**, Roque del Este, tel. 928-510175, fax. 928-510202. Elegant, traditional.

⑨⑨ **La Geria**, Playa de los Pocillos, tel. 928-511908, fax. 928-511918. On the beach.

⑨ **Hostal Residencia Magec**, Calle Hierro 11, tel. 928-513874. Simple accommodation at the harbor.

❌ **Restaurante Los Marineros**, Plaza El Varadero 14, tel. 928-510875. Venetian style, by the harbor, seafood; **Restaurante El Sardinero**, Calle Nuestra Señora del Carmen 9, tel. 928-511939. Popular, by the boccia, fish; **Lani's**: Seven establishments in the *Grupo Lani's* on Avda. de las Playas (pizzeria, ice cream parlor, bistro, grill, etc.).

🚗 *BOAT TRIPS:* Glass-bottomed catamaran **Blue Delfin**, Calle Teide 30, tel. 928-512323, to Fuerteventura, Isla Los Lobos; Motor yacht **César II**, Avda. Juan Carlos I 10, tel. 928-511743, to Fuerteventura and Isla Los Lobos, waterskiing, motor boat trips, waterbikes.

SPORT and DEEP-SEA FISHING: Approx. six-hour-long trip with the **Ana II**, tel. 928-513736.

SUBMARINE: **Aquascope** at the harbor, tel. 928-647467, half-hourly daily 10 am to 8 pm.

HORSEBACK RIDING: **Rancho Texas**, bypass north of Puerto del Carmen, Calle Noruega, tel. 928-173247, fax. 928-173248, daily 10 am to 2 pm, 5 to 8 pm (summer), 4 to 7 pm (winter), also night riding.

WINDSURFING: **F2 Windsurfing Center**, Playa de Matagorda east of Puerto del Carmen, tel. 928-591974. Courses, equipment for rent.

🚗 *MOTORCYCLE RENTAL:* Mopeds to Harleys, Centro Comercial Marítimo, Local 15, tel. 928-512317.

📰 **Foreign Newspapers and Books**: Available at many shops. One good place is **Sus Libros** just above the old harbor, Calle Teide 13, tel. 928-512859, Mon-Sat 10 am to 1 pm, Mon-Fri also 5 to 7 pm.

➕ **Outpatients**: Calle Juan Carlos I, tel. 928-512711; **Red Cross**: Tel. 928-812222; **24-Hour Emergency Service**: Avda. de las Playas 5, tel. 928-513171.

📮 *POST OFFICE:* Calle Juan Carlos I, tel. 928-510 381, Mon-Fri 8:30 am to 2:30 pm, Sat 9:30 am to 1 pm.

📠 *TAXI:* Tel. 928-513634/5/8 and 928-511136.

ℹ **Información Turística**: In the pavilion behind Playa Blanca, Avenida de las Playas, tel. 928-510027, Mon-Sat 9:30 am to 1:30 pm, Mon-Fri 4:30 to 7:30 pm.

Lanzarote

FUERTEVENTURA
Sun, Sand, Wind and Stars

PUERTO DEL ROSARIO

CORRALEJO AND THE NORTH

THE MIDWEST

THE SOUTH AND SOUTHEAST

THE JANDÍA PENINSULA

Fuerteventura

An Island Sahara

With all the sand and rock that makes up most of its largely desolate landscape, Fuerteventura, perhaps the most unspoiled of the Canary Islands, is rather reminiscent of the Sahara Desert. Apart from Maspalomas on Gran Canaria there's nowhere else in the Canary Islands with so many enormous sand dunes and sandy beaches, even though most of the land is stone and rock. One big difference to the Sahara is that this island is volcanic – but then again, the last volcanic activity on Fuerteventura occurred around 7,000 years ago.

Fuerteventura takes quite some getting used to, with its broad, desert-like expanses. If you're naturally inclined towards meditation, you'll appreciate the subtle changes of color in this barren landscape. Broad sand beaches and golden yellow sand dunes attract sun-worshipers, and water sports are also very popular here – though it's best to avoid swimming outside the tourist areas because of the often fierce undertow. Fuerteventura either delights you or leaves you cold. It certainly isn't the "attractive

Previous Pages: Playa del Moro – beach as far as the eye can see. Left: Work of art in the harbor of Puerto del Rosario.

holiday landscape" that many expect to find. Thirty years ago no one could have believed that tourism would catch on upon this solitary island. In 1876, the Spanish government transferred its Foreign Legion to distant Puerto del Rosario, and at the beginning of the 20th century it used Fuerteventura as a place of exile for unwanted politicians and intellectuals. One of these, Miguel de Unamuno, philosopher-dean of the University of Salamanca and poet, was so charmed by the scenery and the warmth of the local population that Fuerteventura very often plays a role in his work.

The island is windy, and has attracted numerous water sports enthusiasts. Divers, windsurfers and body-surfers adore the place. Hikers, mountain-bikers and motorcyclists love the broad landscape, and bicyclists appreciate the well-paved roads. The miles and miles of sand beaches in the south are ideal for families with children.

Arrival

The **Aeropuerto del Rosario** is six kilometers to the south of Puerto del Rosario, and its new terminal hall is one of the most elegant anywhere in the Canary Islands. The airport contains numerous car rental firms, an information office (which also provides bus time-tables), automatic teller machine and a currency exchange office. Because of the exchange rate, large sums of money are best exchanged in tourist resorts like Corralejo, Jandía Playa or Morro Jable.

There's a speedboat connection to the capital from Gran Canaria, and also a car ferry connection to Morro Jable. From Lanzarote take the ferry from Playa Blanca to Corralejo (approx. 30 minutes) or the ship connection from capital to capital (three hours). At the harbor there are buses, taxis and rental cars to continue your journey.

PUERTO DEL ROSARIO

From the airport a well-paved highway leads northwards to the capital of **Puerto del Rosario ❶** (pop. 18,000). To the south of the town is the rather monasti-cally severe-looking **Parador Nacional de Fuerteventura**, with its barred-up balcony *(azotea)* and the white sand **Playa Blanca**, which is so popular with the local population. The hotel is usually patronized by business travelers, and its restaurant is one of the best on the island.

The simple Puerto de Cabras ("Goat Harbor") developed into an important port in the 19th century and was made the capital of the island in 1860 – as the suc-cessor to Betancuria, Antigua and La Oliva, all of them more protected and fur-ther inland. It was only in 1956 that it was given the resonant name of Puerto del Rosario. The town isn't that attractive, however: its harbor installations and the industrial area to the north tend to over-shadow it quite a bit. Anyone traveling into town from Playa Blanca will pass the former red-light district of **Barrio Chino**, still run-down looking today, and also the relics of past industrialization: lime kilns which were fired by English coal until the beginning of the 20th century.

The harbor promenade has been re-built, and oversized sculptures of snails

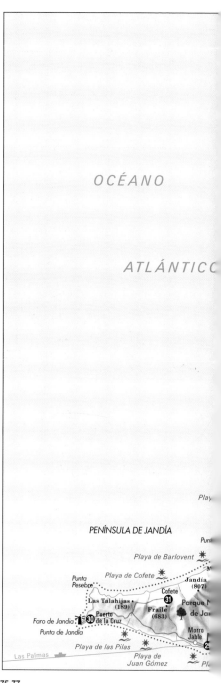

OCÉANO

ATLÁNTICC

PENÍNSULA DE JANDÍA

Playa de Barlovent

Playa de Cofete

Punta Pesebre

Cofete

Las Talahijas (189)

Jandía (807)

Fraile (683)

Parque de Jandía

Faro de Jandía

Puerto de la Cruz

Punta de Jandía

Morro Jable

Las Palmas

Playa de las Pilas

Playa de Juan Gómez

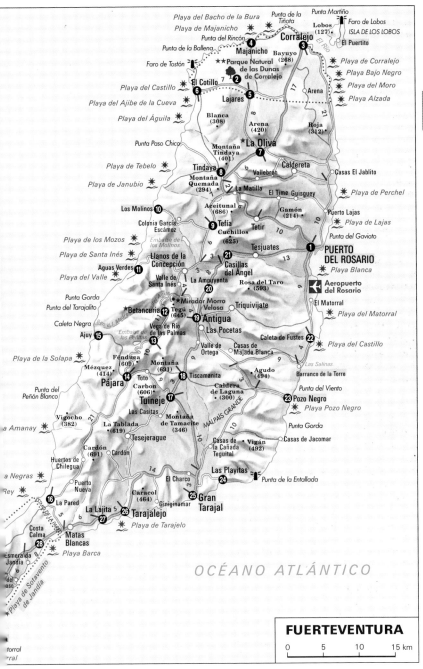

FUERTEVENTURA

0   5   10   15 km

and seashells have given it an artistic edge. The main shopping street, **Avenida León y Castillo**, leads from the **Plaza de España** at the middle of the promenade into the less exciting town center.

There is one highlight worth mentioning on Calle Virgen del Rosario near the church: the former exile home of Miguel de Unamuno now houses the **Casa Museo Unamuno**, which contains several items that belonged to the poet, and reflects the 1920s atmosphere very well. Anyone who speaks Spanish will understand the numerous quotations of the poet arranged as mottoes in several of the rooms, and will be eager to read the forthcoming new edition of his *De Fuerteventura a Paris*. The roofed-over **Arena** for wrestling, located near the church, is also used for major concert and dance events, and the **Casa de la Cultura** (Calle Ramiro de Maeztu) features exhibitions, plays and concerts, too.

Most visitors just take a brief stroll through this town before drinking a coffee at Plaza de España. To make Puerto del Rosario more attractive for visitors, plans are afoot to turn the former red-light district into a tourist quarter and to transform the present foreign legion barracks area into a municipal park.

Anyone traveling round here by bicycle who is also reasonably fit can ride from Puerto del Rosario through the hilly interior of the island via Antigua, Tuineje and Tarajalejo as far as Jandía, passing ploughed fields, valleys with palm trees and cacti, and several excellent views of barren, gently sloping mountain ridges – or the spectacular panoramic stretch via Pájara through the lonely mountain region as far as Istmo de la Pared. If you tend to lack stamina, take a leisurely bike ride northwards along the flat road from Puerto del Rosario through the dunes as far as Corralejo.

Right: The sand dunes near Corralejo have been turned into a national park.

CORRALEJO AND THE NORTH

The most important vacation center in the north of Fuerteventura, Corralejo can be reached along the eastern coast road. The landscape is noticeably barren here and scarcely populated. Around halfway through this desolation is the **Parque Holandés**, a half-completed urbanization with an uncertain future.

A broad and spectacular area of sand dunes extends away to the south of Corralejo. It's a protected area, and very popular with sunbathers and water sports enthusiasts. Shortly before the area was declared the **★★Parque Natural de las Dunas de Corralejo ❷**, the two high-rise hotels of Tres Islas and Oliva Beach were quickly built in the white sand, and the small stores here provide drinks, sun cream and swimsuits, while chaise longues and sunshades can be rented out at the section of beach close by. Small snack bars near the hotels and along the beach also sell delicious food (seafood, shrimp cocktails), ice cream, beer and fruit juice.

Loneliness addicts can find just what they're looking for here, even at the height of the tourist season. Equipped with water bottle, food and sun-hat (and remember there is no shade whatsoever around here) you can walk for miles through the fine, white sand, enjoy the grandiose view across the dunes, build a sand-castle, and wander around naked. If you're not a good swimmer, be careful of the undertow at some sections of beach.

Alongside the hardy, dry vegetation here you'll find plenty of broken snail shells. The strong winds here blow sand regularly across the roads, so be careful when driving. A small train (the *Mini-Tren*) plies regularly between Corralejo and the dunes. If you feel like taking a short walk after sunbathing, why not wander along the beach to Corralejo, between the sand and lava cliffs? There's a good view of the Isla de los Lobos, and

you can end the day in Corralejo with some delicious seafood.

Corralejo ❸ is an unpretentious and attractive vacation resort, and the center has a real village feel to it. It's an international place, and not overly British or German-oriented. There's a pleasant mix of all kinds of vacationers here: surfers, unmarried mothers, beachcombers, bikers with backpacks, and energetic pensioners. There are smaller beaches south of the harbor, and the municipal beach beside the Hotel Hoplaco, located in the middle of subtropical gardens, is ideal for kids. The busy main street, **Avenida Generalísimo Franco**, leads to the center and to the pedestrian precinct.

In the **Centro Atlantico** on this avenue, it's fiesta time the whole year through: in the various pubs here, surfers tend to celebrate until late at night. The cozy **Plaza Felix Estvéez González**, surrounded by restaurants, is a good place to eat out of doors, and every evening there's live music to accompany your meal. In the surrounding streets there are several seafood restaurants, small boutiques and sports stores.

On the **Plaza Pública**, just on front of the tourist office, a **Craft Fair** has established itself, with Canary Islands souvenirs and African mass-produced articles. At carnival time, Corralejo is the liveliest place on the island with all its processions and dancing, and if you're sensitive to noise don't make the mistake of booking accommodation in the town center during that time, because the music goes on right through the night.

Corralejo is also a perfect starting point for motorcycle or mountain-bike tours – the bikes can be rented here without a problem. A day trip is a good way of exploring the **Isla de los Lobos**. Tickets can be obtained at the harbor and in the pedestrian precinct (the boat leaves in the morning and returns in the afternoon, the whole trip takes around 40 minutes and there are also organized tours). The boats arrive at **El Puertito**, a relatively deserted fishing village with a tiny beach bar and restaurant that serves delicious fresh fish

and paella (best ordered in advance, before the trip!).

The safest beach for swimming around here is the **Playa de la Calera**, just a few minutes' walk away to the west, with a view of Fuerteventura. The island is an excellent place for swimming, and can also be hiked around (roughly three hours; bring good shoes, drinking water and sun protection). The local vegetation is relatively sparse and has adapted to the salty seawater.

At the northern tip of **Punta Martiño** you'll arrive at the automatic lighthouse of **Faro de Lobos**. In the west, the 127-meter-high crater rim of the **Montaña Lobos** provides a good view of Lanzarote and Fuerteventura, as well as being the highest point on the island. The waters around the Faro de Lobos – especially the fish-rich straits of **El Río** with their steep reefs – are very popular with divers and anglers.

Above: Windsurfers off the Isla de los Lobos.
Right: Corralejo – a good place to wind down.

Beach and Surfing Paradise

On the way to the northwest side of Fuerteventura you'll start by traveling southwards in the direction of La Oliva. Turn off to the right seven kilometers later in the direction of Lajares. If you happen to like water sports, try taking a detour before you reach it to the surfing paradise on the north coast near **Majanicho ❹**. The winds here make big waves all year round, and the area is so popular with surfers that you won't have any problems finding yourself a board.

Lajares ❺ is surrounded by a region of semi-desert made up of fallow-lying fields. The whole plain is covered by walls to provide shelter from the wind. Dromedaries were still used for field work in this region as recently as two decades ago. Lajares itself is still home to traditional crafts such as the time-consuming *calados*, or hem-stitch embroidery, and there are two shops selling tablecloths, pottery and other craft products. If you follow signs to the **Ermita de**

San Antonio de Padua on the south side of town you'll see two renovated wind-mills: the "male" *molino macho* is the older type, familiar from *Don Quixote*, and the rather thinner "female" one, or *molina*, was developed by a miller from La Palma and is better at grinding. The in-flexible wooden slats on its sails were rather more sensitive to gusts of wind, however, and a miller's apprentice had to keep a permanent eye on them.

Another beach and surfing paradise is **El Cotillo ❻** on the northwest coast. The resort, which looks rather half-built, actu-ally has a long history as a natural fishing harbor, and it also exported its own burnt lime. A new harbor with a massive quay wall is under construction here at present. The old harbor, with its small bars and restaurants, is the most picturesque part of town.

On the coast slightly to the south is the **Torre de San Miguel**, a guard tower built in 1743 to protect the old harbor, and ruined lime ovens can still be seen nearby. A footpath leads down from here to the **Playa del Castillo**, one of the nic-est beaches in this region, located beneath a section of steep coastline.

Further to the south are the beaches of **Playa del Ajibe de la Cueva** and the **Playa del Águila**, both wild and remote; here you'll find nothing but steely blue sky, dark blue ocean with white foam, and fine white sand. There are several nice places for sheltered sunbathing between the lava blocks. This place is perfect for surfers, but even if you're a good swim-mer, only enter the water if the waves are reasonably gentle-looking.

Four-wheel-drive vehicles can easily travel along the coast here, but most of the beaches only have pedestrian access. Bring food along with you, too, and be-ware of the sunshine – there's hardly any shade anywhere, nor drinking water.

North of El Cotillo is a large area of sand dunes with small sandy bays en-closed by lava cliffs, and the housing estate of **Los Lagos** beyond. The modern lighthouse, **Faro de Toston**, on the north-westernmost tip of the island towers above the flat rocky bays with their white sand beaches. Enthusiastic surfers can be seen in the waves here, and beachcombers will enjoy the varied vegetation as well as all the fascinating marine life in the rock pools.

If you feel like going on an extended hike, or a trip in a four-wheel-drive, take the narrow, rather bumpy track along the rough and rocky coast to Majanicho, and either go south from there to Lajares or eastwards to Corralejo. There are plenty of good places to stop along the way, such as the **Playa de Majanicho** or the **Playa del Bacho de la Burra** on the **Punta de la Tinota**, where windsurfers are definitely in their element.

*La Oliva

The village of **La Oliva** ❼ in the interior was the political center of Fuerteventura from the early 18th to mid-19th century, and some (renovated) buildings still survive from that time. In the center of town is the majestic white **Parroquiade Nuestra Señora de Candelaria** church, its square bell tower visible for miles around. The Renaissance portal has a finely-carved wooden door, and highlights inside include the *mudéjar* ceiling, a large painting of *The Last Judgment*, a baroque altar painting by Juan de Miranda (1723-1805) and also some fine trompe l'oeil work.

Not far from the church, towards the northwest along a small side road, the former tithe house of **La Cilla** contains a small exhibition of framing tools. In the eastern part of town is the semi-renovated townhouse **Casa de los Coroneles**, the largest of its type in the entire Canary Islands. This was where the military governors of the islands – the family of Cabrera-Béthencourt, descended from the Norman Jean de Béthencourt – used

Right: The parish church of La Oliva, former power center of Fuerteventura.

to reside. The family coat of arms above the portal is worth noting, as are the artistically-carved wooden balustrades on the front balconies, and the square corner towers. A cultural center is due to be opened here in the year 2000.

Separated by a square from the Casa de los Coroneles is the initially rather inconspicuous **Casa del Capellan**. The stone-masonry on the door and window frames of this former presbytery indicates the Latin American, and particularly Cuban, influence that was brought back to the islands by returning emigrants.

Lovers of local modern art will appreciate the ***Centro de Arte Canario Casa Mané**, located between the church and the Casa de los Coroneles. On the ground level it has rooms for current exhibitions and a sculpture courtyard, while the basement contains a large contemporary art gallery. Not everything is modern here, though – the landscapes by Agulló, for instance, are rather conservative.

From La Oliva the main road carries on towards the south, while a well-paved road branches off westwards to **Tindaya** ❽ at the foot of the volcano of the same name, **Montaña Tindaya** (401 meters). On this reddish-brown mountain, which was held sacred by the islands' original inhabitants, numerous stylized foot imprints have recently been discovered carved into the rock, and their origin is still very much of a mystery. Some assume that there was once a cultic site located on the summit, especially since Tenerife's Mount Teide, the Canary Islands' equivalent of Fujiyama, is clearly visible from there.

A project by Spanish artist Eduardo Cillida (born in 1924) is causing a lot of controversy, but seems to be actually going ahead: he plans to carve a cube out of the mountain with 50-meter-long sides. In Tindaya they think this may attract tourism and earn them rather more than what they're making at present from tomatoes and cheese.

A narrow asphalt road – which later on becomes nothing more than a track – leads from Tindaya to the west coast, with its remote little **Playa de Janubio** surrounded by sand dunes. This is a good place to get away from it all, but be careful if you go swimming: the undertow is said to be quite powerful and no risks should be taken.

To the south of Tindaya, on the **Montaña Quemada** (294 meters), the **Monumento a Don Miguel de Unamuno** was erected in honor of the illustrious exile in 1970. The slightly larger-than-life-sized statue of the philosopher was only officially "opened" after the death of Generalísimo Franco because of fears that the regime would take offense to it. Unamuno was an educator, author and philosopher whose essays had a great influence in early 20th-century Spain. When he publicly supported the Allied cause in World War I he was dismissed as rector of Salamanca University, and his opposition to the Spanish military government in 1924 resulted in his exile

to the Canaries. When General Miguel de Rivera's dictatorship collapsed, Unamuno returned to Spain and got his old job back, but he then denounced Franco's Falangists in 1936 and was placed under house arrest. He died of a heart attack two months later.

The main road leads southeastwards via the villages of La Matilla and Tetir to Puerto Rosario; if you branch off southwards sharply just before La Matilla you'll arrive in **Tefia ❾**. On the southern edge of the village, various old farmhouses and windmills have been renovated using EU funds, and the pretty houses are soon due to provide traditional arts and crafts with a new home.

Take a detour to the west coast and after a while you'll pass another renovated windmill. Shortly after the small settlement of Las Parcelas, the road leads on to the Barranco de los Molinos. The simple harbor village of **Los Molinos ❿** nearby has a pond with geese, and also a pleasantly atmospheric little restaurant with a view of the rocks and surf.

THROUGH THE "MIDWEST"
Betancuria, Pájara and Antigua

From Tefia, the well-paved road continues on its way further southwards. At a roundabout, follow the signs to "Betancuria" off to the right (that is to say, westwards). Near **Llanos de la Concepción** there's a windmill up on a slope. From here you can get to the west coast with its dark basalt cliffs, and to **Aguas Verdes ⓫**, a remotely-situated vacation club on the **Playa del Valle**. Since 1984, the surf here has been smashing against a rusty old wreck – a formerly 100-meter-long freighter that was washed up ashore.

Further to the north are the **Playa de Santa Ines** and the **Playa de los Mozos**. Footpaths lead northwards along the coast to Los Molinos, southwards to

Above: Windmills are a striking feature of the barren landscape (here near Llanos de la Concepción). Right: The fortified church of Betancuria, now a museum.

Ajuy, or back through a *barranco* to Llanos de la Concepción.

From Llanos de la Concepción the road winds its way through the fertile and partially terraced **Valle de Santa Inés** and then onwards into the central hills. At the next fork in the road, keep right (going west) and you'll reach the toll road leading up to the 645-meter-high **Tegú**, with its new **★Mirador Morro Velosa**. From this observation point – and from its telescope – you'll have an astonishing view of the entire northern part of the island. It's also clear how much of the island's surface has been eroded by climatic influences. A restaurant here, which was co-designed by Blanca Cabrera, César Manrique's niece, is ideal for a meal.

★Betancuria – the First Capital

The journey then continues into the valley and to **★Betancuria ⓬**, which was founded by Norman conqueror Jean de Béthencourt in 1405 and remained the capital of the island until 1835. The

Fuerteventura

whole town is a protected site, and its buildings are still thoroughly medieval-looking. Just outside the town is a renovated monastery, the **Convento de San Buenaventura**, erected by Franciscans after the *Conquista*, with outer walls, columns and archways still standing. After secularization in 1836 the building was left to go to ruin, and many stones were used as building material. The badly-weathered tomb slab of the conqueror Diego García de Herrera, who died in 1485, still remains, as does the intact but usually closed **Capilla de San Diego de Alcalá**, built above the cave of Franciscan hermit San Diego de Alcalá.

In the town center is the three-aisled **Iglesia Nuestra Señora de la Concepción** (Calle Alcaldo Carmelo Silvera), originally built in around 1620 as a fortified church and today a museum. The *mudéjar* ceiling is particularly fine, as are the Baroque high altar dating from 1684, with its magnificent colors and fruit motifs, and the choir stalls, separated from the rest of the interior by a painted rood

screen. The entrance fee to the church also includes access to the **Museo de Arte Sacro** behind it, in an old townhouse. The various religious relics on display here include a section of material from the original banner of conquest presented by the King of Castile to his vassal Diego García Herrera.

The attractively restored townhouse **Casa Santa María** (16th century) near the church square is an elegant place to enjoy a good meal. Try walking around the rooms and inner courtyards, too; it's really atmospheric – and the ceramics and local crafts shop in the basement is also well worth a visit.

On the main street, the **Casa Museo Arqueológico de Betancuria**, flanked by cannon, contains a collection of important and fascinating archeological finds. Highlights here include fertility idols, an idol frieze that was discovered near La Oliva, and also numerous farming implements. The **Centro Insular de Artesania**, next to the museum, documents traditional arts and crafts.

Five and a half kilometers south of Betancuria, a turnoff to the west leads to a valley of palm trees containing the simple village of **Vega de Río de las Palmas ⑬**, nestling amid fields that are still largely cultivated. On its main street is the second most important church in the region after the one in Betancuria, the **Iglesia Nuestra Señora de la Peña** (17th century). It contains a *Madonna and Child* made of alabaster which was apparently brought to the island from Normandy by Jean de Béthencourt, and was originally in the Betancuria church. Hidden away during a pirate raid, the alabaster figure was long believed to have been lost for good. Apparently it was rediscovered inside a cave to the west of Vega de Río de las Palmas – the **Ermita de la Peña** marks the site. The *Virgen de la Peña*, the island's patron saint, is believed to bring rain for the crops, and a major pilgrimage

Above: Irrigation is still important in Betancuria, despite the elevation. Right: Steep coastline near Ajuy.

takes place to Vega de Río de las Palmas every year in September.

At the end of the valley is a large embankment and reservoir dating from the Franco period. The shallow water here is attractive to waterfowl and other birds – flamingoes have also been spotted.

Pájara and Environs

The main road winds its way around numerous hairpin bends now as it ascends the **Fénduca** (609 meters, with an observation point at the top) and then continues on to Pájara – rock on one side, a massively steep drop on the other, and very few places for vehicles to pass. The remote terrain is very impressive, especially in spring when the green contrasts sharply with the dark rock and the shadow. Quiet little **Pájara ⑭**, with its population of around 700, has the only freshwater swimming pool on the island. The place is thinking of expanding, but so far it has fortunately had no real idea of how it should do so. The leafy church square and the parks are still idyllic, and there's also a fine old disused waterwheel outside the Town Hall, once driven by dromedaries – whose job today of course is to carry tourists around.

Pájara has one structure that is definitely worth visiting, especially because of its Latin American elements: the **Iglesia Nuestra Señora de la Regla** (built between 1687 and 1711) in the center is quite striking with its extremely fine portico. The stonework here, with all its floral geometrical patterns, clearly betrays Latin American influence. The church is named after the patron saint of Havana, Cuba, and the Virgin at the altar is also thought to have been brought back here by a wealthy emigrant.

From Pájara there's a detour to **Ajuy ⑮** on the west coast, a fishing village still largely untouched by tourism, with two restaurants on its pebble beach and accommodation provided by local boarding

houses. Try the path that leads from the black sand beach northwards via the steep coast to the old harbor of Ajuy. A layer of limestone has risen from the water here, and has some fine natural formations along it.

Steps hewn out of the rock a little further north provide access to the bay of **Caleta Negra**, with its two enormous caves: the first one ends at the sea after around 150 meters, while the second is longer and darker, so bring a powerful flashlight if you plan to explore it – and don't go inside if the surf is up. On the trip back to Pájara there's a worthwhile detour on the left after two kilometers to the **Barranco de la Madre del Agua**, a palm valley with pools and a little stream – ideal for a brief rest stop.

The road leading towards the Jandía Peninsula from Pájara passes through a thinly-populated mountainous region with very little vegetation. Much of the area towards the west has been sealed off by the military. Several high peaks can be seen, including **La Tablada** (619 meters) and the **Montaña Cardón** (691 meters). This trip is at its most spectacular and romantic when made at sunset.

In **La Pared ⑯**, where the road reaches the coast again, a vacation center is being planned, and a golf academy, luxury hotel and real estate office have already been built, along with an incredibly kitschy avenue. The only reasonably remote place around here is the **Playa del Viejo Rey** to the south, on a wild section of rocky coastline.

The name *La Pared* ("The Wall") refers to a land wall that once apparently separated the Jandía Peninsula from the rest of the island during ancient times. Béthencourt's chroniclers refer to it as the wall separating the two kingdoms of Maxorata and Jandía. In 1983, it was apparently used as a source of material by a construction company, and now very little remains apart from a few rocks up at the northern end.

Crossing the **Istmo de la Pared** isthmus in a southerly direction, you'll get your first look at the sand and dune landscape of the Jandía Peninsula. The vegetation here is typical of Fuerteventura, consisting mainly of the *aulaga majorera*, a thorny plant. The southern coast road is reached again by **Matas Blancas**.

If you feel like exploring more of the interior from Pájara, you can take a scenically attractive route via **Toto** to **Tuineje** ⑰. Although the town is the center of a *Municipio*, it's still a very sleepy place. Things were very different in 1740, when 37 farmers – armed with just five muskets and various bizarre agricultural implements – hurried here to fight a 50-man English pirate troop that had arrived with guns and cannon. On the **Montaña de Tamacite** (346 meters) to the south, the farmers actually won by advancing behind their field dromedaries, waiting behind their animals for the first salvo from the English, and then charging before the enemy had time to reload. Thirty Englishmen and five *Majoreros* (the Fuerteventurans' own name for themselves) were killed that day, and two captured cannon can still be seen in front of the museum in Betancuria.

The historic incident has also been immortalized in a painting at the foot of the altar in the **Iglesia de San Miguel Árcangel** (18th century), and a colorful "battle" is still the highlight of annual fiesta (late September/early October).

In the northern village of **Tiscamanita** ⑱, a windmill converted into a museum documents the mills of Fuerteventura. In the **Centro de Interpretación de los Molinos** you can find exhibits and also literature on the subject of windmills.

Antigua – Center of Art

The capital of the island from 1835 onwards was **Antigua** ⑲. Located in a fertile valley, the town – founded in 1485 – is

Right: The chapel of La Ampuyenta with all its fascinating frescoes and paintings.

a center of island culture. At the entrance to the town you can see modern art in the form of iron sculptures. A folklore fair and a large craft market (held on the second Sunday of every month from 10 a.m. to 4 p.m.) underline the creative role played by Antigua.

The single-aisled **Iglesia Nuestra Señora de Antigua** (1785) in the town center has a good *mudéjar* ceiling and also a *Last Judgment* painting.

Leave the town center heading north and you'll come to one of the finer new creations on the island, up on a windswept rise: a renovated windmill is surrounded by the museum village known as **Molino de Antigua**, built under the supervision of César Manrique. There are exhibition halls on art, history and archeology here, a restaurant (usually fully booked) where cookery students can practice on their guests, studios for artists and craftsmen, a craft goods shop, a cactus garden and also a conference hall. The whole place does jar slightly with the more practical, down-to-earth reality of Fuerteventura as a whole.

There's a real artistic jewel five kilometers to the north in **La Ampuyenta** ⑳. Behind a conspicuous hospital building (1891) which was never used lies the carefully renovated little ★**Iglesia de San Pedro de Alcántara**, the interior of which is packed full of frescoes and paintings. Even the pulpit is covered with them. Nowhere else on the island is there such rich and diverse art, and the monumental paintings on the side walls of the transept are breathtaking. The cycle of paintings shows episodes from the life of San Pedro. It is assumed that Juan de Miranda (1723-1805) from Gran Canaria was the artist responsible for these, and also for the baroque trompe l'oeil work by the altar. This is a place you should certainly spend some time: the longer you look at the frescoes and paintings, the more astonishing it is that they could have been created in the first place.

After a brief stop in **Casillas del Ángel** ㉑, with its baroque **Iglesia de Santa Ana** (1781, dark lava facade), the journey continues on to Puerto del Rosario.

THE SOUTH AND SOUTHEAST
Beaches and Fishing Villages

The coast road leads southwards from the capital and passes the airport, and seven kilometers later **El Castillo**, also known as **Caleta de Fustes** ㉒, can be seen on a broad bay. This resort village with its white sand beach is considered exemplary: there are no ugly hotel tower blocks, and accommodation is provided in bungalows built in the Moorish-Canarian style. The landmark of this small community is the domed tower of the harbor building by the marina, which houses the Puerto Castillo Restaurant, a bar and a discotheque. There's a wonderful view of the whole place from the rooftop terrace.

The **Playa del Castillo** is ideal for families with children, with its calm sea and clean water. The harbor mole protects against the surf, so this is a good place to learn the rudimentaries of windsurfing without being repeatedly blown over. Other facilities here include good restaurants, boutiques, sports such as sailing and diving, and excursions with boats, mountain bikes or motorcycles.

Cyclists and pedestrians will enjoy a trip southwards along the coast to the salterns of **Las Salinas** (three kilometers), which is being funded by the EU as an open-air museum. Ancient remains of a settlement were discovered in the **Barranco de la Torre**, south of Las Salinas.

The coast road turns inland at Las Salinas. After around five kilometers you can often see a herd of camels off to the right. This further emphasizes the North African character of the palm-tree-covered landscape, as well as being an ideal distraction for the kids.

Soon the region turns into inhospitable *malpais* ("badlands") where a solidified river of molten lava has made the terrain uncultivable. On the left, a narrow street leads through the Barranco towards the sea, and the fishing village of **Pozo Negro** ㉓. The name means "black well," and the village is primarily visited at weekends, when delicious seafood is served in the restaurants. The **Playa Pozo Negro**, with its dark sand, has colorful fishing boats and nets across it, but isn't that great a place for swimming.

Back on the main road, cross the *Malpais Grande* until you reach a major intersection. A short distance away in the direction of Gran Tarajal is the **Quesería Maxorata** dairy, with its delicious goat's cheese. Southwards, travel a short distance towards the harbor town, and just before you get there turn off left to **Las Playitas** ㉔. This is one of the finest coastal villages on all of Fuerteventura. The cube-like white buildings line the coastal slope, giving the whole place a really Moorish feel. Many wealthy Canarios have their second homes here. At the entrance to the village is a dark sand beach, and there's also a light one a few meters west of the village center. Fishing boats bring in their catches during the afternoon, and the fish is served up shortly afterwards in the seafood restaurant on the promenade.

A detour to the east leads along a narrow asphalt road to the **Punta de la Entallada**. There, roughly 200 meters above the sea, is a massive fortress-like lighthouse (no public access). From the parking lot in front of it you can get a good view of the impressive rocky coastline here.

Gran Tarajal ㉕ is the second-largest town on the island, and owes its growth to the brief heyday enjoyed by its harbor: it was from here that the island's tomatoes were once shipped. Today they are exported from Puerto Rosario instead. The harbor is quite deserted-looking today, apart from the odd fishing boat. The local

kids play soccer on the dark beach, and body-surfers can be seen now and then in the waves with their plastic boards. At first the place seems rather unexciting, but it has a special atmosphere of its own that becomes far more obvious the longer you stay here.

The beach promenade fills up for the *paseo* in the early evening, and business centers around various small shops in the narrow streets. Gran Tarajal isn't trying to be anything special – and this lack of pretension makes it far more authentic than most of the coastal towns on the island of Fuerteventura. Tourists very rarely stray here. One highlight of the town center is a fountain with sea horses spouting water. The church beside it was built in the 20th century, its construction financed by an emigrant returning from Cuba who also introduced metal wind-wheels to the island.

Tarajalejo ㉖ is a strange blend of fishing village and tourist center. Simple, attractively whitewashed and highly picturesque fishermen's houses in narrow alleys are as much a part of the scenery here as modern supermarkets, expensive boutiques, galleries, and the large Club Hotel Tofio with its riding school. The beach, with its imported yellow sand, isn't quite as pleasant as other ones further south, however. Things liven up a lot in the fall, though: there's a fiesta held here from October 8 to 13 each year, known as the *Jurada de San Miguel*.

On the way towards the Jandía Peninsula it's worth stopping at the **Zoo Parque de los Camellos**, near **La Lajita** ㉗. Alongside the apes and birds, the island's flora also takes center stage here. Ponies and dromedaries wait around for vacationers. This is an excellent place to take the kids if you are visiting with your family.

The seaside town is inhabited by fishermen and also by commuters who work in the tourism business on Jandía. Although apartment buildings have been

Right: There are miles of sandy beaches on the Jandía Peninsula.

here for quite some time, the beach still smells far more of sea and fish rather than of coconut suntan oil. Fishermen can often be seen mending their nets, and the marks of the boats in the sand make it clear that they still get used on a daily basis – something that is becoming increasingly rare as tourism gains more of a foothold, and the old traditions gradually die out for good.

THE JANDÍA PENINSULA

The long southwestern point of Fuerteventura, with its broad beaches, desert-like sand-dune landscapes and wild, rocky coasts was made into a nature reserve in 1987, the **Parque Natural de Jandía**. The first large settlement to the west of the Istmo de la Pared is **Costa Calma ㉘**, with an infrastructure largely tailored towards German-speaking visitors. The vacation area lies on either side of the much-traveled road, surrounded by parks with luxuriant foliage and flowers. Most hotels offer a broad range of sports

and entertainment activities, and there are restaurants and bars for the evenings – though it must be said that the standards of cuisine here are generally lower than elsewhere on the island.

The highlight of Costa Calma is the miles-long sandy beach of **Playa Barca** to the southwest, with its clean waters; it's easy to find a quiet, sheltered spot here even during peak season. Windsurfers are particularly fond of this beach.

The ****Playas de Sotavento de Jandía** extend for around 20 kilometers from here, with spectacular golden beaches, sand dunes and sparkling lagoons. Various small urban settlements, bungalows and luxury hotels have sprung up along their length, but without unduly damaging the sense of vastness.

The highlight here is the endless beach near the two large dunes of ***Risco del Paso**, with several lagoons and a sandy promontory. Families with kids really appreciate the clear waters here and the relatively calm sea. Its various greenish-blue tones are further accentuated by the

windsurfers' colorful sails and the white crests on the waves. Follow the signs to the nearby **Mirador** and you can photograph this miniature paradise.

Jandía Playa and Morro Jable

The tourism industry is back in full swing at **Jandía Playa ㉙**: holiday clubs, hotels, bungalows, shopping centers, restaurants, bars and discotheques can be found all over the largest vacation center on Fuerteventura. There are some emptyish beaches around here, too, however, such as the almost 50-meter-wide fine sand beach of **Playa de Matorral** between Jandía and Morro Jable, which has the odd secluded spot along its edges.

Most of the tourists here are German, and water sports, beach ball and beach gymnastics are all very popular. Individualists tend to ride off on bicycle or motorbike tours of the surrounding area. In the

Above: Paella, the Spanish national dish, is a real hit on the beach.

evenings, too, Jandía Playa, with its discos, bars and pubs, is one of the liveliest places on the otherwise rather sleepy Fuerteventura.

The holiday center of **Morro Jable**, located very close by and accessible on foot, developed from a proper town. Naturally the old fishing infrastructure has long since been superseded by hotels, but when the old men of the town play their guitars and timples on the promenade during the evenings, you still get a sense of old Canarian life. The car ferry from Las Palmas de Gran Canaria docks in the large harbor to the west.

Still further to the west is a dusty track that leads 20 kilometers across the inhospitable terrain to the **Punta de Jandía**. Four-wheel-drive vehicles and mountain bikes can be rented in Morro Jable for this trip, and roughly 10 kilometers into it there's a left turn to the **Playa de Juan Gómez**, with its attractive mixture of black and golden sand, plus a path leading off to the equally attractive **Playa de las Pilas** a little further on.

The last place of habitation in the west of Fuerteventura is godforsaken **Puerto de la Cruz ③**, nestling in the shadow of a modern wind-power installation. A bar and a restaurant provide visitors – most of them traveling in four-wheel-drives – with refreshment. The whole place is reminiscent of an American road movie. Out at the Punta de Jandía itself there is a lighthouse.

Things become increasingly desolate and remote – but also more spectacular – as you head north at this point to the striking **Punta Pesebre**, which can be reached along a narrow asphalt road; there's a great view of the coastline from here, and also a good hike along a stony path to the 189-meter-high mountain – or rather hill – of **Las Talahijas**.

On the way back towards Morro Jable a turnoff near Las Pilas leads away northwards to a 400-meter-high pass. There's a very windy **Mirador** up here, but if you can withstand the gusts you'll very much enjoy the view across the north coast of the Jandía Peninsula and the sandy beach of **Playa de Cofete**, with the 12-kilometer-long **Playa de Barlovento** to the east of it.

Cofete ③ consists of just a few houses and shacks with wind wheels and TV antennas, and is another seemingly godforsaken place. Don't lose heart if you're feeling thirsty, however: there's actually a small bar with a terrace here!

The nearby **Villa Winter**, beneath the 807-meter-high **Mt. Jandía**, the highest peak on the island, belongs to the descendants of a mysterious German named Gustav Winter, who enjoyed the protection of Franco during the latter's regime. Some say he ran a secret submarine base in southwest Fuerteventura during World War II for the German navy.

By the way, if you feel like going for a swim at this point to recover from the strains of the journey, don't even consider it – the currents here are exceptionally dangerous.

FUERTEVENTURA

🛬 *ARRIVAL:* **By Plane**: *Aeropuerto del Rosario*, 6 kilometers south of Puerto del Rosario, tel. 928-851250. Rental car, currency exchange. Inter-island flights: *Binter*, tel. 928-860511.

By Ship: *Naviera Armas* shipping company, Puerto del Rosario: tel. 928-851542 and 928-531560. Speedboat Las Palmas de Gran Canaria – Puerto del Rosario, car ferry Gran Canaria – Morro Jable. Lanzarote (Playa Blanca) – Corralejo (30 minutes) Arrecife – Puerto del Rosario (3 hours).

Bus: The bus network run by the *Tiadhe* company connects the larger towns on the island.

ℹ Kiosk in the airport, info about accommodation, transportation, sights, tel. 928-851250.

THE NORTHEAST

PUERTO DEL ROSARIO

🏨 😊😊 **Parador Nacional de Fuerteventura**, Playa Blanca 45, tel. 928-851150, fax. 928-851158. Colonial-style, excellent restaurant, 2 kilometers south of Puerto del Rosario.

🏛 **Casa Museo Unamuno**, near the church, Calle Virgen del Rosario; Tue-Fri 10 am to 1 pm, 5 to 8 pm, Sat and Sun 10:30 am to 1 pm, admission free.

🎵 *DISCOS:* **Taifa**, Calle Juan Tadeo Cabrera 2; **La Fábrica**, in a factory on the road to Tetir.

➕ **Red Cross**: Avda. de la Constitución 3, tel. 928-851376; **Police**: Avda. de Juan Béthencourt, tel. 928-850909.

📮 *POST OFFICE:* Calle Primer de Mayo 58, tel. 928-850412.

🚕 *TAXI:* Tel. 928-850059 and 928-850216.

ℹ **Patronato de Turismo**: Calle Primero de Mayo 33, tel. 928-851024, fax. 928-851812, 928-851695.

THE NORTH

CORRALEJO

🏨 😊😊😊 **Hotel Riu Palace Tres Islas**, Avda. de las Grandes Playas, tel. 928-535700, fax. 928-535858. Large complex near the dunes.

😊😊 **Hotel La Posada**, Calle María Santana Figueroa 10, tel. 928-867344, fax. 928-536352. Pleasant, central, roof terrace pool; **Hoplaco**, Avda. General Franco, tel./fax. 928-866040. Shady garden, simple, comfortable apartments. 😊 **Hotel Corralejo**, Calle Colón 12, tel. 928-535246. Clean, centrally located, popular with windsurfers and backpackers.

❌ **Restaurante / Cantina Méxicana Pancho Villa**, Calle Prim 16, tel. 928-535014, Mexicăn, Tue-Thu 6 pm to midnight; **Sagar**, Calle Lepanto/Avda. Juan Carlos I, tel. 928-867301, Indian, also vegetarian, Tue-Thu 6 to 11:30 pm; **Vicoletto**, Calle La Ballena 6, close to the harbor, nice pizzeria, bar, closed Wed; **Don Juan** and **Café de París**, Avda. General Franco. Two good cafés, centrally located, and they bake their own cakes. **The Big Blue**, Avda. Grandes Playas 3, tel. 928-867411. Blue stylish bar with a sea aquarium, live performances and parties. In summer daily 6 pm to 2:30 am, in winter from 8 pm. Some largely British **surfer bars** in the Centro Atlántico, Ende Avda. General Franco, e.g. **Sandpiper** (English breakfast).

BOAT TRIPS: From Corralejo to the Isla de los Lobos and El Papagayo (Lanzarote) with the **Catamaran Visión Submarina**, tel. 928-509810/820, or the glass-bottomed boat **El Majorero**, kiosk at the entrance to the pedestrian precinct; daily 9 am to noon and 6:30 to 9:30 pm.

DEEP-SEA FISHING: With the catamaran **Pez Velero** daily except Sun from Corralejo, tel. 928-866173.

MOTORBIKES / MOUNTAIN BIKES: **Mal Fun Club**, Avda. General Franco. Motorbikes, scooters, trikes and mountain bikes for rent. tel. 928-867541, 928-535152, Mon-Sun 9 am to 1 pm, Mon-Sat also 6 to 9 pm; **Vulcano Biking**, Calle Acorazado España 10, tel. 928-535706. Cycle hire, tours organized, offers also available for surfers.

DIVING: **Dive Center Corralejo**, tel. 928-866243, Mon-Sat boat trips with two dives 8:30 am to 1:30 pm.

TENNIS: Courses at **Academia Tenis Francisco González**, Avda. Islas Canarias 11, tel. 928-535715, fax. 928-535782.

BODY-SURFING / WINDSURFING: **Ineika Fun Center**, tel. 928-535744. Surfing courses, equipment; **Canary Surfing**, tel. 928-536299. Windsurfing courses, equipment; **Flag Beach Windsurf Center**, tel./fax. 928-535539; **Ventura Surf**, tel./fax. 928-866295; **Fanatic**, Avda. Grandes Playas, tel. 928-866486, fax. 928-866068.

Red Cross: Tel. 928-860000; **Clinica Médica Brisamar**, open 24 hours, Avda. General Franco, tel. 928-536402; **International Medical Center**, Avda. General Franco 13, in the Hotel Duna Park, tel. 928-536432, also house calls daily 9 am to 8 pm.

POST OFFICE: Calle Lepanto 31, tel. 928-535055.
VOYAGES: **Naviera Armas**, office at harbor, tel. 928-867080; **Líneas Fred Olsen**, at harbor, tel. 928-535090.

EL COTILLO

Apartamentos Cotillo Lagos, tel. 928-175388/389, fax. 928-852099. Near the beach, Urbanización Los Lagos.

Panadería/Pastelería Los Cabezones, Calle Santo Tomás, tel. 928-538668, good bread; **Bar Restaurante La Marisma**, Calle Santo Tomás, tel. 928-538543, good paella, seafood, fish.

DIVING: **El Cotillo Diving**, Coto Grande de Mascona, 3, tel./fax. 928-175011, courses, equipment.

POST OFFICE: Calle Santo Domingo, tel. 928-538539.

LA OLIVA

Museo La Cilla, Tue-Sun 10:30 am to 6:30 pm; **Centro de Arte Canario Casa Mané**, tel. 928-868233, daily 10 am to 5 or 6 pm.

Caminata, Villaverde near La Oliva, tel. 928-535010. Organized hiking tours.

Casa Marcos, in Villaverde, north of La Oliva, tel. 928-868285. Ceramics, Canarian crafts, Fri-Wed 9:30 am to 3 pm and 4 to 7 pm; **La Ermita**, ceramic workshop outside La Oliva, Mon-Sat 9 am to 6 pm.

POST OFFICE: Calle Franco 14, tel. 928-868065.

LAJARES

Café Central, surfers' hangout with live music. **La Casa del Artesano y del Calado**, tel. 928-868341. Crafts shop with restaurant (La Caldera), goat's cheese sold; daily 9 am to 7 pm; **Artesanía Lajares**, crafts center in the middle of the village.

THE MIDWEST

AGUAS VERDES

Club Aguas Verdes, tel. 928-878350, fax. 928-878360. Quiet, remote, sports facilities, fitness.

ANTIGUA

Molino de Antigua, north of the town center, tel. 928-851400, with restaurant, daily 10 am to 6 pm.

POST OFFICE: Calle Peña Brito 11, tel. 928-878516.

TAXI: Tel. 928-878011.

BETANCURIA

Restaurante Casa Santa María, tel. 928-878782. In a renovated manor house, one of the best on the island, not exactly cheap though. Lamb, smoked salmon, crafts, ceramics, agrarian products.

Mirador Morro Velosa, observation point, Canarian restaurant; daily 10 am to 6 pm; **Iglesia/Museo de Arte Sacro**, Calle Alcalde Carmelo Silvera; Mon-Fri 9:30 am to 5 pm, Sat 9:30 am to 2 pm; **Museo Arqueológico**, Calle Roldán, tel. 928-878241, Tue-Sat 10 am to 5 pm, Sun 11 am to 2 pm.

TAXI: Tel. 928-878094.

LA PARED

☒ **Bar Restaurante El Camello**, tel. 928-549090/1. Spanish regional dishes, Tue-Sun 1 pm to midnight.

🏌 *GOLF:* **Driving Range**, tel./fax. 928-161052/62, for professionals and beginners, daily 10 am to 6 pm.

PÁJARA

☒ **Bar Restaurante La Fonda**, in the center, Calle Nuestra Señora de Regla 23, tel. 928-161625. Grill specialties Tue-Thu 9:30 am to 11 pm.

TISCAMANITA

🏛 **Centro de Interpretación de los Molinos**, windmill museum, tel. 928-851400, daily 10 am to 6 pm.

VEGA RÍO PALMA

➕ **Centro de Salud**, Calle San Sebastián, tel. 928-878455.

THE SOUTH AND SOUTHEAST

CALETA DE FUSTES

🏨 😊😊 **Barceló Club Castillo**, east of the harbor, tel. 928-163046, fax. 928-163042. Pleasant, well-tended bungalow complex, with tennis, squash, windsurfing and diving.

☒ **Bar Restaurante Puerto Castillo**, at the harbor, first floor, tel. 928-163100/101. Excellent international cooking, also vegetarian food, open Tue-Sun 6 to 11 pm.

🤿 *DIVING:* **Dressel Divers Club International**, tel. 928-163554. Diving courses, free beginners' lessons. Similar offers: **El Castillo** diving center, on the mole, tel. 928-878100.

WINDSURFING: **Escuela de Windsurfing del Castillo**, tel. 928-163100.

SUBMARINE TRIP: The **Nautilus** makes trips from the harbor.

COSTA CALMA

🏨 😊😊😊 **Risco del Gato**, Polígono D2, tel. 928-547 175, fax. 928-547030. Bungalow hotel with pool, sauna, tennis, golf, gourmet restaurant.

😊😊 **Bungalows Bahía Calma**, tel. 928-547158. Pretty bungalows on the beach.

🚕 *TAXI:* Tel. 928-547032.

GRAN TARAJAL

🏨 😊 **Hostal Tamonante**, Calle Juan Carlos I, tel. 928-870348, 928-162472. Small, clean, the only place to stay, popular with backpackers.

➕ **Centro de Salud**, Calle Tindaya 2, tel. 928-870 889.

🚕 *POST OFFICE:* Plaza de la Candelaria, tel. 928-870334.

🚕 *TAXI:* Tel. 928-870059.

JANDÍA PLAYA

🏨 😊😊😊 **Hotel Club Jandía Princess**, Urbanización Esquinzo, tel. 928-544089, fax. 928-544097. Andalusian-Moorish style, six pools, six tennis courts, 20-kilometer-long sand beach; **Hotel Iberostar Palace**, Urbanización Las Gaviotas, tel. 928-540444, fax. 928-540405. Slightly outside, long sand beach, three pools, squash, sailing, windsurfing, diving.

☒ **Restaurante Don Carlos**, Edificio Don Carlos, tel. 928-540485. At the Robinson Club good servings, Spanish cuisine, closed Tue.

🤿 *ROBINSON CLUB:* Tennis, diving for guests of the **Robinson Club**, windsurfing courses, catamaran excursions also for non-guests, tel. 928-541375/376. Similar offers available in the **Club Aldiana**, tel. 928-541447/448.

DIVING: **Barakuda Club**, next to Residencia Atlántic, main street, tel. 928-541418, fax. 928-541417.

WINDSURFING / MOUNTAIN BIKING: **Pro Center**, Hotel Sol Gorriones, tel. 928-547025/026/050, fax. 928-870850.

➕ **Centro Médico**, tel. 928-540420 and 928-541543.

ℹ **Oficina de Turismo**: Avda. del Saladar, tel. 928-540776, fax. 928-541023.

LA LAJITA

🏛 **Zoo Parque Los Camellos**, dromedary and pony rides, tel. 928-161135, daily 9 am to 7:30 pm.

MORRO JABLE

🏨 😊😊😊 **Hotel Riu Calypso**, Carretera General, tel. 928-541522, fax. 928-540730, on the beach.

😊 **Hostal Maxorata**, Calle Maxorata 31, tel. 928-540725, 928-540474, simple, popular with backpackers; **Pensión Omahy**, Calle Maxorata 6, tel. 928-541254, for backpackers.

☒ **Restaurante La Gaviota**, on the beach promenade, fish, Canarian live music.

🚕 *POST OFFICE:* Plaza Pública, tel. 928-540373.

🚕 *VOYAGES:* **Naviera Armas**: Tel. 928-542113 and 928-542457.

TAXI: Tel. 928-541257.

ℹ **Oficina de Tourismo**, in the Centro Comercial, Avda. del Saladar, tel. 928-540776.

TARRAJALEJO

🏨 😊😊 **Hotel Tofio**, on the beach, tel. 928-161001, fax. 928-161028, pool, disco, sports facilities. Riding in the hotel's own **Centro Hípico**, tel. 928-161351.

GRAN CANARIA
Holiday Island to Suit All Tastes

BEACHES IN THE SOUTH
THE IMPENETRABLE WEST
THE MILD NORTH
LAS PALMAS DE GRAN CANARIA
THE ARID EAST
THE INTERIOR

Gran Canaria

Broad Beaches, Craggy Coastline

After Tenerife, Gran Canaria is the biggest tourist attraction of the Canary Islands. Germans are top of the tourist list, making up almost a third of the visitors, followed by the British and Spaniards from the mainland. Most of the vacationers stay in the large hotel and apartment regions on the south coast of the island. Lonely beaches are few and far between around here, but if you appreciate a beach holiday with a mixture of relaxation and variety, visit the attractive sand beaches and the magnificent dune landscape of Maspalomas, and then indulge in all the water sports facilities before plunging into the nightlife.

The island's capital, Las Palmas de Gran Canaria, is also growing increasingly popular. It has good hotels and boarding houses, the municipal beach of Las Canteras, elegant stores and a broad range of cultural activities. A new kind of tourism is also developing to cater for travelers with individual tastes: you can live in the renovated fincas, for instance, that are strewn all over the island. The

Previous pages: Maspalomas – mini-Sahara in the south of Gran Canaria. Left: Calle Mayor de Triana – stylish shopping street (Las Palmas de Gran Canaria).

green north of the island is also very popular now: bike tours and hiking trips can be taken through places like the pine forest of Tamadaba. Traditional buildings with carved wooden balconies and richly decorated churches can still be found in towns such as Gáldar, Teror and Telde.

Gran Canaria's beauty is mainly evident in the central mountain region, with the 1,949-meter-high Pico de las Nieves and the 1,817-meter-high Roque Nublo. Cragged rock formations at the summits, resembling prehistoric steles, were considered holy by the islands' ancient inhabitants; to today's visitors they are more reminiscent of Wild West movies. Deep gorges *(barrancos)* and glittering reservoirs add to the attraction of this breathtaking mountain scenery.

Arrival

If you're traveling to Gran Canaria by ferryboat, you usually arrive in Las Palmas harbor; the ferry from Tenerife also travels to Puerto de las Nieves, the harbor of Agaete. Most international visitors arrive at the only major airport, the **Aeropuerto de Gando** in the east of the island. Located 22 kilometers from the capital, the airport is a hub of international, national and interinsular air traffic, and provides all modern amenities, from banking services to rental cars. A well-paved highway connects the Aeropuerto de Gando with the capital and the tourist centers to the south. Buses leave for Las Palmas every 20 minutes, and there are numerous taxis available, too.

BEACHES IN THE SOUTH

Most vacationers take their package holidays in the hotels that line the sun-soaked south of Gran Canaria. It's not surprising, therefore, that the apartment complexes along the beaches here are usually booked out in high season.

You can lie in the sand and relax, take part in the extensive hotel activity programs, or try your hand at sports: windsurfing, diving, water-skiing, paragliding, horseback riding and golf are just as much on offer as tennis, squash, mountain biking and volleyball. There's also a lively multinational pub scene.

Once you've grown accustomed to the uniform-looking phony urbanity of it all, you'll soon realize that life in the hotel complexes is comfortable, and that the attractive, subtropical parks and gardens are often a colorful way of concealing an odd architectural eyesore. Naturally, there are some regions that stand out positively from the rest, one of them being Puerto de Mogán (see p. 87) on the southwest coast, where planners were careful to harmonize the new buildings with the old town center and the surrounding landscape. This kind of success, however, is rare, and the homogeneity of Manrique's Lanzarote is conspicuous by its absence. He did give local architects pause for thought, however, and even though financial considerations still tend to outweigh esthetic ones, there seems to be a gradual realization among planners that landscape must play a part.

Highway GC1 from the airport to the south runs along a broad and almost desert-like strip of coast, nearly parallel to the road. Barren, rocky mountains can

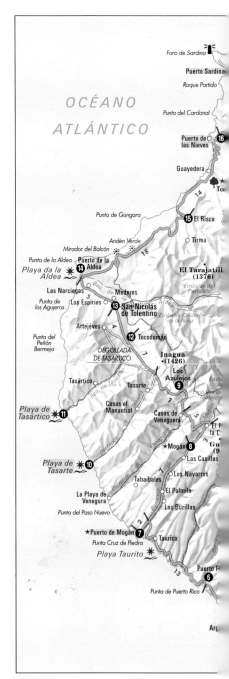

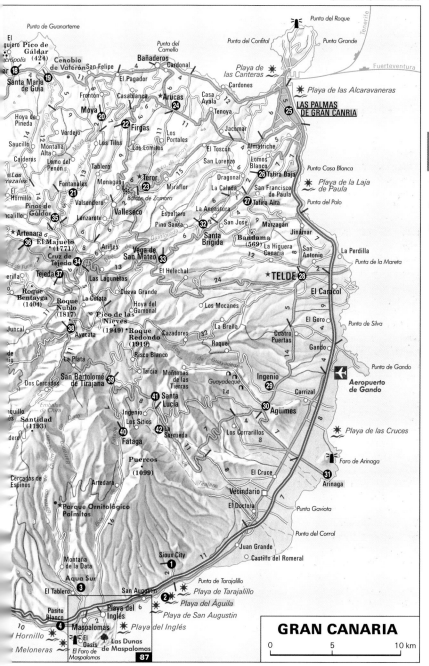

Gran Canaria

GRAN CANARIA

0   5   10 km

83

be seen along the horizon to the west. Shortly before the **Playa de Tarajalillo** you can change from the highway to the main road. The airplane beside it indicates the presence of the **Aeroclub de Gran Canaria** flying club.

Branch off to the right through the **Cañon del Águila** to the western town of **Sioux City ❶**, where visitors tired of beaches can enjoy Wild West shows (the buses run from Playa del Inglés and Maspalomas; closed Mondays).

The **Playa del Águila ❷** marks the start of a series of beaches connected to each other by promenades, and extending a distance of around eight kilometers as far as Playa del Inglés and the dunes of Maspalomas.

The father of surfing champion Björn Dunkerbeck has set up a surfing school on the Playa del Águila. The small, sandy beach with its clear water mainly attracts

Above: Playa de San Agustín – sun, sand and hordes of people. Right: Maspalomas – just perfect for surfing in a steady breeze.

young people. This whole stretch of coast, with its steady winds, is ideal for windsurfing. Even if you're a beginner, just go and ask for a lesson – you'll wobble around and get wet for the first hour or so, but it's astonishing how quickly you learn. Don't forget to wear sun protection, though – things can get very hot once you've learned how not to fall in all the time!

Next door, on the very neat and tidy **Playa de San Agustín**, all generations join together to relax in the sun. This part of the coast is especially popular with Germans. The beach extends for about two kilometers, and there are numerous apartment blocks and hotels with leafy parks around them. Guests can either swim in the sea or in the hotels' own pools. Pedestrian footbridges provide access to the beach from the hotels on the other side of the main road. As far as nightlife is concerned, the discos and bars of the hotels provide evening entertainment, and there's a casino in the luxurious *Melia Tamarindos Sol* beach hotel.

Gran Canaria

Playa del Ingles and Maspalomas – The Tourist Machine

If the beaches mentioned so far were reasonably quiet and peaceful, the **Playa del Inglés** ❶ is busy and loud. Either you love it or you hate it – some people come here only to leave in disgust, others spend years returning to the same place and can't seem to get enough of it. No worries about having to do without your local newspaper from back home, or not being able to speak Spanish: the waiters and shopkeepers are real linguistic geniuses. A seemingly endless stream of visitors moves along the beach in both directions all day long. You can watch windsurfers fighting the wind, and yachts doing risky maneuvers.

Of course, this vacation location has a very busy nightlife, with bars, discos and amusement arcades. You can play bingo, eat Black Forest cake, drink Guinness and yodel with Bavarians. The massive shopping centers – especially the **Kasbah** ❷ on the Plaza del Teide and the **Yumbo** ❸ on Avenida de España – are packed full of jewelry, fashion, electronic articles, souvenirs and groceries from all over the world. It's strange that the built-up conglomeration of restaurants, souvenir shops and amusement arcades should be so close to an astonishingly beautiful and relatively unspoiled area: the Playa del Inglés is almost seamlessly connected with the magnificent, kilometer-wide dune area known as ****Las Dunas de Maspalomas** ❹. This is where all those masses of tourists get lost, and in the middle of the golden yellow sand dunes the (often nude) sunbathers are greeted by relaxing silence. Wandering through this protected natural park is like being in a miniature Sahara Desert – especially when a "camel caravan" moves by.

The area on the western edge of Maspalomas is called **El Oasis**. **La Charca** ❺, the remains of a lagoon with reeds around the edge, borders a grove of palm trees. Entering the lagoon area is forbidden, because the reeds are home to nesting waterfowl. The highest lighthouse in all the Canary Islands, **El Faro de Maspalomas** ❻ (65 meters), marks the southernmost point of the island. Hotels, restaurants and stores have spread out beneath it. To the north of the lagoon is the starting point for the camel safaris, as well as the gold course and the squash courts. The **Holiday World** ❼ amusement park and the **Océano Parque Acuatico Maspalomas** ❽ water park are both ideal for families with children.

To the north of Maspalomas, in the suburb of El Tablero, you'll find the water park of **Aqua Sur** ❸ (on the right after you've passed under the highway), and an excursion high up into the rocky Barranco de Chamoriscan leads 12 kilometers later to the *Parque Ornitológico Palmitos** (served regularly by bus from Playa del Ingles). This 200,000-square-meter area is an artificial biotope with around 1,000 palm trees, a cactus garden, an orchid and butterfly house, a seawater aquarium and 230 exotic species of bird, some of which have been allowed to fly freely. There's an amusing parrot show for the kids which should not be missed – the birds are trained to do all sorts of amazing feats, such as pedaling on unicycles, lying in deck chairs and actually doing some relatively simple math – and of course there's a souvenir shop and a snack bar here, too.

Six kilometers to the north of the Playa del Inglés (follow the signs to Fataga; there's also a bus connection), up on a hill, there's the "archeological show-park" of **Mundo Aborigen**, introducing visitors to the way the ancient inhabitants of the Canary Islands used to live, in an area covering 100,000 square meters. This place is definitely worth a visit. A village has been reconstructed, as have typical scenes from Canarian aboriginal life, along with their pets, plants and crafts. The whole thing is explained in several different languages, and there's also a live show in which the praises of the brave warriors are sung in their battle

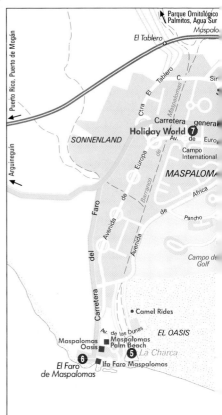

against the Spanish intruders. The usual snack and souvenir stands can also be found here.

Back at the coast you can either take the highway or the well-paved asphalt road, the 812, westwards. Near **Pasito Blanco** ❹ there is a yacht harbor and sailing school, as well as a private campsite. The quieter beaches between Maspalomas and Arguineguín are the **Playa de las Meloneras** and the **Playa del Hornillo**. The highway ends shortly before Arguineguín, and traffic now has to pass along the narrower coast road.

The one-time fishing village of **Arguineguín** ❺ does contain the usual hotel blocks, but its original center has remained largely intact – the only eyesore

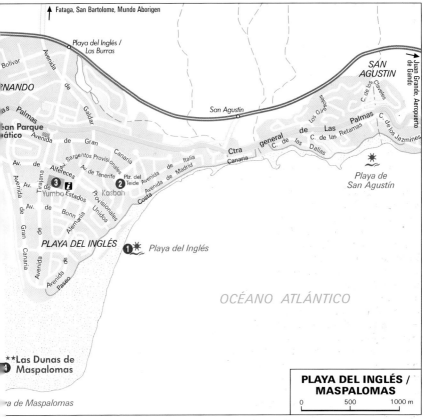

Fataga, San Bartolome, Mundo Aborigen

Playa del Inglés / Las Burras

Bolivar

ʔNANDO

as Palmas

San Parque
ático

Av. de

Playa del Inglés / Las Burras

SAN
AGUSTIN

Juan Grande, Aeropuerto de Gando

San Agustín

Las Giras

Palmas

Avenida de Galdar

Gran Canaria

Sargentos Provisionales

Av. de Tenerife

Italia

general de Las

C. de las Retamas

C. de los Claveles

C. de los Jazmines

Av. de Alférez

Tirajana

Yumbo Estados

Plz. del Teide

Avenida de Madrid

Ctra
Canaria

C. de las Dalias

Kasbah

Provisionales

Costa

Avenida de Av. de Bonn

Alemania

Unidos

PLAYA DEL INGLÉS

Playa del Inglés

Playa de
San Agustín

Avenida de

Gran

Canaria

Avenida de

Paseo

OCÉANO ATLÁNTICO

**Las Dunas de
Maspalomas

a de Maspalomas

**PLAYA DEL INGLÉS /
MASPALOMAS**

0   500   1000 m

Gran Canaria

to speak of being the nearby cement works. At the harbor there is a great restaurant, the *Cofradia de Pescadores*, which serves delicious seafood. A boat makes the Arguineguín – Puerto Rico – Puerto de Mogán trip several times a day (travel time about 90 minutes).

After Arguineguín it's one bay after another. The buildings at **Puerto Rico** ❻ are particularly striking: the apartment complexes here have been packed together quite tightly on the mountain slopes, and it's astonishing how rigorously the tourist industry has exhausted the possibilities of this piece of real estate. The monotony is alleviated somewhat by the luxuriant greenery, which has successfully concealed a great deal of ar-

chitectural evil all over the island. Puerto Rico also has a yachting harbor and a broad sand beach, both of which provide numerous opportunities for different water sports, including windsurfing, sailing and waterskiing.

*Puerto de Mogán

Shortly before Puerto de Mogán, you can reach the grayish-black **Playa Taurito** by going through a barranco with small plantations. This beach, a favorite with backpackers and easy-going sunworshipers, is gradually being developed, but still has a pleasant relaxed atmosphere. Attempts have been made to create a kind of alternative holiday location

at the end of the Barranco de Mogán, the **Puerto de Mogán** ❼. Apart from a tower-like structure at the harbor exit, all the buildings have been kept purposely low, and are connected via promenades and little bridges. The colorful doors and window frames of the holiday apartments blend in very nicely with the gardens and parks. The harmony of the architecture is pleasantly refreshing after the numerous eyesores elsewhere.

One section, closed to cars, has been flooded with seawater to create what is locally referred to as "Little Venice." The pubs, bars and cafés are generally owned by non-residents. The local fishermen live slightly outside the village, up on a slope. The harbor, protected by a mighty quay wall, contains an armada of luxury yachts. The 300-meter-long, gently sloping sand beach of **Playa de Mogán** is actually artificial, even though it looks extremely realistic.

Above: Puerto de Mogán – a Canarian "Little Venice." Right: Not the smallest of tuna!

THE IMPENETRABLE WEST
Craggy Mountains, Remote Beaches

The west of Gran Canaria is one of its wildest but also most impressive regions. The road leads north from Puerto de Mogán through the Barranco de Mogán, and then heads up inland. This thinly-populated area contains banana, mango and papaya plantations. Before you reach the pretty town of Mogán you'll see some oversized – sometimes man-sized – household utensils at the roadside, such as coffee pots, coffee mills and irons. They stand there almost all year long and are sometmes carried along on parades. There are also the remains of an old wind-mill – just the renovated shell. Foreign residents and artists have created their own individual refuge in the various elegant houses dotted around ★**Mogán** ❽.

This town, idyllically situated on the slopes of the 932-meter-high **Guirre**, is a popular starting point for tours and hikes in jeeps through the surrounding area. One good excursion leads along a narrow track with hairpin bends, through the Barranco de Mogán, and to the reservoirs of **Embalse de Mulato**, **Embalse de Cueva de las Niñas** (with a cave), and **Embalse de Soria**. The track then continues inland as far as Ayacata (see p. 115). A word of warning, by the way – this stretch of road seems to be a permanent construction site, so beware of potholes and other obstacles.

The 810 bends dramatically westwards just past Mogán and then winds its way through some very rugged mountain scenery, with numerous barrancos all leading to the sea. The first one, the **Barranco de Veneguera**, has become a political issue because environmentalists want to protect it and its beach from tourists. The island government has, however, given the go-ahead for a project to build holiday apartments here, with accommodation for up to 20,000 people. At the present time it looks increasingly unlikely that the real estate developers can be stopped.

Carry on in the direction of San Nicolas de Tolentino, and beneath the 1,426-meter-high **Inagua** you'll reach a place known as **Los Azulejos** ❾, so named because of its resemblance to the blue tiles that often adorn Portuguese buildings. This is a fascinating geological formation: iron has colored several rock and pumice strata here bluish-green. There's a bar to quench your thirst, and information on a number of other hikes where you can see even more colorful rocks is also available here.

The next turnoff in the direction of the sea leads through the fertile Barranco de Tasarte as far as the black **Playa de Tasarte** ❿. Huts and fishing boats make the place extremely idyllic. The water is also quite shallow here, and is suitable for young bathers, too. Locals come here at weekends and the beach bar gets extremely crowded.

It's (still) a lot less busy at the neighboring **Playa de Tasártico** ⓫, which can

Gran Canaria

be reached via the Degollada de Tasártico Pass (550 meters) shortly before Tocodomán. The new road down in the valley will soon make the beach easily accessible. Getting into the water for a swim here is difficult because of the slippery rocks, though. At **Tocodomán** ⓬ there's a **Cactus Garden** with around two million specimens from all over the world.

San Nicolás de Tolentino

San Nicolás de Tolentino ⓭ is the main tomato-growing region on Gran Canaria. The fields, with their plastic sheets protecting the plants, can be seen from a long way off. Apart from the houses, the whole valley looks like something produced by Christo, the packaging artist.

San Nicolás is one of the oldest settlements on the island, and was the destination of numerous Christian missionaries from Mallorca during the 14th century. In a squabble over land rights which lasted for over 300 years, the villagers finally

managed to defeat the noble family of Villanueva del Prado in 1911 and obtain land for their own private cultivation.

From San Nicolás you can take a spectacular tour of the interior. A narrow asphalt road with plenty of bends (often with just one lane) leads through the canyon-like Barranco de la Aldea, one of the most impressive of its kind on the island. The route then continues through a craggy section of mountain landscape and past a chain of reservoirs before finally arriving at Artenara, at 1,250 meters the highest village on Gran Canaria.

If you prefer to stay at the coast, visit the pebble beach of **Playa de la Aldea**, located south of the fishing village of **Puerto de la Aldea ⑭**. Small restaurants serve delicious seafood, and the view of the sun setting behind the silhouette of Tenerife in the evening is very impressive. The only time this place gets busy is during the *Fiesta del Charco* (September

Above: A profusion of cacti in Tocodomán.
Right: Luxuriant vegetation near Agaete.

11) and on weekends. The fiesta involves standing in a pond and getting sprayed with water.

Puerto de las Nieves and *Agaete

The road now passes several observation points with fantastic views across the rocky coast and the sea. At the **Mirador del Balcón** (with kiosk) the cliffs fall 400 meters down to the sea below; a little further on, near the observation point of **Andén Verde**, the rocks are even higher. It's worth taking a closer look at the sea through binoculars here – you may see the odd large fish just below the surface.

The small village of **El Risco ⑮** with its *Bar Perdomo* is a good place to refresh yourself before continuing the trip down into the valley. On the sea below you can usually see at least one of the ferry boats that ply between Gran Canaria and Tenerife. They're headed for **Puerto de las Nieves**, the harbor of Agaete (see next page), reached via a left turn just before you reach Agaete. Ever since the ferry connection was established here, the place has become busier; beforehand the only excitement was the fiesta in honor of the *Virgen de las Nieves*. Restaurants serve fresh seafood down by the harbor; the black sand and rocky beaches here and beneath the mountain slope take a bit of getting used to. The steep rock formation known as the **Dedo de Díos** ("Finger of God") is popular with photographers, and is especially attractive when viewed from the harbor.

The most valuable artifact in this town is the triptych in the **Ermita de Nuestra Señora de las Nieves**, possibly the work of the Flemish painter Joos van Cleve (1485-1540), which shows the "Virgin of the Snows" with the infant Jesus at its center. During the festivities celebrating the *Bajada de la Rama* on August 4 each year, a copy is carried in a solemn procession to the main church of Agaete and put on display there. The festival probably

dates back to an ancient rain ritual, and includes a water-thrashing ceremony in the harbor as a punishment for lack of rain. It's the perfect way to release frustrations, though whether it's effective is quite another matter.

★**Agaete ⓰** is distinctive for its intact center, white houses and narrow alleys. Note the arches on the old bridge across the barranco, and the red cupola on the 19th-century **Iglesia de la Concepción**. Festivals are celebrated in the leafy plaza opposite, otherwise Agaete is a rather sleepy place.

There's a good detour inland at this point, from Ageate to the thermal baths at **Los Berrazales**. The road passes through the Barranco de Agaete with its banana, citrus, mango and avocado plantations, and Los Berrazales can finally be reached via the **Ermita de San Pedro**. The buildings of this former spa are now ruined, but the mineral water can still be used for a cure in the *Princesa Guayarmina* hotel complex. This is just the place to wind down after all that busy sightseeing.

THE MILD NORTH

The northern part of the island is very different from the arid south and the craggy west. Because of its high moisture levels, the north is greener, often cultivated up to high elevations, and dotted with terraced fields. The coastal strip as far as the capital is dominated by plantations and small towns. This high population density has brought a lot of traffic in its wake. Inland things are quieter. The little roads wind their way through the barrancos in hairpin turns, and journeys can take longer than expected. It's worth taking the trouble, however, for the idyllic views across the highly varied mountain and valley scenery.

Gáldar – Guanche Caves

If you leave Agaete and head in the direction of Gáldar, there's a turnoff to the left (signposted) to the **Reptilandia** reptile park, with over 1,000 turtles, snakes and spiders. Shortly afterwards you'll reach the outskirts of Gáldar. If you feel like visiting a beach or enjoying some seafood, turn off to the left before the center to **Puerto Sardina** ⓱. Six kilometers further on you'll reach a black sand beach in a partly built-up bay. Tourists stray here very rarely – and the restaurants on the beach and in the village serve fresh and very delicious seafood.

The signposted **Necropolis de Gáldar** is easier to find by following the signs in the center of Gáldar rather than through the labyrinth of plantations. It's located between the beach of **El Agujero** and a large banana plantation. Near three structures referred to as mausoleums there are the ruins of some buildings thought to have been the apartments of royal advisors *(guaire)*, the ceremonial hall of the high priest *(faicán)*, and rooms occupied by unmarried sacred women *(harimaguadas)*. The necropolis can usually only be inspected from the outside, and there are no regular opening times.

The town of ★**Gáldar** ⓲, on the slopes of the Pico de Gáldar (424 meters), was inhabited as far back as Guanche and Canario times. This is where the kings, known as *guanarteme*, lived in a palace-like structure which later had to make way for a Spanish chapel. The role played by the **Cueva Pintada**, a cave discovered in the town center in 1873, is still unclear. Clay pots and shards were discovered inside it, and are thought to be funerary offerings. There were also several human skeletons. The large geometrical patterns are unusual – there are no comparably well-preserved cave paintings anywhere else on the Canary Islands. The area is closed indefinitely for restoration purposes, unfortunately – but the Museo Canario in Las Palmas contains a copy of a cave wall.

Gáldar is a busy town with a leafy plaza, outside the portals of the mighty

Right: The flower cheese (queso de flor) in Guía is mild-tasting.

three-aisled church of **Santiago de los Caballeros** (1778), which – despite its baroque elements – was the first neoclassical structure on the Canaries. It lies above the foundations of an old Canario palace. A green-glazed font dates from the time the islands were conquered by Spain, and the subjugated population was forced to convert to Christianity. The church also contains an organ with a scale of 4,776 different tones. The statues of the *Purisima*, *Nuestra Señora de la Encarnación*, *Nuestra Señora del Rosario*, of *Nazareno* and *San Sebastián* are all the work of local master Luján Pérez.

If you take a look inside the inner courtyard of the neoclassical **Ayuntamiento** (Town Hall) on the plaza you'll see a very fine 300-year-old **drago** (dragon tree). The **Casa Museo Antonio Padrón** is in honor of one of the city's sons. The artist Padron (1920-68) termed himself a "moderate Expressionist," and the museum is worth a trip just to see his strange paintings on Canarian themes.

Santa María de Guía

Santa María de Guía ⓳, a former suburb of Gáldar, has now become a town in its own right. It was here that the most famous and also most prolific of Canarian sculptors, Luján Pérez (1756-1815), grew up. The **Iglesia de la Santa María de Guía** (begun in 1607) in the old part of town here contains many of his works, from the altar painting to various statues of Christ and the Virgin Mary, including *El Crucificado, El Cristo Predicador, El Cristo de la Columna, El Cristo en el Huerto, La Dolorosa* and *Nuestra Señora de las Mercedes*. The whole church is like a private Luján Pérez museum, in fact. The sculptor presented the clock on the right-hand church tower to the local community. On the church facade, a plaque commemorates a famous visitor: the French composer Camille Saint-Saëns (1835-1921), who stayed here at the end

of the 19th century and composed his "Valse Canariote" after hearing some impressive Canarian folk music. He first arrived here incognito, posing as a wine merchant, but a missing persons announcement in a French daily newspaper finally revealed his identity.

Guía is best-known for its *queso de flor*, or "flower cheese." Artichoke leaves are used in its preparation. You should definitely visit two excellent cheese shops here: the one by the church (Marqués del Muni 34) and the other right on the main street (Carretera General, near the gas station). The owner, who's been working here since he was a child, also sells honey, rum, tapas and craft items.

If you travel east from Guía in the direction of Las Palmas, a road branches off after three kilometers in the direction of something pleasantly mysterious with a special atmosphere all of its own: the ***Cenobio de Valerón**, a refuge with a rear wall honeycombed with caves. The islands' original inhabitants must have

kept a communal granary here under this rocky overhang, where grain was kept in around 300 different caves. Since there was also a place of assembly *(tagoror)* above the caves, it is assumed that the place must also have had a cultic significance, but as with many Guanche sites, its real purpose remains uncertain. Just take some time to soak up the atmosphere of this strange place.

Moya – Gateway to the Hinterland

Further along the 810 in the direction of the capital you'll cross two very fine bridges – one of them is 125 meters above a barranco, and is actually the highest bridge in Spain. Shortly afterwards there's a turnoff southwards into the mountains and **Moya ⑳**, where the gentle hinterland begins. The landmark of this village is its church, the **Iglesia El Pilar**, which was built during the 1940s. It majestically dominates the nearby Barranco de Moya. The church contains a *Virgen de la Candelaria* which was

brought from Tenerife to Moya in the 16th century. Opposite the church square is the **Casa Museo Tomás Morales**, inside the birthplace of Modernist poet Tomás Morales (1884-1921). A doctor by profession, he became famous for his collection of poems entitled *Las Rosas de Hercules*. Poetry readings are held regularly in the museum here, attracting the literarily inclined from all over the islands to this rural location.

The once-majestic building housing the former "water exchange" *(Heredad de Aguas de Chorro)* is in a pitiable condition today. In the old days, those who owned water rights were influential and wealthy, and shares in water were attractive investments. The water was here thanks to extensive laurel forests, most of which have now been removed to make way for fields and farmland. You can still see some of the old trees in the **Barranco**

Above: Cenobio de Valerón – a granary and cultic site of the Guanches. Right: The Virgen del Pino with her intriguing face.

de Laurel, south of Moya. If you turn down the high road from Moya to Guía, a narrow mountain road branches off to the left 2.5 kilometers later near **Los Tilos**, heading south into the barranco. Because of the unpaved road, it's better for environmental reasons to drive to (**San Bartolomé de) Fontanales** ㉑ further south, leave the car there and wander up inside the barranco on foot. In the upper part of it you'll cross some fields, and at the bend there's a good view of the laurel forest located further down.

In **Firgas** ㉒, to the east of Moya, a large mineral water company is profiting from the springs in the region. In the town center this source of wealth has been provided with a suitable monument in the shape of the **Paseo de Gran Canaria**. At the center of a promenade leading down a flight of steps, decorated with tiled coats of arms and island maps, a small stream rushes downwards into the valley. At the bottom end of the promenade is a **cultural center**, and the plaza beside it – flanked by the Town Hall and the **Iglesia**

San Roque – is where everyone, young and old, meets up.

From Firgas, a road winds its way southwards up to an elevation of around 900 meters before going back down shortly before the **Balcón de Zamora**, an observation point with a large restaurant, providing a view of Teror and its surrounding landscape from above.

★Teror – Attractive and Historic

With its old-fashioned renovated facades and balconies, **Teror ㉓** is possibly the most attractive village on the island, and its entire center has been listed as protected since 1979. This peaceful little village is the heart of popular religion on Gran Canaria. The **★Basílica de Nuestra Señora del Pino** (18th century) contains a Madonna figure with an interesting face, one half of which seems to be crying and the other laughing – so it's perfect for the worshipers, who can read anything into it they want. It always seems to show understanding.

Every year on September 7 the *Virgen del Pino* is placed in front of believers under the dome. Before the spectacular robbery of its emeralds in 1975 it was counted among the most valuable Madonna statues in Spain. Strangely enough, the statue is considered so special that it holds the rank of *Capitán General* in the Spanish army – an honor bestowed on it by King Alfonso XIII in 1929 – and because of this, the processions of believers are regularly accompanied by high-ranking soldiers.

The most recent alterations to the appearance of this neoclassical, three-aisled basilica date from 1811, when Lúján Pérez changed the western facade. The church is the third to be built on this site. Its octagonal side-tower survives from the previous structure, which was destroyed in a fire. Inside, the gray basalt columns with their honey-brown capitals look very striking. Alongside figures of

Gran Canaria

saints by Luján Pérez the church also contains the five most important rococo paintings on the island, one of which depicts an angel and several believers roasting in purgatory – among them a pope.

A 17th-century townhouse on the central square contains the **Casa Museo Patrones de la Virgen del Pino**. The Manrique de Lara family, the nobles who own the house, have been the custodians of the Virgen del Pino for four generations. The rooms convey a sense of the former elegance of Gran Canarian culture, and the exhibits range from historical photos and paintings to antique furniture and porcelain. The former stables contain saddles and also the state coach of Alfonso XIII, used when he traveled through the island's capital after his coronation in 1906. There is also an English Triumph dating from 1951 on display. The Lower Silesian painter Georg Hedrich (born 1927), who moved to the Canary Islands in 1957 and now lives in Teror, has had a hall of the mu-

seum devoted to his works. His studio, opposite the basilica, is open to visitors.

The small **Plaza Teresa de Bolívar** next to the cathedral is named after the wife of South American freedom fighter Simón Bolívar. It contains a bust of the liberator of the colonies from Spanish domination and also the coat of arms of the Rodríguez del Toro family, from whom his wife was descended. On a raised plaza above the church is the **episcopal palace**, with a **cultural center** in one section of it. At the front is the **Town Hall**, which is decorated during festivals.

This whole region is a very good place to go for extensive walks and hikes, and Teror is an ideal starting point for rambles through the surrounding countryside – you can take a detour to the Balcón de Zamora, for instance, or a longer walk to the traditional villages of **Vallesco** and **Lanzarote** off to the west. A more ex-

Above: Teror in festive mood. Right: Well-nourished goats being driven to market at Cardones near Arucas.

hausting hike, which takes a full day to complete, is to go from Teror via Vallesco through the fertile plain to **San Bartolomé de Fontanales**, then from Vallesco to **Valsendero**, and onwards along partially ruined paths in a westerly direction, then downhill through rather varied vegetation, with some excellent views extending as far as the coast. Once you've had a well-deserved rest in Fontanales you can either return by the same route or else continue northwards via **Tablero** and **La Laguna** back into the valley of Teror (3.5 hours each way).

*Arucas – Rum Production Center

Teror produces a mineral water that is famed across the island, and towards the sea in **Arucas** ㉔ you can sample some rather strong rum. It is produced by the firm of *Arehucas*, on the outskirts of Banaderos, in the largest rum factory on the archipelago. Around 3.5 million liters of this 90 proof drink are made here each year. The *aguardiente*, thinned down to

around 70 percent alcohol content and less, is kept in 6,000 barrels before being turned into various types of rum. One of the most popular products is the 12-year-old *ron añejo*. The 24 percent *ron miel*, with added honey, is often drunk in place of a liqueur. A **museum** documents the history of rum production in Arucas. You can also see barrels signed by famous visitors, such as the King and Queen of Spain, the Gran Canarian operatic genius Alfredo Kraus, Nobel Peace Prize winner Willy Brandt, artist César Manrique and tenor Plácido Domingo.

Arucas, the third-largest town on the island with a population of 27,000, possesses one of the most unique churches on the archipelago: the ★**Iglesia Parroquial de San Juan Bautista**, a massive and yet filigree Neo-Gothic structure made of dark basalt. Its church tower is 60 meters high, making it the tallest in the Canary Islands. A major role in the construction of this church was played by Manuel Vega March, a student of the Catalan architect Antonio Gaudí. The

construction of this church extended over decades: it was begun in 1909, consecrated in 1912, completed except for the main tower in 1932, and finally had the main tower finished in 1977. The project received financial support from the owners of the rum factory, the Gourié family, who also bequeathed their former residence to the town, the **Casa del Mayorazgo**, for use as a municipal museum, together with the **Parque Municipal** in front of it.

From Arucas it's worth taking a detour (via a turnoff northwards) to the 412-meter-high **Montaña de Arucas**. Here a **Mirador** provides a fantastic panoramic view, and in the restaurant *El Mesón de la Montaña de Arucas* grown-ups can indulge in excellent food and good wine while their kids romp about in the playground outside.

Leaving Arucas in the direction of the capital, you have two options: the faster route, via the coast road, or the more arduous journey along the 813 parallel to it, which runs through the villages. The coast road leads into the most modern section of La Palma, while the village route reveals the rather less successful side of the city.

LAS PALMAS DE GRAN CANARIA

No other city in the Canary Islands is as metropolitan as **Las Palmas de Gran Canaria** Ⓞ, which together with Santa Cruz de Tenerife is the capital of the autonomous region. With a population of over 356,000 it is a large harbor city, jammed into the rather narrow confines of the northeastern coast, with non-stop real estate construction and several traffic tunnels through the volcanic rock. Las Palmas de Gran Canaria has everything a modern metropolis should have: a historic Old Town with a cathedral, elegant shopping streets, leafy squares, and an exciting cultural life with plenty of museums, galleries and festivals. A shopping trip will take you past attractive emporiums, elegant boutiques and all kinds of other smaller places; there are street cafés and restaurants to relax in and also the magnificent golden-yellow beach of Las Canteras. Alongside all this, however, there are areas of new development with concrete apartment blocks, an area of slums in the outskirts, a drugs scene and also a crime rate that is becoming increasingly disturbing.

Las Palmas de Gran Canaria was founded in 1480, to the south of the Barranco del Guiniguada which is almost entirely obscured today. The Ermita de San Antonio Abad (see p. 102) still stands at the original location, however. In 1515, Las Palmas was the first community on the Canarian archipelago to be accorded municipal status, and over the decades that followed the San Antón Abad district started to grow. In the 19th century the town began expanding north-

Right: Las Palmas de Gran Canaria – the Canarians' metropolis.

wards rapidly in the direction of La Isleta, and in the 20th century the houses had already started to appear up on the slopes. Access to La Isleta used to be blocked by high tide, and the land had to be reclaimed. The harbor of Puerto de la Luz now lies on the site.

The Old Town Center

Don't bother looking for the city center of Las Palmas de Gran Canaria – because there isn't one. From the La Isleta peninsula, the Canteras beach and modern suburbs in the north, the city extends southwards for kilometers along the sea. The most important sights are in the old center, in the southern part of town. The latter consists of the three districts of **Vegueta**, **Triana** and **Ciudad del Mar**, and you can easily spend a whole day, if not more, exploring their delights.

*Vegueta – Medieval Streets

The most striking building in Vegueta, the oldest section of the city, is the three-aisled cathedral of ***Santa Ana** ❶. It's much larger than any other church on the Canary Islands – its facade alone measures 100 meters across. The church was started around 1500, and the dark-gray late Gothic basalt columns along the nave are part of the original structure. In 1599, the capital was plundered and burned by the Dutch pirate Van der Does and his men; they stole all the icons and pictures from the cathedral and destroyed the choir and pulpit. Since they also burned the entire cathedral archives, very little is now known of the building's early history. Santa Ana owes its present-day appearance to alteration work that lasted from 1852 into the 20th century. The neo-classical facade, with its arched portal, rose window, stone baldachin above the central section and two towers (the left of which is a belfry as well as a clock tower) all date from that time.

Renovation of the entire interior was completed in 1998, and the difference is remarkable: the once rather dimly-lit interior is now flooded with light, and the cathedral has gained a new and special magnificence. A section on the north side is due to be turned into a sanctuary. On the south side of the cathedral is the *Patio de los Naranjos*, a courtyard of orange trees, which can be admired during a visit to the Museo Diocesano de Arte Sacro – the courtyard is pleasantly shady, and also makes the whole place somewhat reminiscent of Seville.

The interior of the cathedral has side-chapels off to the left and right, and the side aisles are separated from the central nave by impressive, 20-meter-high rows of pillars. The side-chapels contain the tombs of several bishops, as well as of the first proper chronicler of Canarian history, José Viera y Clavijo, the poet Bartolomé Cairasco de Figueroa, and the politician Fernando León y Castillo. Beneath the dome, on the crossing, there are 16 larger-than-life wooden statues of saints, all painted gray to make them look like stone. These are the work of sculptor and architect Luján Pérez, who also made the changes to the facade during the 19th century. More of his works can be admired in the side-chapels, including a *Redeemer* and the *Virgen de la Antigua*.

The most impressive works by Luján Pérez are inside the **Museo Diocesano de Arte Sacro** (entrance at Calle Espiritu Santo 20), located in the southern part of the cathedral complex. Five halls contain religious works by various artists, and in the chapter hall on the first floor you can see Luján's deeply moving *Dolorosa*. It is carried through the streets of Las Palmas every Easter, together with a statue of Christ (also by Luján). The floor of the chapter hall is covered with hand-made ceramic tiles; the only mosaic of its type anywhere in the Canary Islands.

The large, slightly sloping **Plaza de Santa Ana ❷** in front of the cathedral is surrounded by attractive townhouses and several historic structures. The cast-iron black dogs on the eastern side of the

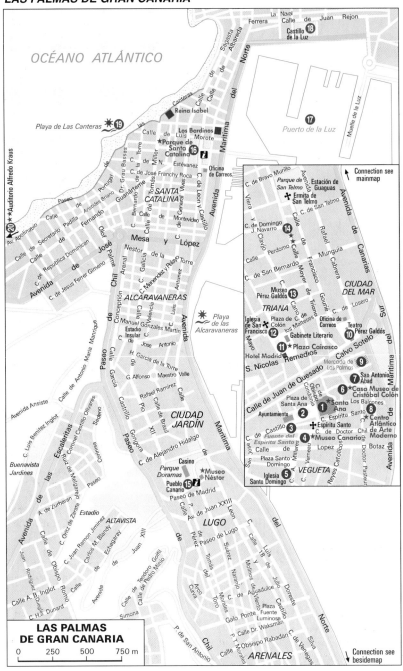

LAS PALMAS DE GRAN CANARIA

OCÉANO ATLÁNTICO

Playa de Las Canteras

SANTA CATALINA

Puerto de la Luz

Castillo de la Luz

Parque de Santa Catalina

Auditorio Alfredo Kraus

Mesa y López

ALCARAVANERAS

Playa de las Alcaravaneras

CIUDAD JARDÍN

Casino

Parque Doramas

Museo Néstor

Pueblo Canario

ALTAVISTA

Buenavista Jardines

LUGO

ARENALES

LAS PALMAS DE GRAN CANARIA

0   250   500   750 m

Connection see mainmap

Connection see besidemap

(inset map)

Parque de San Telmo

Ermita de San Telmo

Estación de Guaguas

CIUDAD DEL MAR

TRIANA

Museo Pérez Galdós

Iglesia de San Francisco

Plaza de Colón

Oficina de Correos

Teatro Pérez Galdós

Gabinete Literario

Plaza Cairasco

Hotel Madrid

Remedios

S. Nicolás

Mercado de Las Palmas

San Antonio Abad

Casa Museo de Cristóbal Colón

Los Balcones

Centro Atlántico de Arte Moderno

Plaza de Santa Ana

Ayuntamiento

Santa Ana

Espíritu Santo

Castillo de Fuente del Espíritu Santo

Museo Canario

VEGUETA

Plaza Santo Domingo

Iglesia Santo Domingo

Calle de Juan de Quesada

Calvo Sotelo

100

square, directly opposite the cathedral facade, are a popular meeting point. These dogs are meant to be reminders of how the Canary Islands got their name: according to Roman historians, large dogs had apparently been found on newly-discovered islands in the eastern Atlantic. Whether the name "Canary" really comes from *canis*, the Latin word for dog, or whether it is derived from the name of a Berber tribe (as claimed by the author James Krüss, who died in 1997) is still a subject of some controversy.

Cross over to the north side of the square and admire the monastery-like **Episcopal Palace**, built in the Renaissance style in 1630. It's still in use today and so, unfortunately, is closed to visitors. Beside it is the impressive 16th-century **Casa del Regente**, with its Renaissance facade. Once the seat of the Spanish governor, it houses the law courts today.

On the south side of the square there are several other buildings, some with Art Nouveau ornamentation. The chronicler José Viera y Clavijo lived and also died in one of them (marked with a plaque on the facade), and today the building houses the **Archivo Histórico Provincial**, where scientists can inspect private and official documents about population censuses, land sales, water rights, the slave trade, goods transportation and numerous other archives.

On the western side of the square, opposite the cathedral facade, is the neoclassical building that was once the **Ayuntamiento**, or Town Hall. It stands on the site of the former Town Hall which burned down in 1842, and has now grown too small as well.

To the south of the plaza, between the Town Hall and the cathedral, on Calle del Doctor Chil, there is a triangular square with the **Fuente del Espíritu Santo ❸** at its center. This neoclassical fountain was created by Manuel Oraa. Next to it, the simple chapel of **Ermita del Espíritu**

Santo, services were once held for Africans who had been brought here to do forced labor during the days of slavery.

On Calle del Doctor Chil (on the corner of Calle Verneau), the excellent ★**Museo Canario ❹** contains important finds from the pre-Hispanic era, including mummies with grave goods, and also a collection of skulls with a list of the various recognizable diseases, injuries or operations their former owners once had; among the exhibits you can also see a reconstruction of the Cueva Pintada in Gáldar, along with items of jewelry, idols, clay stamps, ceramics, weapons and tools. A library with a large selection of archeological and ethnographic literature is also available. The museum, based on the collection of the doctor Gregorio Chil y Naranjo, is financed by a private foundation and is the oldest in the city. Naranjo started the collection in 1880 before bequeathing the building and all the scientific documentation inside it to Las Palmas. The museum is certainly worth spending some hours in, and gives a good insight into the history of the islands before the Spanish arrived.

A detour southwards via Calle Agustín Millares leads to the shady **Plaza Santo Domingo**. This is where the conqueror Pedro de Vera once had a country estate with a sugar-cane plantation. The **Iglesia Santo Domingo ❺** (early 16th century) survived the fire attack by Dutch pirates and still contains a fine baroque altar, as well as works by Luján Pérez and one of his pupils, Fernando Estévez. The latter created the *Virgen del Rosario*, and works here by Luján Pérez include the statue of Christ in the side altar. The square outside the church was where non-believers were burned at the stake, and is still familiarly known as the *Plaza de la Quemada*, or "Square of the Burned."

Behind the cathedral to the east stands the ★**Casa Museo de Cristóbal Colón ❻** (Calle Colón 1; entrance at the side), with its impressive, richly ornamented Gothic

Gran Canaria

portal, finely carved balconies and leafy inner courtyard. The museum is entered through a side door. According to legend, Christopher Columbus stayed in this imposing building while two of his three caravels were being repaired. The fascinating museum deals with topics such as pre-Hispanic America, the life and times of Christopher Columbus, the situation of the Canary Islands between continents, and the development of the city of Las Palmas. There is a very fine reconstruction of Columbus's cabin on board the *Santa Maria*, and it gives a good impression of what life must have been like at sea in those days. Another department contains some excellent etchings and paintings from the Prado, including several works by Goya.

The chapel **Ermita de San Antonio Abad 7** (see also p. 98) a short distance

further away to the northeast was completed at the end of the 15th century and renovated in the 18th century. According to legend, this is where Columbus is supposed to have prayed to God that his venture would succeed.

Further south is Calle de los Balcones. Modern art and architecture have found an impressive new home in a converted townhouse on this street: the **★Centro Atlántico de Arte Moderno (CAAM) 8** presents alternating exhibitions on a variety of themes, mainly with an emphasis on the cultural situation of Gran Canaria between the continents of Europe, Africa and the Americas. A permanent modern art exhibition is planned for the building next door. The rooftop terrace of this ultra-modern and functional building provides a pleasantly romantic view of the cathedral and the houses of the Old Town.

After all this art and history it's a good idea to take a well-deserved break in the roofed-over **Mercado de Las Palmas 9**, on the northeastern corner of Vegueta.

Above: The Casa Museo de Cristóbal Colón is a jewel of Canarian architecture. Right: The Mercado de Las Palmas – a landmark of the capital.

Gran Canaria

This is the oldest market hall in the city, and is a paradise of sights, sounds and smells. If you want to buy any fresh seafood, this is the place to come.

*Triana – Bourgeois Magnificence

The suburb of **Triana**, with its numerous small stores and boutiques, begins to the north of the Juan de Quesada highway. In contrast to the rather feudal-looking Vegueta with all its alleyways and old buildings, the Triana quarter is extremely varied. Formerly inhabited by Andalusian, English, Maltese and Danish merchants, it has much less homogeneous architecture; in fact, almost every architectural style of the 19th and 20th centuries, including postmodernism, can be found here. This variety makes the whole area quite fascinating, however, and it's interesting just to stroll past the different buildings and guess their architectural styles.

From the market hall in the Vegueta quarter, cross the main road towards the outwardly rather dusty-looking **Teatro Pérez Galdós** ❿. The building was first named after the Spanish dramatist Tirso de Molina in 1888, but it was destroyed by a fire in 1918. After its reconstruction the theater received its new name in honor of writer and dramatist Benito Pérez Galdós (1843-1920), a native of the city who spent the first 19 years of his life here. He became famous for his cycle of romances *Episodios Nacionales*, in which he painted a fascinating portrait of the morals of his time.

The theater building was reconstructed under the supervision of architect Miguel Martín Fernández de la Torre. He got his brother, Nestor de la Torre, a famous artist and stage designer, to decorate the rooms with drawings, paintings and wood carvings. Part of the building is dedicated to the French composer Camille Saint-Saëns, who stayed on Gran Canaria incognito and, to everyone's surprise, commented expertly on the rehearsals of the local philharmonic orchestra (see also p. 93).

One of the most pleasant squares in this quarter of the city is the ***Plaza Cairasco** ⑪, named after the poet Bartolomé Cairasco de Figueroa. Its charm derives mainly from two important buildings: the **Gabinete Literario** and also the **Hotel Madrid**, where General Franco stayed on July 17, 1936, at the beginning of the Spanish Civil War, determined to undertake a military putsch against the lawfully elected government of the Republic. He flew from here to Morocco in a private English plane and then took over as supreme commander for the attack on the motherland. The bar on the ground floor of the hotel has tables outside in the palm-lined square.

The Gabinete Literario was originally the Teatro Cairasco, but the latter soon proved to be too small. In 1884, the graceful, stuccoed house with its little towers

Above: African traders are a part of the scene. Right: Spanish Art Nouveau pavilion in the Parque de San Telmo – a good place for an extended coffee break.

and balconies thus became a cross between a private gentlemen's club and a literary salon, and locals refer to it as the *Casino*. Only members have access, and visitors are merely allowed to peek inside the roofed-over inner courtyard. The brief glimpse of the large staircase and three-storied arcades is definitely worth the trouble, however.

On the raised **Plaza de Colón** ⑫ there is the **Busto a Colón**, a pillar bearing a bust of the great explorer Columbus. The long church behind it is the three-aisled **Iglesia de San Francisco de Asís** (17th century). Alongside a floor made of white Carrara marble and the typical *mudéjar* ceiling, it also contains two important statues by Luján Pérez: one of *St. John* and also a *Señor del Huerto*. The *Virgen de la Soledad* here is also interesting from an art historical point of view: some experts believe her features are the same as those of Isabella of Castile, the founder of the church.

Calle de los Malteses leads to the **Museo Pérez Galdós** ⑬ on Calle Cano. This almost cute little birthplace of the famous author contains memorabilia of his life – from his cradle to his deathbed to his death mask. Items of furniture designed by Galdós from his apartment in Madrid and his bedroom can also be seen here. A library contains original copies of his works as well as translations, correspondence and scientific papers.

The main destination of this stroll is the ****Calle Mayor de Triana** ⑭, because the renovated facades of the buildings here are true masterpieces. The Art Nouveau buildings also have several contemporary elements – from the optician to the bank, and from the boutique to the fast food outlet. There's a pleasant leafy café at the end of the pedestrian precinct in the **Parque de San Telmo**. You sit in a pavilion filled with colorful tiles, the **Quiosco Modernista* of Valencian architect Rafael Masanet Fau. It's worth coming to the park for this little jewel alone. The late baroque **Ermita de San Telmo** chapel at the western corner of the park is consecrated to the patron saint of fishermen, as is evident from the many votive pictures inside. To the east of the park, on Avenida Rafael Cabrera, is the bus station **Estación de Guaguas**.

Ciudad del Mar and Pueblo Canario

It's a lot more modern altogether in **Ciudad del Mar**, because parts of the terrain around here were only reclaimed from the sea as recently as the 1960s. The narrow strip between the coastal highway and the Triana quarter is packed with tall administrative tower blocks and corporate buildings.

To the north of the Triana quarter and of Ciudad del Mar are the less attractive suburbs of **Arenales** and **Lugo**. Cross over to the villa district of **Ciudad Jardín** in the **Parque Doramas** and you'll find the **Pueblo Canario** 15. This ensemble of buildings has been designed as a modern interpretation of traditional Canarian architecture. There are stores selling art and craft items and souvenirs, a café and a tourist information center. On Thursday afternoons and Sunday mornings there are folklore performances held here. Otherwise, the patio is a popular place for celebrations and marriages.

A key role in the creation of the Pueblo Canario was played by Gran Canarian artist Néstor de la Torre (1887-1938), who with amazing foresight was predicting tourism as the future role of the Canaries as long ago as 1934. Like César Manrique later on, he wanted to preserve the islands' cultural identity and independence. The small but excellent ***Museo Néstor** is dedicated to his attitude to art and his own works. It contains an exquisite selection of the incredible amount of material this highly versatile artist produced. Alongside several of his early works there are also sections from his painting cycle *El Poema del Atlántico*

on display. His interests ranged from folkwear and costume design to stage design, and also construction plans for tourist facilities.

A further highlight of his creative output is the unfinished cycle of paintings *El Poema de la Tierra*, in which he embeds the erotic shapes of two lovers inside the exotic forms of plants native to the Canary Islands. Néstor de la Torre is seen as an exponent of *Modernismo* (an art movement in Spain influenced by the French Romantics and Symbolists).

The Parque Doramas was originally the grounds of the Hotel Santa Catalina, one of the best in the city (which includes a casino). The park is rather neglected now, but contains several modern statues illustrating the history of the Guanches. Nearby are a swimming pool and also a tennis club.

The elegant side of Las Palmas opens up in the boutiques and sophisticated department stores on Avenida de José Mesa y López, on the northern edge of the district of **Alcaravaneras**. The presence of

Gran Canaria

department store giant *El Corte Inglés* is very obvious, with its two buildings on either side of the tree-lined avenue. This is where you'll sometimes see limousines with liveried chauffeurs taking diplomats and their wives out to shop. Unless you're feeling especially rich, it's probably a good idea to keep your wallet closed around here.

Santa Catalina and the Harbor District

The clientele in the bars and restaurants is quite colorful in the streets and squares of the **Santa Catalina** district, located between the harbor to the east and the municipal beach of Las Canteras to the west. The heart of this area is the large green square known as ***Parque de Santa Catalina** 16. Couples, sailors, old-age pensioners and tradesmen walk along

Above: Life's a game in the Parque de Santa Catalina. Right: The Playa de Las Canteras is the city's Copacabana.

here past the souvenir shops, bars and newsstands; tourists collect information material from the **Casa de Tourismo**, and the *aficionados* of dominoes, chess and cards all play their games here. This whole area is busy at the best of times, but becomes astonishingly active when the annual carnival reaches its climax.

The harbor of **Puerto de la Luz** 17, completed as a means of creating employment at the end of the 19th century, is considered the largest in Spain. It is now the most important container shipping port in the North African region. The yacht harbor bordering it to the south attracts plenty of sailors eager to participate in the international transatlantic regattas.

In the old days the harbor, and the ships lying here at anchor, had to be protected from attack from British, French and Dutch pirates, who were usually sent here by their monarchs and had some very powerful fleets. The mighty defensive bulwark in such situations was the **Castillo de la Luz** 18, on the south bank of the **La Isleta** peninsula, which was

built above the foundations of a fort dating from the days of the *Conquista* and had eleven batteries. The fort failed to withstand the attack in 1599 by the pirate Pieter van der Does, with his 84 ships, and was completely razed to the ground. Today it is used for cultural purposes. A word of warning, by the way: avoid the park area beside it, which has now become a center of the drugs scene. The streets north of the fort are hectic and businesslike: between the bars and bodegas, various shipping and trading companies have established themselves, and Calle de Juan Rejón contains numerous Indian and Chinese shops with a whole range of exotic goods for sale. There are even shops tailored to the special requirements of Russian sailors.

Near the harbor, the bars generally cater to the many mariners who visit here regularly, and the whole area is reasonably seedy: there are snack bars here, fast food outlets, and also traditional tapas bars, closely followed by dubious-looking nightclubs and sex shops. Near the ★**Playa de Las Canteras** ⑲ things get slightly better, with several good restaurants and cafés.

The yellow sand beach, protected by a rocky reef from the sea, is one of the most popular on the island. During the week it is reasonably full, but on weekends all the Palmeros come here with their extended families and have a relaxed beach holiday weekend, which can involve anything from a simple picnic to a small-scale soccer tournament. There is a sailing school here, too, teaching young people in small boats.

On the beach promenade, street cafés and restaurants with terraces of all different kinds lie one beside the next, from the *Cafetería Mozart* – a popular meeting place for local families – to the elegant restaurant in the five-star *Reina Isabel* hotel, and also the American-style *Off Shore*, where young people gather in the evenings to drink tropical cocktails and listen to English crooners.

If you feel like combining a visit to a **flea market** with a visit to the beach and the restaurant and bar area beyond it, it's best to visit Santa Catalina on a Sunday morning: near the city highway, behind the hotel tower of Los Bardinos and almost as far as the Castillo de la Luz, you'll find all kinds of junk, artistic and otherwise, on sale. It's easy to spend several hours here without noticing how the time goes by – and the prices are often very reasonable, too, which of course adds to the enjoyment. Beware of pickpockets, by the way – flea markets are a favorite haunt of theirs.

In the southwest, beyond the Paseo de las Canteras, a new business district has appeared with several shopping centers. This is where you'll find a building that has become the talking point of the classical music fraternity ever since it was opened in December 1997: the **★★Auditorio Alfredo Kraus** ⑳, a modern palace made of massive natural stone, which was designed by the Catalan architect Óscar Tusquet. Leading international orchestras, soloists and conductors all perform here – indeed the building has done an enormous amount to enhance the quality of classical music in the Canaries, and has placed Las Palmas de Gran Canaria on a par with many other leading musical locations in the world.

The special architectural feature here is that the back of the stage in the main concert hall provides a view of the sea – a unique feature which makes for regularly inspiring performances. This building, with its total of 10 concert halls, represents the fulfillment of a lifetime dream for opera star Alfredo Kraus, and is now the city's top cultural address. Make sure you fit attending at least one concert here into your itinerary.

Near the Auditorio you'll reach the municipal highway, westbound section, with a **rock statue** by Tony Gallardo dedicated to the lost continent of Atlantis.

Right: Tafira Alta with its Italian-style manor houses.

THE ARID EAST

Tafira

For a detour inland, take the coast highway heading south, following the turnoff to Tafira while still inside the capital; it leads between the districts of Vegueta and Triana and into the mountains. After several hairpin bends you'll arrive in **Tafira Baja** ㉖, which has developed into a kind of suburb for wealthy commuters. The streets here all have suitably opulent-looking villas along them. At the entrance to the town is the **University of Gran Canaria**, founded in 1989. It was built in a simple neoclassical style, but also has a few Bauhaus elements to it.

One special highlight of Tafira Baja is the **★Jardín Botánico Canario Viera y Clavijo**. You can already hear the birds singing as you park your car. From the restaurant and from an observation platform there's a good view of the area. Most of this botanical garden was laid out on the steep wall of a barranco, with surfaced footpaths and cascades leading past it in the direction of the valley. The main attraction featured here is the flora of the archipelago: each Canarian plant species has its own little reserve, even the Canarian laurel forest; and there are also lots of different kinds of succulents for cactus aficionados.

Tafira Alta ㉗, which adjoins the garden to the southwest, is distinctive for its mainly Italian-style villas with their magnificent gardens, terraces and verandas. If the through traffic weren't so noisy and irritating it would be nice to take a leisurely stroll past these fine buildings. A very striking one is the **Villa María,** built in the Andalusian-Moorish style and right next to the main road.

At the end of the village the road bends away in the direction of the **Caldera de Bandama**. It passes through vineyards, where the popular *Vino del Monte* grows. The winding road also passes several

wine estates before it reaches the famous Bandama Crater (569 meters), which is 200 meters deep. A farmer is still tilling fields right at its base. From an observation point above the Caldera you can see the coastal strip from La Isleta beyond Las Palmas all the way to the airport. To the west of the crater there is a golf course.

*Telde – Traces of the Guanches

To reach Telde, it's best to go back up the main road to Tafira Alta and carry on towards Las Palmas from there until you reach a right turn (easy to miss) that will take you to **Marzagán**. The narrow, winding side road leads past vineyards and, just before Marzagán, goes by the hemispherical building housing the American School of Gran Canaria. Next you'll pass the weird concrete jungle of **Jinámar**, with its tedious apartment buildings lined up one after the other against the hilly landscape. Since this place has the same social problems as other similar areas all over the world, attempts are being made to offer a comprehensive cultural program – but the people who usually attend the events come here from the city center.

*Telde ㉘ – in pleasant contrast to Jinámar – possesses a historic center. To look at this place it's hard to believe that it has a population of around 90,000. Across to the right, beyond the valley, the picturesque suburb of San Francisco is huddled around the church of the same name, and can be reached by a footpath from the plaza at the Basílica San Juan Bautista that leads across an old aqueduct. The streets of San Francisco are cobbled with dark-gray, oval basalt stones, and here you can still see the old, dark street signs which have been replaced by more modern, Guanche-ornamented ones nearly everywhere else.

To the left is the broad square in front of the **Basílica San Juan Bautista**. This church contains a Gothic altarpiece from Flanders with six scenes from the life of the Virgin Mary, a statue of John the Bap-

tist by Fernando Estévez from Orotava (Tenerife), and a statue of the martyr *San Pedro de Verona* by Luján Pérez. The baptismal chapel contains a font of Carrara marble and also frescoes by Gran Canarian artist Jesús González Arenciba, painted in 1948. The crucified Christ at the main altar is a bizarre work by Mexican Indios. Because the 1.85-meter-high statue was made from maize paste, it only weighs seven kilograms. The color of Jesus's face changes with the seasons, a fact ascribed to a wood-stain derived from seeds. Beyond the church, on the left, a promenade leads to the **historical archives** and to the **public library**. There's a choice of cafés on the plaza in front of the **Iglesia San Gregorio**.

By the way, don't miss a visit to the **Casa Museo León y Castillo**, which can be reached from the church square by fol-

Above: Replica of the "Idol of Tara" in the church square of Ingenio. Right: Hem-stitch embroidery – a local specialty (Museo de Piedras y Artesanía, Ingenio).

lowing the main street. The museum contains the estate of the diplomat Fernando León y Castillo, which ranges from a collection of walking sticks to a Paris Opera ticket, and also a collection of Impressionist and contemporary paintings. It's quite astonishing what he managed to collect, and the exhibits provide a fascinating insight into what life was like during the late 19th and early 20th century.

Telde is definitely historic ground, as proven by old documents. The Italian fortress builder Leonardo Torriani claims in his 16th-century report that he counted 14,000 Guanche houses here. The Guanche symbolic figure known as the *Idolo de Tara* was found in the part of town called **Tara**: the torso of a clay figure with noticeably thick upper arms and thighs. The figure is on display in the Museo Canario in the capital, and copies of it are popular souvenirs.

Most of the archeological sites in this section are in appalling condition, and to get a proper sense of the history of this region it's best to visit the area called **Cuatro Puertas** south of town, roughly halfway towards Ingenio. On a hill that was sacred to the Guanches, you'll see a former "residential cave" with four door openings. If you cross around from the cave, which is on the shady side of the hill, to the sunny side, you'll find further relics from Guanche times, including a complex of caves and also a piece of rock with carvings that is thought to have once formed part of a sacrificial altar. This place is very atmospheric, especially around dusk.

Ingenio, Agüimes, Arinaga

The name **Ingenio ㉙** ("Sugar Mill") indicates the former importance of this place for the sugar-cane industry. The **Museo de Piedras y Artesanía** in the suburb of **Mejías** is actually a sales exhibition of Canarian arts and crafts. In the entrance area there's a collection of stones on display, and you can also watch women as they embroider. The chapel at the center of the complex is jam-packed with devotional material; its prominent visitors included Maria Callas (1967) with the Greek shipowner Aristotle Onassis. In the part of town called **Las Rosas**, across to the east in the direction of the highway, a former manor house contains a similar exhibition of crafts for sale. An old mill can also be seen there.

There's a generously-sized church square at the center of Ingenio. The church itself, with its two towers and white dome, can be seen far and wide, and it houses the statue of the patron saint of the Canary Islands, the *Virgen de la Candelaria*. Beneath the church, a copy of the *Idolo von Tara* has been set up. Many of the house walls have large-sized pictures of village scenes on them, and there is also some Guanche ceramic ornamentation on several buildings. At the eastern end of the village in the direction of Carrizal, someone has placed an full-scale model of a sugar mill in the middle of a traffic island.

The central church of **Agüimes ③** also clearly dominates the town, with its pastel-colored houses up on the steep slope of the Barranco de Guayadeque. The buildings are all closely huddled together, and together with the narrow streets give the place a distinctly medieval look. The three-aisled **Parroquía San Sebastián**, declared a "historic cultural monument of Spain," contains three statues by Luján Pérez: a *Virgen de la Esperanza*, a *Santo Domingo* and a *San Vincente*.

The entrance to the village of Agüimes marks the start of the always green ***Barranco de Guayadeque**, which was one of the most populated places on the island in former days. The road winds its way along the bed of the (largely dried-out) stream at the bottom of the ravine, and up into the hinterland. You won't only see caves dating from the Guanche period here – some modern cave dwell-

Gran Canaria

ings and also a chapel have been cut out of the rock as well. The main attraction here, however, is the regular series of folklore performances held in the caves. Busloads of tourists arrive here for them all the time. The nicest time of day in the barranco is the peaceful period just after sunrise, because carousing tends to go on until very late at night here.

If you travel from the Agüimes plateau down to Arinaga, you'll see nothing but modern buildings stretching away to the south. **Arinaga ③**, beside the sea, looks half-finished in several places, but tourism should soon transform it into yet another holiday paradise. The sandy beach, with its promenade, faces the sea in a half-moon shape. The sunny spots of the south can be reached very quickly via the nearby highway.

HIGHLIGHTS OF THE INTERIOR

The center of Gran Canaria contains the most spectacular mountain ranges anywhere on the island. Striking mono-

patch which the locals cultivate for their own use. The dry seasons are successfully bridged with the help of several reservoirs located nearby.

If you leave Las Palmas in the direction of Tafira, you'll reach a historic section of mountain ridge just after you've passed through Tafira Alta. On the **Monte Lentiscal** the Dutch pirate Pieter van der Does had to abandon his plan to subjugate the entire island: with his 4,000-man troop he was beaten back by a courageous horde of just 500 militiamen. In nearby **Santa Brígida ㉜** this event is celebrated with a special festival (ask about dates and times at the local tourist information center). The village lies 500 meters up, and is perhaps the most exclusive residential area near the island's capital. It was valued for its slightly cool climate at the turn of the century, mainly by wealthy English visitors who used it as a summer spa. Outside the old center there are several neoclassical and postmodern villas inside leafy grounds. Breathing the fresh air here after the heat of the beaches makes one wonder whether tourism may soon concentrate more on health and relaxation rather than on suntans and sand. Then again, judging from the age and elegance of the houses here, it's pretty easy to tell what has lasting importance in the long run.

liths and rock formations rear up out of volcanic cones and mountain ridges into the azure-blue sky. As a rule these are volcanic vents that have withstood erosion for millions of years. Looking at them, it's easy to understand why the Guanches worshiped these storm and rain-lashed shapes as gods. There are new and even more breathtaking views at each bend in the road, and it's hard to understand why many people who have never visited Gran Canaria automatically assume that the scenery here has nothing very special about it, and that the whole island is covered with tourist areas.

The table mountains and plateaus up here have corn growing on them; it gets turned into *gofio* (roast flour; see p. 230), and is supposed to give the Canarios (what they claim is) their immense strength. Between the cornfields you can also see the odd cabbage and vegetable

The road rises another 300 meters to reach the rather modern-looking village of **Vega de San Mateo ㉝**, an agricultural center with regular cattle markets. This water-rich high valley contains not only fruit and vegetables but also special herbs used in traditional medicines. Shortly after you enter the village, Canarian entrepreneur Jesús Gómez has created the **Casa Museo Cho' Zacarias** on his estate, some parts of which are 300 years old. The exhibition documents the traditional, fast-vanishing everyday culture of the island world. Since there is also a very good restaurant here, be prepared for a crush at weekends.

Above: Donkeys and mules are still used in the mountains. Right: Artenara – old caves, new accommodation.

112   *Map pp. 82-83, Info pp. 116-119*

Gran Canaria

While the high valley of **Las Lagunetas** still looks reasonably cultivated, you'll soon notice that the landscape gets very rough and barren as you approach the rocky heights of the central Caldera Massif. The next place you reach is the **Cruz de Tejeda ㉞**, a stone cross, around which restaurants, souvenir shops, children's donkey rides and a country hotel have all sprung up. If you're traveling with kids, this is a good place to distract them. From the *Parador Nacional* on the edge of the crater (closed for overnight stays at present) and from various other locations close by you'll get magnificent views of the mountains and valleys of Gran Canaria. By the way, if you don't like having a lot of people around, it's best to avoid this place on weekends.

To get to know the volcanism on Gran Canaria from another angle, travel from here in a northwesterly direction to the **Pinos de Gáldar ㉟**. From an observation point you can look down into a crater full of reddish and black volcanic ash. You'd

think there had been a recent eruption if it weren't for the green foliage all around. The crater was formed at least 3,000 years ago, when the island was still relatively uninhabited.

Now we're approaching the region of Canaria where numerous cave dwellings from the pre-Christian era are still in use. From a long way off you'll already notice ★**Artenara ㊱**: a statue of Jesus reminiscent of the one in Rio de Janeiro welcomes visitors with its arms outstretched. This is the highest village on Gran Canaria (1,250 meters) and in the surrounding hamlets as far as Juncalillo and beyond, people have built dwellings and granaries, but also churches and chapels underground.

A short cobbled path for pilgrims leads eastwards from the village center to a cave chapel, where the shrine of the *Virgen de la Cuevita* has been carved from the reddish-brown tuff. West of the village, a pedestrian tunnel leads to the *Méson La Silla* restaurant, where you can eat on a terrace and enjoy a magnificent

view of the mountain scenery at the same time.

From Artenara, even in bad weather, it's worth taking a detour to the largest intact forest area on the island, the nature reserve of the ***Pinar de Tamadaba**, 12 kilometers to the west. A paved road leads around the Tamadaba Massif (1,444 meters), affording impressive views of the Caldera de Tejeda, the coast in the west and also of Tenerife with Teide. In foggy weather the pine forest is transformed into something straight out of a fairy tale. The whole place is extremely mysterious: enormous chunks of rock lie strewn among the trees, and water glistens on the greenish-yellow lianas that hang from the branches. The forest is an ideal place to go for a hike or a picnic. Spending the night in the idyllically-located camp and picnic site in the north-

Above: Mountain-bikers in the "petrified storm" (Miguel de Unamuno). Right: The monumental beauty of barren mountain scenery south of Karge Fataga.

west is free of charge, but no services are provided apart from a water supply. Travel back by car from the Pinar de Tamadaba in the direction of Artenara. A few kilometers outside the town a winding road branches off to the west, in the direction of Acusa and San Nicolás de Tolentino, which are among the highlights of any island tour (see p. 89 ff.).

If the road from Artenara to **Tejeda ③** has become impassable – and this often happens after rockfalls caused by rain – you'll have no choice but to make a detour via Pinos de Gáldar and Cruz de Tejeda. Surrounded by terraced fields of corn, and fruit and vegetable fields, Tejeda is located 1,000 meters up on the slopes of the enormous crater of the same name. Without the tourist boom this place would have been deserted long ago, because surviving from agriculture in this barren landscape is very difficult. Around 50 percent of the villagers have turned their backs on this place in the past.

A few kilometers further on in the direction of San Bartolomé de Tirajana, a

Gran Canaria

road branches off to the ***Roque Bentayga** (1,404 meters). This basalt cliff is part of the **Parque Arquéologico del Bentayga**, which provides information on archeological finds and sites in the region. Signposted hiking routes, providing views into the neighboring barrancos, lead to a series of caves that also includes the great **Cueva del Rey**, or the "King's Cave."

If you follow the 815 further southwards, you'll arrive in the small town of **Ayacata ㊳**. Here the access road to the ***Roque Nublo** (1,817 meters) – the most famous landmark on the island – branches off towards the northeast. A good, well-marked hiking route starts at a parking lot beside the road and winds its way up to the "Cloud Rock." Several broken boulders, cracked by erosion, lie strewn across the slopes; these once formed part of the massif, and all that remains of it now are the Roque Nublo and several smaller rocky fingers, such as **El Fraile** ("The Monk") further to the south. The names go well with the rocks, and if

you stare long enough at El Fraile it really does look like a monk.

From Ayacata you can take a nice detour to the highest mountain on the island, the **Pico de las Nieves** (1,949 meters). In the car, follow the road past the Roque Nublo and turn southeast at the next intersection near Cruz Llanos de la Paz; a few kilometers later a road branches off to the right through pine forests to the summit, which can also be reached on foot. A picnic area has been built here, and from the observation point you can see the southwest of the island with the neighboring **Caldera de Tirajana** crater.

From Pico de las Nieves you can either continue on to Telde and Teror, or drive back to Ayacata. From there, a winding stretch of road leads on to Mogán and to the southwest coast (see p. 88). If you decide to take the 815 southwards from Ayacata, you can go via the pass of **Cruz Grande** to **San Bartolomé de Tirajana ㊴**. The **church** in this town contains folk art: on the right of the altar there are two equestrian statues, showing St. Jacob

(*Santiago*) triumphing over the "heathen" Moors: one of them is large and aggressive-looking, the other small and rather naively done.

Just after San Bartolomé de Tirajana the road makes a fork: a scenically attractive stretch of road leads off southwards via the picturesquely situated town of **Fataga ⑩**, and then on to the coast and Playa del Inglés. The landscape round here becomes very monumental yet again, with broad barrancos and massive, barren mountain ridges. To really appreciate the scenery, and especially if you have kids in tow, try visiting one of the three camel stations here, which provide rides through this astonishing, desert-like region, with its handful of palm-lined oases. Camel riding isn't that difficult, and it's a very memorable experience.

If you go left at the fork in the road you'll arrive in **Santa Lucía ⑪**, where the white church with its dome looks rather like a mosque when seen from a distance. Near the *Restaurante Hao*, a castle-like structure contains the private **Museo del Castillo de la Fortaleza**, in which archeological finds from the surrounding area are on display. Around one kilometer to the south of the village, a right turn leads to the palm forest of **La Sorrueda ⑫** and to a historically important rocky ridge. This was the former site of the Guanche mountain fortress of *Alsite*, renamed **Fortaleza Grande** by the Spanish. It was here that the Guanches made their last stand, until they were finally forced to surrender; two of their leaders jumped from the rocks to their deaths. On April 29 each year a ceremony is held on the plateau behind the fortress in honor of them. Access to the coastal highway is very fast from here, via Agüimes. After this tour into the interior with its stunning scenery it's rather difficult to believe the common misconception about Gran Canaria being an island destroyed and made ugly by touristic development.

GRAN CANARIA

🛬 *ARRIVAL:* **By Plane:** The *Aeropuerto de Gando* is 22 kilometers south of the capital, tel. 928-579000. Tourist information, rental cars, currency exchange. Bus transfer every 20 minutes.

By Ship: *Transmediterránea*, tel. 928-260070, feries several times a week to and from Tenerife, jetfoil several times a day. *Naviera Armas*, tel. 928-474080, ferries to and from Tenerife, Lanzarote, Fuerteventura.

By Bus: Bus terminal *Estación de Guaguas*, opposite the Parque de San Telmo, Avda. Rafael Cabrera. It's very useful to have a working knowledge of Spanish here. The firm for the capital and the southeast is "Salcai," tel. 928-381110, and "Utinsa" does the capital and the northwest, tel. 928-360179.

THE SOUTH

MASPALOMAS AND ENVIRONS

🏨 😊😊😊 **Hotel Maspalomas Oasis**, Avda. del Oasis, tel. 928-141448, fax. 928-141192. The most luxurious hotel on the island, with a park right next to the dunes; **Helga Masthoff Park and Sport Hotel Los Palmitos**, Barranco de los Palmitos (above the Parque Palmitos), tel. 928-142100, fax. 928-141114. Gardens, tennis, golf, pool, excellent restaurant.

❌ **Restaurante Amaiur**, Avda. Neckermann 42, tel. 928-764414. Next to the golf course, Basque fish specialties, good wines, desserts closed Sundays; **Restaurante Orangerie**, Avda. del Oasis, tel. 928-140806. Excellent restaurant in the Hotel Maspalomas Oasis, modern Canarian cooking, wines closed Thursdays and Sundays.

⛳ *GOLF:* Avda. Neckermann, tel. 928-762581, fax. 928-768245. 18-hole course, driving range, restaurant.

GO-CARTS: **Gran Karting Club**, Tarajalillo (Maspalomas), Carretera General del Sur, Km 46, tel. 928-760090. The longest go-cart track in Europe, daily 10 am to 9 pm (winter), 11 am to 10 pm (summer).

AMUSEMENT PARKS: **Holiday World**, Campo Internacional, Lote 18, tel. 928-767176. Ferris wheel, shows, sideshows, daily from 6 pm; **Aqua Sur**, Carretera los Palmitos, Km 3, tel. 928-141905. Waterpark with slides, wave pool, daily from 10 am; **Parque Aquático**, at highway exit 47, tel. 928-764361. Waterpark, wave pool with water slides, daily from 10 am.

➕ **Red Cross**: In Maspalomas, tel. 982-762222; in Arguineguin, tel. 928-735911; **Police**: Tel. 928-141571; **Emergency**: Tel. 062.

📮 *POST OFFICE:* Avenida de Tirajana 37.

PLAYA DEL INGLÉS

📧 😊😊 **Hotel Eugenia Victoria**, Avda. de Gran Canaria 26, tel. 928-762500, fax. 928-762260. Oldish building, centrally located, inexpensive; **Sandy Beach**, Avda. Alfereces Provisionales, tel. 928-772726, fax. 928-767252. Near the beach, children welcome, group activities, tennis.

😊 **Apartamentos Royal Playa**, Avda. Alfereces Provisionales, tel. 928-760450. Near the beach.

❌ **Restaurante Tenderete II**, Avda. Tirajana, Edificio Aloe, tel. 928-761460. Small but excellent, vegetables from the garden, fish, kid.

🏛 **Mundo Aborigen**, culture park, Carretera Playa Inglés – Fataga (after 6 km), tel. 928-172295; daily 9 am to 6 pm, free bus.

🚴 *MOUNTAIN-BIKING:* **Happy Biking**, Centro Yumbo, tel. 928-768298. Bicycles and rollerblades for rent, tours organized, Mon-Sat 9:30 am to 1 pm and 6 to 9 pm.

DIVING: **Gran Canaria Diving Club**, Apart. Iguazu, tel./fax. 928-774539, courses, dives, daily 9 am to 8 pm.

🍸 *DISCOS:* Near the *Kasbah* shopping center **Joy**, **Pacha** and **Garage** (from 11 pm till dawn).

🧵 **Tienda de Artesanía del Cabildo Insular**, Avda. de España/corner Avda. de los Estados Unidos, crafts, Mon-Fri 10 am to 2 pm and 4 to 7 pm.

🚌 *BUS:* **Salcai**, Centro Yumbo, tel. 928-765332.

ℹ️ **Centro Insular de Turismo**, Avda. de España/corner Avda. de los Estados Unidos, tel. 928-767848, fax. 928-771050; Mon-Fri 10 am to 2 pm and 4 to 7 pm, Sat 10 am to 1 pm.

PLAYA DEL TAURO

📧 **Camping Guantánamo**, between Puerto Rico and Puerto de Mogán, tel. 928-560207. A square enclosed by a concrete wall, right next to the road, has sanitary facilities.

PUERTO DE MOGÁN

📧 😊😊 **Hotel Club de Mar**, at the yacht harbor, tel. 928-565066, fax. 928-565438. Comfortable, with pool.

😊 **Pensión Salvador**, Calle de la Corriente 13, tel. 928-565374. Simple and clean.

❌ **Bodeguilla Juanana**, Local 390, tel. 928-565579. Popular restaurant at the harbor with good Canarian cooking and good wines; **Seemuschel**, at the harbor, tel. 928-565486. fish for gourmets, daily from 7 pm, closed in July and August.

🚤 *BOAT TRIPS:* Excursions in a submarine, from the harbor, tel. 928-565108.

➕ **First Aid**: Tel. 928-569222; **European Clinic Mogán**: Tel. 928-565090; **Emergency**: Tel. 062.

🚕 *TAXI:* Tel. 928-735000.

AIRPORT TRANSFER: Tel. 928-574141.

SAN AGUSTÍN

📧 😊😊😊 **Hotel Gloria Palace**, Calle Las Margaritas, tel. 928-768300, fax. 928-767929. Modern establishment, beach access by road or footbridge; **Hotel Meliá Tamarindos Sol**, Calle Las Retamas 3, tel. 928-774090, fax. 928-774091. By the beach, with swimming pool.

😊😊 **Hotel Costa Canaria**, Calle Las Retamas 1, tel. 928-760220, fax. 928-761426, pool, park, near the beach.

❌ **Restaurante Buganvilla**, Calle Los Jazmines 17, tel. 928-760316. International cuisine, specialty is grilled perch (*cherne a la brasa*), dinners only.

🏛 **Sioux City**, Cañon del Águila, tel. 928-762573, 928-762982, Tue-Sun 10 am to 5 pm.

🍸 **Casino** in the Hotel Meliá Tamarindos Sol, tel. 928-762724. Dinner show, French restaurant, admission fee, daily 9 pm to 4 or 5 am.

🚤 **Nautico** diving school, tel. 928-770200, fax. 928-141805. From beginner to advanced.

➕ **Red Cross**: Tel. 982-762222; **Emergency**: Tel. 062.

🚕 *TAXI:* Tel. 928-763688.

THE NORTHWEST

AGAETE

📧 😊😊 **Apartamentos El Angosto**, Paseo del Obispo Pildaín 11, tel. 928-554194.

❌ **Bar-Restaurante El Dedo de Dio**, Puerto de las Nieves, near Agaete, tel. 928-898000. Moderate prices, fish. View of the "Finger of God" rock formation, daily 10 am to 11 pm. Also organizes apartments.

🚤 **Reptilandia Park**, tel. 928-551269, turn off from the Agaete – Gáldar road, daily 11 am to 5:30 pm.

🚕 *TAXI:* Tel. 928-898020.

LOS BERRAZALES

📧 😊😊 **Hotel Princesa Guayarmina**, at the end of the Valle de Agaete, tel. 928-898009, fax. 928-898525. Spa hotel with old-fashioned charm, garden, pool, restaurant. Dogs allowed.

PINAR DE TAMADABA

📧 **Camping Tamadaba**, Magnificently situated campsite in the northwest of the nature reserve, only a water connection, but free of charge.

SAN NICOLÁS DE TOLENTINO

📧 😊 **Hotel Los Cascajos**, Calle de los Cascajos 9, tel. 928-891165. Simple bed and breakfast.

➕ **Red Cross**: Tel. 928-892222.

🚕 *TAXI:* Tel. 928-898020.

117

THE NORTH

ARUCAS

Restaurante El Mesón de la Montaña de Arucas, on Arucas' local mountain, tel. 928-601475. Canarian and international cuisine, good desserts.

Red Cross: Tel. 928-601838.

TAXI: Tel. 928-600095.

FONTANALES

Hotel Rural El Cortijo, Camino de Hoyas del Cavadero 11 (2 km outside, in direction of Pinos de Gáldar), tel. 928-610285. Country hotel 1,080 meters up, ideal for hikers and families. 7 double rooms, pool, restaurant, good Canarian cuisine, tel. 928-610283.

GÁLDAR

Casa-Museo Antonio Padrón, Calle Drago, tel. 928-551858, Mon-Fri 8 am to 2 pm, admission free.

Red Cross: Tel. 928-552004.

TAXI: Tel. 928-881059.

GUÍA

CHEESE: **Queso de Guía** is available from two stores – at Marqués del Muni 34 (tel. 928-881875) and on the Carretera General, near the gas station.

Red Cross: Tel. 928-882222.

TAXI: Tel. 928-882846.

MOYA

Casa-Museo Tomás Morales, Plaza de Tomás Morales, tel. 928-620217, Mon-Fri 9 am to 2 pm, admission free.

Red Cross: Tel. 928-610222.

TAXI: Tel. 928-620083.

PUERTO SARDINA

La Fragata, on the harbor mole, tel. 928-883296, fish, seafood, very good quality, high prices, Tue-Sun 11 am to 11 pm; **Bar-Restaurante Vistamar**, above the beach, inexpensive, seafood, daily noon to 11 pm.

TEROR

Bar-Restaurante Balcón de Zamora, tel. 928-618042. Dining room has a view of Teror, large delicious helpings, simple Canarian food, moderate prices, Sat-Thu 8 am to 11 pm.

Casa-Museo Patrones de la Virgen del Pino, Plaza Nuestra Señora del Pino 3, Mon-Sat 11 am to 6 pm, Sun 11 am to 2 pm; **Studio** of the artist Georg Hedrich, in the house on the corner opposite the cathedral, tel. 928-631716. Visits Tue-Thu 11 am to 5 pm.

Red Cross: Tel. 928-630190.

LAS PALMAS DE GRAN CANARIA

Hotel Reina Isabel, Calle Alfredo L. Jones 40, tel. 928-260100, fax. 928-274558. On Canteras beach, two excellent restaurants, pool on the rooftop terrace, fitness center, comfortable rooms; **Hotel Santa Catalina**, Calle León y Castillo 227, Parque Doramas, Ciudad Jardín, tel. 928-243040, fax. 928-242764. Built in the neo-Canarian style, with a casino.

Hotel Los Bardinos, Calle Eduardo Benot 3, tel. 928-266100, fax. 928-229139. Hotel tower in the Canteras quarter. Functional, balconies with sea view.

Hotel Madrid, Plaza de Cairasco 2, tel. 928-360664. Built in the colonial style, located in Old Town.

Restaurante La Casita, Calle León y Castillo 227, tel. 928-243831. Delicious food, closed Sun; **El Novillo Precoz**, Calle Portugal 9, tel. 928-221659. Grilled specialties, Tue-Thu 1 to 4 pm and 8 pm to midnight; **Bodegon Biberon**, Las Canteras, Pedro del Castillo 15, good pub, daily noon to 4:30 pm and 7:30 pm to 2:30 am; **Café del Real**, Calle Doctor Chil 19, tel. 928-318299. Café with tapas, Mon-Sat 7:30 am to 10 pm; **Terraza A Bordo**, Parque Alonso Quesada, open-air bar, July-Dec daily noon to 4:30 am; **Bar-Restaurant Off Shore**, Alonso de Ojeda, tel. 928-461555. At north end of Canteras Beach, American-style, families meet here during the day and young people at night, daily 11 to 2 am, Fri and Sat 11 to 4 am; **Terraza Horizonte**, Plaza de los Escritores (at Parque de San Telmo), open-air bar, Mon-Thu 11 to 2 am, Fri-Sun 11 to 4 am.

Museo Canario, Calle Doctor Chil 25, tel. 928-315600, Mon-Fri 10 am to 5 pm, Sat 10 am to 1 pm, Sun 10 am to 2 pm; **Casa-Museo de Colón**, Calle Colón 1, tel. 928-312373, Mon-Fri 9 am to 6 pm, Sat and Sun 9 am to 3 pm; **Centro Atlántico de Arte Moderno** (CAAM), Calle Los Balcones, tel. 928-311824, Tue-Sat 10 am to 9 pm, Sun 10 am to 2 pm; **Museo Pérez Galdós**, Calle Cano 6, tel. 928-366976; Mon-Fri 9 am to 1 pm and 4 to 8 pm; **Museo Diocesano de Arte Sacro**, Calle Espíritu Santo 20, tel. 928-314989, Mon-Fri 10 am to 5 pm, Sat 9 am to 2 pm; **Museo Néstor**, Pueblo Canario, tel. 928-245136, Tue-Fri 10 am to 1 pm and 4 to 8 pm, Sun 11 am to 2 pm.

Teatro Pérez Galdós, tel. 928-361509. Theater, dancing, music; **Centro Insular de Cultura**, Calle Pérez Galdós 5, tel. 928-371011. Exhibitions, readings, theater, film, Mon-Fri 11 am to 2 pm and 5 to 8 pm.

La Librería del Cabildo Insular de Gran Canaria, Calle Cano 24, tel. 928-381539/594. Well-stocked bookstore, books about the archipelago; **Librería Archipiélago**, Calle Constantino 9, tel. 928-380006; **Tienda de Artesanía del Cabildo Insular**, Calle Domingo J. Navarro 7, tel. 928-369661, crafts, Mon-Fri

9:30 am to 1 pm and 4:30 to 8 pm, Sat 9:30 am to 1 pm; **Main Shopping Streets**: Calle Triana (pedestrian zone and Avda. de José Mesa y López with side streets. Bargains can also be found in the harbor district and at the **Flea Market**, on Sundays near the Mercado del Puerto.

⊕ **Red Cross**: Tel. 928-222222.

🚌 *BUS*: City and southeast, **Salcai**, tel. 928-381110; city and northwest, **Utinsa**, tel. 928-360179.

TAXI: Tel. 928-462212.

BREAKDOWN SERVICE: Tel. 928-368761.

ℹ️ **Patronato de Turismo de Gran Canaria**, Calle León y Castillo 17, tel. 928-362222, fax. 928-362822; **Casa de Turismo**, Parque de Santa Catalina, tel. 928-264623, Mon-Fri 9 am to 1:30 pm and 5 to 7 pm.

THE EAST

AGÜIMES

🛏️ **Turismo Rural de Agüimes S. L.**, tel. 928-124183, fax. 928-783663. The agency organizes renovated country houses in the medium to luxury categories.

❌ **Bar-Restaurante Tagoror**, end of the road in the Barranco de Guayadeque, tel. 928-172013, inside a cave, Canarian cuisine, daily 10 am to midnight.

⊕ **Red Cross**: Tel. 928-182222.

🚌 *TAXI*: Tel. 928-180774.

ARINAGA

🏛️ **Parque de Cocodrillo**, inland from Cruce de Arinaga, tel. 928-784725. Crocdile park, menagerie, feeding and shows, Sun-Fri 10 am to 6 pm.

INGENIO

🏛️ **Museo de Piedras y Artesanía**, Mejías, Cam. Real de Gando, tel. 928-781124. North of Ingenio, stones, crafts, Mon-Sat 8 am to 6 pm, Sun 8 am to noon.

⊕ **Red Cross**: Tel. 928-782222.

🚌 *TAXI*: Tel. 928-781585 and 928-782848.

TAFIRA ALTA / TAFIRA BAJA

🛏️ **Hotel Golf Bandama**, near the Caldera de Bandama, tel. 928-353354. Small, with garden, next to the oldest golf course in Spain. Near Tafira Alta.

❌ **Restaurante La Masía de Canarias**, Calle Murillo 36, tel. 928-354040. Canarian cuisine.

🏛️ **Jardín Botánico Canario Viera y Clavijo**, Tafira Baja, tel. 928-351645. Botanical garden with restaurant, Mon-Sun 9 am to 6 pm.

TELDE

🏛️ **Casa-Museo León y Castillo**, Calle León y Castillo 43/5, tel. 928-691377, Mon-Fri 9 am to 2 pm; **Casas**

Consistoriales, old Town Hall, Pl. de San Juan 1, work by regional artists, Mon-Fri 8 am to 3 pm, 5 to 9 pm.

⊕ **Red Cross**: Tel. 928-682222.

🚌 *BUS*: Tel. 928-690518.

TAXI: Tel. 928-694908.

SANTA BRÍGIDA

🛏️ ⊕⊕⊕ **Hotel-Escuela Santa Brígida**, Monte Lentiscal, tel. 928-355511. Prospective hotel cooks can practice on guests here – the food is superb.

❌ **Restaurante Mano de Hierro**, Vuelta del Pino 25, tel. 928-640388. German cuisine with a Canarian touch, closed Sun, Mon evenings; **Restaurante Mallow**, Calle José Antonio, 5, tel. 928-641309. Traditional dishes, breakfast, tapas, daily 6 to 2 am.

🚌 *TAXI*: Tel. 928-640371.

THE CENTER OF THE ISLAND

CRUZ DE TEJEDA

❌ **Hostería Cruz de Tejeda**, tel. 928-666050. Parador restaurant, specialties include pumpkin soup, roast kid, almond cake, expensive, closed in the evening.

FATAGA

🛏️ ⊕⊕ **Hotel Rural Molina del Agua**, above Fataga, tel. 928-172089. Rooms, bungalows, pool, restaurant. Gofio mill, camel rides.

🐪 *CAMEL RIDES:* **Camel Safari Park La Baranda**, Fataga valley, tel./fax. 928-798680, daily 9 am to 6 pm.

SANTA LUCÍA

🏕️ **Camping Temisas**, on the right of the road from Temisas towards Santa Lucía. Small, peaceful site, sanitary facilities are rudimentary.

❌ **Restaurante Hao**, main street, tel. 928-798007. Grill specialties, delicious Canarian cuisine, open daily until 6 pm.

🏛️ **Museo del Castillo de Fortaleza**, on main street, tel. 928-798 007, Mon-Sat 8 am to 8 pm, Sun until 5 pm.

🥾 *HIKING* in small groups: Guido Miltenburg, El Papalillo 22, tel. 928-798693, fax. 928-798319.

VEGA DE SAN MATEO

🛏️ **RETUR**: Vega de San Mateo, Calle Lourdes 2, tel. 928-661668, fax. 928-661560. Renovated country houses on offer, all categories.

🏛️ **Museo Cho-Zacarias**, Carretera del Centro 22, tel. 928-660627, Mon-Sat 9:30 am to 1 pm. Has a good restaurant, Tue-Sun 1 to 4 pm, Sat, Sun reservations.

⊕ **Red Cross**: Tel. 928-661049.

🚌 *TAXI*: Tel. 928-660345.

Gran Canaria

OCÉANO ATLÁNTICO

TENERIFE

La Orotava · Santa Cruz de Tenerife

Arucas

LA GOMERA

Las Palmas de Gran Canaria

San Nicolás

Los Abrigos

San Sebastián de la Gomera

GRAN CANARIA

TENERIFE
A Continent in Itself

THE SUNNY SOUTHWEST
THE NORTHWESTERN TIP
THE OROTAVA VALLEY
THE NORTHEAST COAST
ANAGA MOUNTAINS
SANTA CRUZ / LA LAGUNA
THE ARID SOUTH

Tenerife

"Isle of Hell" with Ten Climatic Zones

Tenerife towers above all the rest. The summit of Mount Teide, covered with snow or sulfur depending on the time of year, can be seen from far and wide. The highest mountain in Spain braves the trade winds, absorbing life-giving moisture from the clouds that crowd around its peak. Gran Canaria has been referred to as a "continent in miniature," but this applies more to Tenerife. There are up to 10 climatic zones on the "Isle of Hell," as Tenerife was known to medieval writers; four differently-shaped mountain ranges make up the relief, extensive forests turn into deserts of boulders and scree reminiscent of moonscapes, and there are broad sand beaches here too.

Tenerife has become so popular that formerly unspoiled and beautiful regions – such as the Oratava Valley that was praised so highly by Alexander von Humboldt – have now been turned into large built-up areas. Formerly barren coastal strips have been transformed into large vacation centers. Tenerife is the largest of the Canary Islands, and has a

Previous Pages: Snow-capped Mount Teide, the "Mount Fuji of the Canaries." Left: The carnival in Santa Cruz provides strong competition for Rio de Janeiro.

good traffic infrastructure – so finding your way around and exploring in a rental car is a good idea. Luckily, though, there are regions that can still only be properly explored by hikers, and for many they make up the real Tenerife.

Like most of the Canary Islands, Tenerife has two sides to its climate: there's the one sheltered from the wind, where it's almost always summer, and the one towards the wind where climatic conditions are rather more spring-like. The south is warm and dry, and the north is pleasantly moderate – but also cloudy and damp, especially in the winter months. Hikers therefore prefer the north and the center, while beach fans head south. Watersports and paragliding can be indulged in all over the island.

Arrival

The main port of entry to the island for vacationers is the international **Aeropuerto Reina Sofía** in the south. There are car rental firms here, public buses and taxis; you can exchange money at the bank, and the tourist information office can provide information on accommodation and sights.

If you're arriving by plane from the other islands, you'll usually land at **Los Rodeos** airport, near La Laguna in the

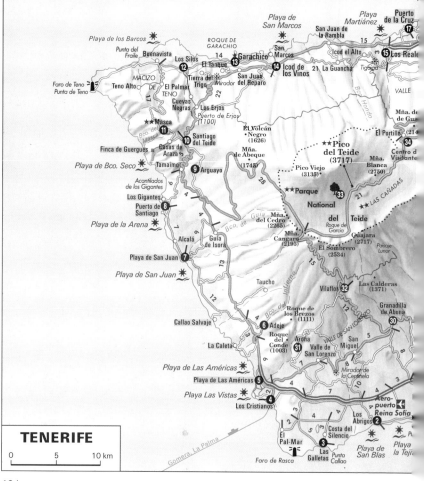

OCÉANO

ATLÁNTICO

Playa de los Barcos ✳
Punta del Fraile
Buenavista
Los Silos ⑫ El Tanque
ROQUE DE GARACHIO
Garachico ⑬
San Marcos
Playa de San Marcos
Playa Martiánez ✳ Puerto de la Cruz ⑰
San Juan de la Rambla   15
Icod el Alto ⑮ Los Reale
Faro de Teno ➤=
Punta de Teno ➤=
MACIZO DE TENO
Teno Alto
El Palmar TENO
Tierra del Trigo
Mirador
San Juan del Reparo
Icod de los Vinos
La Guancha   21   Tigaiga
VALLE
Cuevas Negras
Los Erjos
Puerto de Erjos (1100)
22
El Volcán • Negro (1626)
Mña. de Gua
El Portillo (21-
③④
★★Masca ⑪
Santiago del Teide ⑩
Mña. de Abeque (1745)
★★Pico del Teide (3717)
Mña. Blanca (2750)
Centro d Visitante
Finca de Guergués
Casas de Araza
Tamaimo
⑨ Arguayo
Pico Viejo (3135)
Playa de Bco. Seco
Acantilados de los Gigantes
6
Los Gigantes
Puerto de Santiago ⑧
★★Parque
National
del Teide
Roque del Garcia
★★LAS CAÑADAS
Playa de la Arena ✳
Alcalá
Guía de Isora
Mña. del Cedro (2265)
Mña. Cangaro (2195)
Guajara (2717)
Paisaje Lunar
El Sombrero (2534)
28
21
Bco. de Guía
13
Playa de San Juan ⑦
Playa de San Juan ✳
Taucho
12
Las Calderas (1371)
Vilaflor ㉜
Granadilla de Abuna
㉚
Callao Salvaje
⑥ Adeje
Roque del Conde (1003)
Roque de los Brezos (1111)
Aroña ㉛
VALLE DE SAN LORENZO
San Miguel
La Caleta
Valle de San Lorenzo
Mirador de la Centinela
Playa de Las Américas ✳
Playa de Las Américas ⑤
Aero-puerto Reina Sofía
Playa Las Vistas ✳
④
Los Cristianos
Los Abrigos ②
P.
El Pal-Mar ➤=
③
Costa del Silencio
Playa de San Blas
Playa la Teji
Las Galletas
Punta Callao
Faro de Rasca

Gomera, La Palma

TENERIFE

0   5   10 km

124

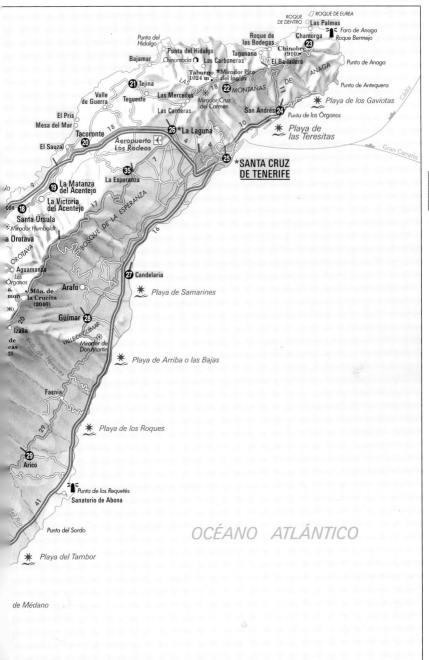

OCÉANO ATLÁNTICO

north. There, too, you'll find car rental firms, buses and taxis. The ferries from Cádiz and Gran Canaria arrive at the capital Santa Cruz de Tenerife, while the ones from Gomera and La Palma dock at the harbor of Los Cristianos. Here, too, there are plenty of taxis and buses around.

THE SUNNY SOUTHWEST

El Médano

If you're crazy about surfing wind and waves, then **El Médano ❶**, located east of the international airport, will be like paradise. It consists of modern buildings grouped around a small sandy beach and a broad plaza beyond it, which is used for fiestas and which becomes the social center after siesta time. On the western side is a small beach promenade with ice cream parlors, cafés and restaurants. There are

Above: El Médano is one of the world's top 10 windsurfing centers. Right: Golf del Sur, one of the four golf courses in the south.

more restaurants on the eastern side of the plaza and also down at the fishing harbor, where the narrow streets make everything more atmospheric.

The main attraction here, however, is definitely windsurfing. El Médano is one of the 10 top addresses in the world for windsurfers, and international competitions are held here every year. Accommodation, courses and equipment are all provided here – and there's no better feeling than surfing across the bay with your eyes on the **Punta Roja**, a red volcanic cone at the end of it!

If you only come here to swim, there's an endless sand beach just 10 minutes' walk away from the western side of the town: the **Playa de la Tejita** (nudity is also partially tolerated here, by the way) with its light sand that has been baked into tuff at some locations. There are no plants and no shade as far as the eye can see, and hardly any protection from the wind either. Miniature "dust devils" are a common sight here. A little farther west, **Los Abrigos ❷** has made a name for it-

Tenerife

self as a provider of seafood specialties. The rocky bay here which forms a natural harbor is lined with an astonishing number of fish restaurants, all with views of the sea. On nice weekends they're usually packed, especially the *Perlas del Mar*, which is magnificently located up on a rock on the eastern side of the harbor. If you're lucky, freshly-caught fish may just be arriving down at the harbor – and it will arrive on your plate very shortly afterwards, garnished beautifully and utterly delicious.

To reach the next coastal village to the west you first have to turn inland. After a golf course, the green grass of which contrasts markedly with the dark, earth colors of the desert-like landscape here, you'll arrive at **Costa del Silencio**, a chessboard-like conglomeration of hotels and apartment blocks, with a few stores and restaurants of its own. The town of **Las Galletas ❸**, which replaced the former fishing huts here, is also full of new buildings. Behind a narrow, dark pebble beach there's a pedestrian promenade

with ice-cream parlors, cafés and restaurants that is actually the only place people can walk here. The name of the apartment village, *Ten-Bel* (short for "Tenerife-Belgium"), makes it clear that a lot of Belgians spend their vacations here.

An enormous, brightly-painted quay wall encloses the bay of Las Galletas. Anyone looking for a bit of a change can watch the fishermen landing their catches here, or stroll past the anchored yachts. The protected harbor is ideal for windsurfing beginners who find the waves at El Médano too difficult to negotiate – you can wobble around on your board a lot more easily here without having to fall in all the time!

Incidentally, if you feel like exploring the underwater world of this volcanic island massif, try visiting the diving schools at Costa del Silencio and in Las Galletas, which also provide useful lessons for beginners. Golfers and golf hopefuls will find a golf school near the turnoff to El Palm-Mar, with a nine-hole course.

Los Cristianos and Las Américas – The Tourist Centers

In early photographs, **Los Cristianos** ❹ looks like a sleepy little fishing village at the end of the world. The fishermen are still here, but no one is sleepy any more, least of all the tourists returning from the all-night discos. Los Cristianos now takes up an entire inhospitable stretch of barren coastline, and its apartment buildings, hotels, restaurants and stores extend high up the surrounding slopes. In the town center, the modern **Plaza del Carmen** is the center of social life for the inhabitants as well, so Los Cristianos doesn't appear half as sterile as many similar towns. The light sand beach is protected by the large harbor wall and is very popular with families. Fishing boats, ferries and excursion ships coming and going also ensure that there's always something to see.

Above: The daily bustle on the kilometers-long beach promenade of Playa de Las Américas. Right: Surfing in wintertime.

The newly laid out sand beach to the west of the center, the **Playa Las Vistas**, is larger and a lot more cosmopolitan. Its pedestrian promenade leads as far as the northern end of the **Playa de Las Américas** ❺, the town's far busier rival when it comes to filling beds and pampering streams of visitors.

While Los Cristianos still has an old-fashioned, relaxed edge to it, Las Américas is action 24 hours a day. Not a lot of sleeping goes on around here. The pubs and discos are often open at any time of the day or night, ready to cater to the wishes of excitement-hungry guests. The most notorious center of all this action is **Las Verónicas**, with its continuous thumping music. There were several battles here in the past between very violent and mainly British youths and the island police, who at first were not equipped to deal with them.

You usually have to look twice to realize that life in Las Américas, which has several beaches protected by breakwaters, is not that bad after all. Plenty of wa-

ter from the mountains ensures that the plant life here thrives, and many a tedious-looking modern building has been esthetically rescued as a result. Some of the hotels are miniature botanical gardens in their own right. Hotel buildings in every modern style also constitute the main sights of Las Américas. One very striking establishment is the exclusive *Bahia del Duque*, with its blend of super-modern and Canarian traditional architecture.

Playa de Las Américas caters to every spare-time activity you can think of, and a lot more besides: there are swimming pools and tennis courts at virtually every hotel here, and entertainers and "animators" work tirelessly to keep the guests fit and merry. Water parks, sailing, diving, parascending – everything marketable or merely "in" can be found here.

The tourist boom in Las Américas also resulted in the construction of numerous modern buildings in **Adeje** ❻, which until the 1980s used to be an inconspicuous but picturesque small village in the hinterland. An avenue lined with laurels

passes through the historic center, and numerous restaurants and bars have their tables outside. At the end of this main street there's a freshly-renovated little church, the two-aisled **Iglesia Santa Úrsula**. Alongside its Mexican-style belfry and a remarkable ceiling construction in the presbytery dating from the 17th century, the church also contains a special relic from the feudal era: a barred balcony above the sacristy from which the former lords of Adeje – members of the influential Genoese family of Ponte, who also owned Gomera and Hierro at some time or other – used to listen to Mass being celebrated.

The Ponte family's fortified residence dating from the 16th century, the **Casa Fuerte**, is only a ruin today. The former manor house can be found to the northwest of the church, at the start of the hiking path into the Barranco del Infierno. A cannon once used against pirates stands on a small hill nearby.

For hikers, the ***Barranco del Infierno** is a nice, easy introduction to the special qualities of the landscape on Tenerife. From Adeje, a well-surfaced path leads to an 80-meter-high waterfall, which can be very or not so wet depending on the time of year. In peak season this ravine gets quite full of people, so you can't expect it to be that peaceful (the hike there and back takes around three hours altogether).

Along the West Coast

As you continue driving along the coast road in a northwesterly direction, you'll pass banana plantations and newly claimed land, revealing that the real estate boom in the southwest of the island still hasn't peaked. Tourist enclaves such as La Caleta or Callao Salvaje will probably grow together one day.

Playa de San Juan ❼ has been around for quite a while, but its white buildings look very modern. The most interesting feature of the place is the harbor, protected by a large harbor mole, and also a dry dock. There's always something going on here: fishermen can be seen mending their nets, and boat-builders painting their ships.

A detour inland leads to **Guía de Isora**, where the almond trees blossom very beautifully every spring. The large amount of water and the fertile soil in this region have made it a center of potato and tomato cultivation. The church of **Virgen de la Luz** contains not only a renovated Artesonado ceiling, but also two Madonna statues by José Luján Pérez, the famous baroque woodcarver from Gran Canaria.

The next village to the north of Playa de San Juan, **Alcalá**, is rather a rarity in this part of Tenerife – it's one of the very few places in the southwest not to have sold out to tourism. The village is located right next to the sea with a view of

Right: The attractive black sand of the Playa de la Arena, with a view of Gomera.

Gomera, and has a harbor inside a small bay on the steep coast. The central plaza still retains the relaxed atmosphere of the good old days, and it's definitely worth soaking up that feeling for a short while.

At the end of the coast road is the former fishing harbor of **Puerto de Santiago ❽**, which has long since been transformed into a vacation resort and has grown together with its modern satellite town of Los Gigantes. The main attraction here is the well-tended, dark sand beach of **Playa de la Arena**, where wooden planks protect your feet from the scorching sand. Some fishermen still leave from here, but most of them seem to earn more taking tourists out on boat trips to the bays outside all the local barrancos and back again.

In **Los Gigantes**, large and sprawling apartment complexes can be seen all over the slopes. The quiet streets are full of luxuriant vegetation, and wind their way gracefully through this hilly town. Los Gigantes is named after the up to 600-meter-high and 10-kilometer-long **★steep coast**, which is worth a boat trip on its own. You can find a boat at **Puerto Deportivo** (yacht harbor) at the foot of the enormous rocky cliffs, where various attractive ships lie at anchor – and the voyage to the steep cliffs is definitely worthwhile. The dark beach is protected by quay walls, so children can bathe quite safely there.

While you're winding your way up around the hairpin bends to **Tamaimo** and looking down at the terraced tomato fields below, you may catch sight of a paraglider coming down from the Ladera del Bicho if the thermals are right. It's a sport which has become increasingly popular in recent years, and the conditions around here are especially suitable. Some paraglider pilots are so skilled that they can use thermals to fly upwards rather than down, and soar around for hours on end. Tamaimo is an ambitious little place that is doing its best to earn

money from the tourists by selling craft products like embroidered cloths.

Just before the plateau of Santiago del Teide there's a turnoff to **Arguayo** ❾, near which you'll find lava dating from the last eruption in 1909. Today you can still see which fields the lava covered and which ones it spared. Arguayo used to supply the entire southwest of the island with clay vessels, and traditional pottery (without the use of a wheel) has recently been revived as part of a state-financed project. In the **Centro Alfarero**, a small museum on the main street, you can see the latest generation of potters at work.

THE NORTHWESTERN TIP
Rocky and Unspoiled

Santiago del Teide ❿, picturesquely surrounded by vineyards and cornfields, nestles among the foothills of Teide and the Teno Mountains. Several large wine presses (*lagars*) rotting away at the side of the road make it clear that we're in a wine region. A few pleasant stores on the main road and a tasting center cater to the tourists. At the center of Santiago there's a Moorish-style whitewashed church, built in the early 20th century, with a small domed roof. A pass road in front of it leads off to the west, and to one of the landscape highlights of Tenerife: first of all there's a fantastic view from the top of the pass, the ***Degollada de Cherfe**, back down across the Santiago Valley, dominated majestically by the summit of Teide. You can clearly see the black tongues of lava from the last eruption here, up on the Teide Massif. Across to the west and the north are the jagged Teno Mountains, La Gomera can be seen across the ocean, and in good weather you can even make out La Palma to the northwest. Don't miss this amazing panorama. It's not far from here to Tenerife's most attractive village, either!

Masca – Finest Village on the Island

A narrow, winding road leads to ****Masca** ⓫, the location of which re-

sembles the bottom of a well-shaft. It consists of several small hamlets; their houses are made of natural dark stone and are located on the few relatively flat areas of the rocks. A series of pleasant restaurants fits into the landscape nicely, so you can enjoy the excellent combination of delicious food and amazing panoramic view. Before the tourist boom this place was considered by many to be the finest village on the island, and could only be reached along mule paths. These days it's far too overcrowded with visitors, because the **Barranco de Masca** has become a very popular place in which to go hiking.

The hike down the winding path into the ravine is one of the most exciting things you can do on Tenerife. Depending on your stamina it can take from two to three hours (and almost twice as long to

Above and Right: The hike through the bizarre Barranco de Masca (above) from the picturesque village of Masca (right) is now one of the most popular walking routes on Tenerife.

get back up), but the weird ravine rewards all the trouble you take with a whole series of plants endemic to the island, all of which are protected. On hot afternoons the air here can be incredibly hot – so don't forget to bring along enough to drink. When the tide is out a black beach appears by the sea, but swimming in strong surf is very dangerous, and there are also hidden rocks beneath the water. If you don't feel like making the tiring return journey, you can arrange for a fisherman from Playa de Santiago to pick you up in advance – just decide on a price and a time with him.

If you don't feel all that athletic, a less arduous hike leads to a deserted farmstead, the **Finca de Guergues**. It is located on a sloping plateau to the south of the Barranco de Masca and affords impressive views of the Barranco Seco and as far as Las Américas. You start the hike near the **Casas de Araza**, visible directly below from the Degollada de Cherfe, and stay on the path which first leads up to the southern edge of the Barranco de Masca

so you can get several great views of its depths. On foot, one way, this trip takes around two hours. The former threshing floor is a good place to have a picnic.

In the Teno Mountains

A well-paved road with a few dangerous narrow sections leads up to the top of the pass, beyond which you'll see the high valley of **El Palmar**. There are a few hamlets dotted across this broad green valley, with its wonderful scent of eucalyptus and wild fennel. The area's main town, El Palmar, nestles beneath a volcanic cone which has bits cut out of it in several places, rather like a cake, to provide fertile volcanic earth for the banana plantations.

From El Palmar the journey continues westwards to a high plateau and to **Teno Alto**. Although there's actually a restaurant here now as well as a store, this place is like going back hundreds of years. The farmers in the small hamlets around here, who have to make do with a few goats and

a tiny plot of land, do not have an easy time of things. It's not surprising that a lot of young people are deserting the villages up here. The old people use scythes to cut animal fodder from the roadside and then carry the heavy bundles home on their heads, accompanied by their dogs. By the way, there's a great route through this unspoiled landscape for weatherproof hikers: a path leads slightly downhill from Teno Alto and westwards to the edge of the Teno Massif, from where you can see the lighthouse on the Punta de Teno; and you can also reach it via a steep path that goes down the edge of the massif (about five hours there and back).

Back in El Palmar, keep traveling north and go down the coast as far as **Buenavista**, a town still largely untouched by tourism. There's a small harbor for fishing boats here, and the **Playa de los Barcos** with its rough pebble beach sometimes gets visited by tourists. The large village square has an inviting coffee pavilion for a well-earned rest. This is the other, peaceful side of Tenerife, where

time oftens seems to be standing still. The nearby **Iglesia Nuestra Señora de los Remedios**, built in 1513 and the most important historic building in Buenavista, was unfortunately destroyed in a fire in 1996. Renovators are trying to reconstruct the interior again, with its fascinating *mudéjar* ceiling.

If the road happens not to be closed because of rain, there's a good detour at this point to the lighthouse on the **Punta de Teno**. Travel along this spectacular steep coast and through two tunnels, and you'll reach the **Faro de Teno** and several small bays that are used for swimming when the sea is calm, despite a rather uncomfortable descent to get there. The color contrast between the crystal-clear turquoise of the sea and the reddish-brown volcanic rock is also very pleasant, even if swimming isn't possible.

Above: The whole place relaxes during a Romería, here in Buenavista. Right: Garachico – architectural jewel in the northwest of Tenerife.

East of Buenavista, in the midst of banana plantations, is **Los Silos** ⓬, which like the entire northwestern corner of Tenerife has fortunately remained largely undiscovered by tourism as yet. People don't come to Los Silos for impressive sights, nor for the rather eclectic, wedding-cake-style church of **Nuestra Señora de la Luz**. They come here for the idyllic and shady square at the center of the village with the obligatory coffee pavilion in the middle – all of it reached along a bumpy road.

For hikers, the **Laurel Forest** in the mountains to the south of Los Silos is a real treat. Leave the village at the church and soon you'll pass through a deserted hamlet called **Cuevas Negras**, where "hippies" (the name the locals give to dropouts) sometimes live. At Los Erjos on the high road, curve away to the west in order to get back to Los Silos. This round hike, which takes all day, leads through the largest intact laurel forest on the island and is an unforgettable experience for nature lovers.

Tenerife

*Garachico – Past Glory

Garachico 🔞 is a real jewel. Hardly any other place on the island has remained so homogeneously intact as this town, which was once the largest trading harbor on the island. In 1706, the wealthy little community was rendered totally insignificant after the worst volcanic eruption in the island's history: lava poured through large parts of the town, burying whole districts and much of the harbor. Garachico never recovered economically from this catastrophe – but it still has several houses in the simple, traditional style and several historic buildings as well, and overall presents a rare picture of architectural unity.

Even before you reach the town – by the bend in the road with the **Monumento al Emigrante Canario** ("Monument to the Canarian Emigrant"), where the statue has a hole in its chest in place of its heart – you will see the central parish church of **Santa Ana**. Its predecessor was destroyed by fire in the 1706 eruption,

approximately 200 years after it was first built, but today's church still contains the first retables ever made on the island – because an artists' workshop for altarpieces has been doing good business in prosperous Garachico ever since the 17th century.

Beyond the church is the shady **Plaza de Arriba** with its monument in honor of Simón Bolívar, liberator of South America, and the pavilion so typical of the island. The gloomy-looking **Palacio de los Condes de la Gomera** ("Palace of the Counts of Gomera"; 17th century) is made of dark-gray basalt, and looks like it could do with some renovation work. It takes up almost the whole south side of the square.

The **Convento de San Francisco** (Franciscan monastery, 16th century) on the **Plaza Glorieta de San Francisco** is now a cultural center, and is also worth a visit. Its rooms contain alternating exhibitions of works by local artists. Photographs and documentation about the town's history are on display here, to-

and numerous works by local artists can be seen here. Concerts here are highly recommended by the way; it's certainly hard to think of a better setting for chamber music.

Hikers who also like history will enjoy the cobbled former bridle path that leads to **San Juan del Reparo**, and which starts beyond the harbor park. The two-hour walk provides hikers with a rewarding view of Garachico, towering above the sea like a huge balcony of lava.

Icod de los Vinos

Ancient myths relate that the first settlers here in the pre-Hispanic era arrived on the island close to the region around today's **Icod de los Vinos** ⓮, 200 meters above the sea. Located right beneath the peak of Teide, the town gets an awe-inspiring view of the "Fujiyama of the Canaries."

gether with several liturgical instruments and a collection of stuffed sea animals, birds and butterflies.

The former harbor gate, or **Puerta de Tierra**, was dug out of the section of harbor that was buried by the lava, and is now surrounded by an attractive park. Hidden away in back of it is an old wooden wine press, and the **Castillo de San Miguel** (17th century) is a relic from the days of pirates. Once built to defend the harbor, it now contains an interesting exhibition of rocks, fossils and shells. On the terrace next door you can enjoy a meal with a view of the seawater swimming pool, best appreciated at sunset.

On the eastern edge of town is the former **Dominican Monastery**, which today is an old people's home. The chapel attached to it is a museum of modern art,

Icod de los Vinos, as its name suggests, is surrounded by a very fertile wine growing region. Efforts made over past years to keep quality steady have won this region the right to a special indication of region of origin (*Ycoden Daute Isora*). The undisputed main attraction in Icod, however, is its legendary dragon tree known as the ***Drago Milenario**, which, though reputed to be 1,000 years old is probably "only" half that age. Despite all its concrete and metal supports it is still very much alive, however. Since a dragon tree isn't really a proper tree at all, its real age can't be measured by counting its rings. There is no more mighty specimen of this endemic plant anywhere else in the Canary Islands, however. The tree was sacred to the Guanches, who used its sap for curative purposes and embalmed their dead with it, and today it is a protected species.

On the church square and the nearby Plaza de la Constitución there are more interesting plants, including ornamental banana and jacaranda. The three-aisled

Above: This attractive Canarian balcony in Icod de los Vinos clearly shows Andalusian influence. Right: The main attraction in Icod de los Vinos is the Drago Milenario, seen here with San Marcos in the background.

Tenerife

*Iglesia San Marcos (15th-century) with its late Gothic, Renaissance and baroque elements contains fine retables and Artesonado ceilings. Its church treasure includes liturgical implements, Mass clothing and a cross made of Mexican silver. It weighs 47 kilograms and is two meters high, and is thought to be the largest filigree silver cross ever made (on display in the mornings in the sacristy).

The **Plaza de la Constitución**, located a little higher up, still looks the same as it did 200 years ago. With its centuries-old traditional-style buildings and its mossy well in the middle, it's one of the most homogeneous places on the island. Winetasting cellars and shops selling wines and cheeses from the region ensure that visitors can feast more than their eyes on what this place has to offer.

Every year on the night of November 29 the town comes alive. The bodegas celebrate the end of the wine harvest, and there's a big fiesta out in the streets with hot chestnuts, barbecued meat on skewers and plenty of wine to wash it all down.

Young people race down the steep streets of Icod on improvised wooden sleds at amazing speeds. Although a high pile of car tires brakes their descent at the bottom, the crazier ones always race past and often get injured quite badly.

The ***Playa de San Marcos** is a far quieter place altogether, indeed it's one of the safest swimming bays in the north. The black sand beach lies below the town, and is protected by enormous rocky projections. In the summer most of the visitors here are locals, but in the winter they find the water too cold, and leave the tourists to themselves.

Anyone who wants to go back from Icod de los Vinos southwards will find themselves on a high road that leads through several hamlets to **El Tanque** and from there, via the 1,100-meter-high **Puerto de Erjos** pass, into the high valley of Santiago del Teide (see p. 131). On the western edge of El Tanque Alto (the upper section of the village), on the road to Tierra del Trigo, there's a *Mirador* with a good view of Teide and the coast. A cooking school restaurant here is a good place to stop and enjoy some fine Canarian food. The simple Canarian-style building on the turnoff to the observation point with the bizarre sculptures serves as a studio for the Italian artist Antoine Manfredi.

From Icod de los Vinos, the round-trip tour of the island can either run along the main route, which leads directly to the highway at Puerto de la Cruz, or along a rather more complicated mountain route that passes through La Guancha to La Orotava, located in the higher reaches of the Orotava Valley.

On the coast road from Icod to the Oratava Valley, you'll pass a series of small villages, with restaurants and stopping off places. The larger villages are off to the side closer to the sea – one of these is **San Juan de la Rambla**, a nice place with a recently refurbished center. The church and surrounding buildings have all been newly whitewashed, and many houses still have old Canarian wooden balconies, shady patios and red tiled roofs.

One of these buildings has been rented out by an international group of artists, who have founded the **Biblioteca Expresión Contemporánea Antonín Artaud**, in which exhibitions, lectures, discussions and workshops are held. If you're interested in local art, this is one of the top addresses.

The country road leads into a rural region just after Icod and then up to **La Guancha**, and is far less traveled than the coastal route. Leaving the modern and rather too tidy village behind you, drive up to the observation point on the **Ladera de Tigaiga**, just after Icod El Alto. Here you'll see the entire Orotava Valley at your feet. Once praised by German natu-

ralist and writer Alexander von Humboldt for its gentleness and varied flora, this strip of land is now one of the most built-up on Tenerife. There's a larger-than-life statue of Bentor here, the son of the Mencey of Taoro, who jumped off the edge of the Ladera to his death after the Guanches were defeated at La Victoria del Acentejo (see p. 143).

THE OROTAVA VALLEY

Although **Los Realejos** ⓯ seems close enough to touch from the Mirador, there are several more hairpin bends to negotiate before you reach the upper part of it (Realejo Alto). Realejo Bajo and several settlements down near the coast combine with Realejo Alto to make up Los Realejos, the name of which is derived from the Spanish conquerors' royal camp (*real* = "royal"). Even though this is an old town – it was one of the first ever towns founded by the island's new overlords – the atmosphere is anything but old-fashioned. Both historic sections of it are full of modern buildings, and the churches are now almost the only reminder of its past. It was in today's lower town that the Spaniards finally managed to break the resistance of the Guanches of Taoro, and the defeated aboriginal population were forced to be baptized in the upper town.

The **church** in the upper town was completed as long ago as 1498, and is therefore the oldest on Tenerife. It was built on the site of Alonso de Lugo's military camp. The choir at the main altar is 17th-century, but not much remains of the church's original structure now. A tower was added in 1774 during one of the frequent periods of alteration work. Highlights inside the building include a statue of Christ by Martín de Andújar, and a Flemish *Santa Lucía*.

Outside the church is a monument honoring the enlightened cleric and thinker Viera y Clavijo (1731-1813), the town's

Right: Flowers carpeting the streets and festive flags and pennants at all the windows mark the route of Orotava's Corpus Christi procession.

Tenerife

most famous son, who was the first person to write a detailed history of the Canary Islands, the *Noticias de la Historia General de las Islas Canarias,* which has been the official work of reference for the past two centuries. Clavijo, an enlightened theologian and a friend of Voltaire and other free thinkers, died in Las Palmas in 1813.

*La Orotava – Old Trading Town Steeped in History

At the eastern end of the Orotava Valley, 400 meters above the sea, lies the town of **La Orotava** ⓰. The showpiece of this fast-growing municipality is its well-preserved historic *Old Town, all of which has been put under a preservation order. This is also where most visitors come, rather than to the busy eastern part of town with all its stores, apartment blocks and industrial estates. The old Town Hall square is still the center of life here. The famous carpet of colorful volcanic earth and blossoms is laid out here

and in the narrow lanes along the path of the annual Corpus Christi procession.

Orotava's Old Town, which reveals just how wealthy the merchants in this municipality were in former days, is best explored from the **Plaza de la Constitución**. Enjoy a coffee in the pavilion, and the view of the remarkable buildings around the square. The former **Augustinian Convent** dating from the 17th century has a freshly renovated monastery church, containing retables (shelves or frames enclosing decorated panels behind altars) from various epochs and an artistic Artesonado ceiling.

The **Liceo de Taoro**, reminiscent of an Italian country house, was formerly a school and today is used as a casino by a private cultural association. To the right, beyond the Liceo, you can see the marble mausoleum of the Ponte family (designed by French artist Adolphe Coquet in 1882) in the **Jardín Victoria**, a renovated public park. The view of the old section of La Oratava from the mausoleum is the best in town.

To the west of the plaza stands the baroque **Iglesia Nuestra Señora de la Concepción**. It was built in 1788 above the foundations of a previous structure that was destroyed by an earthquake in 1705. The church contains a fine *Dolorosa* and a statue of St. John by José Luján Pérez from Gran Canaria; the *Candelaria* and St. Peter statues are by Fernando Estévez, a native of La Orotava. The neoclassical marble pulpit is Genoese, and the marble tabernacle on the main altar is by the Italian master Giuseppe Gagini. There are also two very good paintings: *The Marriage of the Virgin Mary to St. Joseph* by Cristóbal Quintana, and an *Immaculate Conception* by Gaspard de Quevedo.

Many of the townhouses and manors in La Orotava proudly bear familial coats of arms carved in stone above their main doorways. Some of the historic buildings

Above: The patio of the Casa de los Balcones in Orotava. Right: Puerto de la Cruz – coastal resort with a cosmopolitan character.

have long balconies of dark Canary pine, and have shady patios and wooden verandas surrounded by much luxuriant foliage. Good examples of these can be found in the steep Calle San Francisco at the 17th-century ***Casa de los Balcones** (above the church). Inside the houses, various Canarian craft products are on display and for sale.

There are simpler houses from earlier epochs in the mill district of **Farrabo** above the Old Town. Even though the old watermills have been replaced by motorized ones, many of the old implements still survive and are happily shown to visitors. The mills can be recognized by their round structure, and usually (but not always) have damaged-looking water pipes leading to them.

On the way from the Casas de los Balcones to the Town Hall is **El Pueblo Guanche**, a small ethnographical museum inside a renovated townhouse. The Canarian food served here in traditional surroundings is almost more remarkable than the exhibition of finds from the pre-Hispanic era.

Behind the neoclassical Town Hall is a park called **Hijuela**. It is part of the Botanical Gardens of Puerto de la Cruz, which has plants native to the Canary Islands, as well as several species that were introduced later.

Back at the Plaza de la Constitución, you can see the church tower of the Monastery of Santo Domingo towering above the jumble of rooftops. If you're keen on seeing a very nice museum, visit the ***Museo de Artesanía Iberoamericana** inside this attractively restored monastery building. Several exhibition halls on two levels contain collections of Latin-American musical instruments, ceramics, woven products, textiles and a series of prize-winning items of furniture designed by local artists.

The upper Orotava Valley is an ideal place for lonely walks and long hikes. Good starting points are **La Caldera**, a

Tenerife

picnic site inside a small crater, or the nearby **Aguamansa** with its fishponds. It's also rewarding to go on a roughly three-hour-long tour around Los Órganos, a rock formation resembling organ pipes that you can see peeking through the trees at La Caldera. Another possibility is to follow the pilgrim route to Arafo (about five hours), signposted 200 meters to the east of La Caldera, which leads along the Cumbre Dorsal and down to the south.

Puerto de la Cruz – Bastion of Tourism

From a distance **Puerto de la Cruz** ⑰ may appear rather forbidding because of the endless line of horrid skyscrapers along the coast. Nevertheless, the former harbor of La Orotava has retained a few little corners that visitors have kept returning to over the years. The harbor is used by just a handful of fishermen, whose boats provide a welcome dash of color against the grayish-black pebble shore. Beyond the harbor, the crowded **Plaza del Charco**, with its shady Indian laurel, is definitely the heart of the town.

Across to the west is the most unspoiled quarter, **La Ranilla**, with its small but excellent restaurants. The main tourist street begins over to the east. It leads past the **Iglesia San Francisco** (1608), which is used as an art gallery today, and the slightly elevated church square to the **Punta del Viento**, where a short promenade above the steep coast begins. From here you can see the *★Lago Martiánez**, the seawater swimming pool designed by César Manrique, using only natural materials from the island. The tourist street ends at the newly-created **Playa de Martiánez**, where restaurants playing international pop oldies suddenly seem to be all over the place.

Relics from the time when Puerto rose to become the most important trading harbor in the northern part of the island after the destruction of Garachico can be found all over this tourist center. From west to east, they are the **Castillo San**

Felipe (early 17th century), which puts on good exhibitions and has even better concerts than the Playa Jardín; the former **Customs House** at the harbor; severable respectable-looking merchants' houses, such as the **Casa Iriarte** on Calle San Juan; or the town villas that have now become the **Marquesa** and **Monopol** hotels.

The two hotels stand opposite the ***Iglesia Nuestra Señora de la Peña de Francia**, a church popular for weddings. This church, with the small park beside it and the swan fountain in the plaza, is especially picturesque on moonlit nights. Inside it, local artist Luís de la Cruz has created paintings for retables and pulpits; there is also a *Dolorosa* by José Luján Pérez and a statue of St. Peter by Fernando Estévez.

One recent jewel is the wild and romantic ***Playa Jardín** in the west, which

Above: Puerto de la Cruz is a great place to indulge in Mediterranean-style food. Right: The dolphin show in the Loro Parque.

was designed by César Manrique. This black sand beach has brought Puerto de la Cruz a new clientele: while surfers display their talents offshore, people can bathe in the gentle surf, protected by submerged breakwaters. The park-like area beyond is a real eye-opener.

Just a short distance away to the southwest in the suburb of Punta Brava is the internationally-renowned ***Loro Parque**. This efficiently-run 125,000 square meter "parrot park" contains the largest parrot collection in the world, with over 300 species and sub-species. The entrance hall contains an "original" Thai village, while a Gambian market on the site gives the whole place an African feel. Parrots with little roller skates strapped to their feet perform tricks in the parrot shows here, and there are also shows with sea lions and dolphins. A shark aquarium which can be walked through along a transparent underwater tunnel is a special attraction of the park.

Those more interested in plants should visit the ***Jardín de Aclimatación de**

Orotava in the La Paz district. This botanical garden was originally an intermediate storage location for tropical plants, which it was hoped could be trained to weather the climate of mainland Spain. As you can see, the plants are really flourishing here in Puerto, while in Spain they regularly withered away.

If you feel like leaving the hustle and bustle of Puerto de la Cruz and finding a nice, quiet and relaxing beach, go to **El Rincón** east of the town and walk down into the rocky bay at **Playa Bolullo**, with its beautiful black sand beach. No one knows how long this serene little place will last because investors are already planning a vacation complex with a golf course for this region.

On the edge of the Orotava Valley is **Santa Úrsula** ⑱, one of the sunniest towns in the north, and located on a busy through route. Innumerable stores, restaurants, banks, drugstores and repair shops have settled here. One of the few remaining historic buildings is the **parish church** dating from 1628, which contains

a sculpture of St. Rita by Fernando Estévez. At the **Humboldt View**, an observation point halfway to Santa Úrsula, you can read the praises heaped on this region by the famous German scholar as you peer down on this still very slightly gentle-looking valley.

Traveling Through the Acentejo

Travel through the Acentejo and you are moving through a very important historical region: this is where the decisive and dramatic war of resistance between the Guanches and their Spanish conquerors was played out. The first village on the route, **La Victoria del Acentejo**, derives its name from the Spanish victory. Decimated by disease and exhausted from their long struggle, the Guanches were forced to surrender on Christmas Day in 1495. A wind-blown pine tree next to the church (above the main road) is thought to date from that time. Inside the church there's an artistic Artesonado ceiling in the *mudéjar* style, and the architecture of the main chapel is Portuguese-colonial. Several families in the village itself are continuing the tradition of pottery making without the use of a wheel, as practiced by the Guanches.

The martial-sounding name of the neighboring village to the northeast, **La Matanza del Acentejo ⑲**, refers to the last victory of the Guanches before they were finally subjugated. The "bloodbath" of Acentejo, as the Spanish refer to their defeat, relates to a legend whereby the Guanches were not only very tough warriors but very cunning ones as well. Apparently they lured the Spanish into an ambush, and then broke up their battle lines by whistling loudly, thus getting a herd of goats to charge among them. After the hail of lances and rocks had ended the Spaniards had lost 900 mercenaries, the majority of them Canarian. The Spanish conqueror Alonso de Lugo was very lucky to escape alive.

THE NORTHEAST COAST AND ANAGA MOUNTAINS

The backbone of the northeast is formed by the Anaga Mountains, with fertile valleys to the west and northwest. The coastline in this part of Tenerife is rough and unsuitable for swimmers; hikers and wine lovers are more in their element round here. The latter should definitely visit **El Sauzal**, with its attractive ensemble consisting of the neo-Canarian Town Hall with its large flight of steps and the domed white church. There's a great view of the steep northern coast from the church square and also from an observation point just below it.

Just outside this town, near the highway exit, there's another jewel in the shape of **★Casa del Vino**. This renovated country house in the La Baranda district is a center of Tenerife wine, which

Right: The Anaga Mountains are a paradise for hikers.

goes extremely well with the substantial Canarian food. This blend of museum, wine-tasting hall, bar, restaurant and store was voted the best restaurant on Tenerife by the island's newspapers in 1995.

The busiest wine town around here is **Tacoronte ⑳** on the far western edge of the high plateau of La Laguna (500 meters above sea level). Its vintners have had their wine officially recognized and were the first on the island to fulfill the EU norms. **Bodegas Álvaro**, with their large selection of wines, organize tastings and is visited by numerous bus groups. The building is two kilometers outside the town center on the road to La Laguna, and is definitely worth a brief stopover if you feel like familiarizing yourself with the archipelago's greatest wines.

The two church squares are oases of peace in this busy small town. The churches that go with them – the **monastery church** of the Augustinian Order near the center and the **Iglesia Santa Catalina** located a little lower down, are the most important sights to be seen around here. The ornamentation on the retables inside reveals a distinctly Latin-American influence.

Mesa del Mar and **El Pris**, two small towns on the coast reached via steep roads, should be visited by anyone who really enjoyed the view of the steep coast near El Sauzal. While the cliffs are far more attractive than the buildings in Mesa del Mar, El Pris is a sleepy little fishing village which unfortunately has not totally escaped the tourist trade. Beyond the large tunnel in Mesa del Mar there is a sheltered bay with black volcanic sand that is especially suitable for families with children who want to swim.

Valle de Guerra, in the steep valley of the same name, is surrounded by agriculture of all kinds, from banana plantations to fields of cut flowers. On its outskirts there is an agrarian institute researching into possibilities of improvement in culti-

vation methods so that they suit conditions on the island better. Nearby is the **Museo Etnográfico de Tenerife**, housed in an old building dating from the 17th century; it provides a glimpse into what country life was like in the past.

Also very agricultural is **Tejina ㉑**, on the eastern edge of the Valle de Guerra. Until the 1950s sugar cane was the main crop here, and was used to make rum in the local factory *Cocal*. Rum production is still here today (the factory is in the lower part of the town, and can produce up to 70,000 liters a day during its three-month season), but these days the sugar cane is imported from South Africa. The factory also produces the delicious, sweet "honey rum" (*ron miel*) as well as a banana liqueur.

From Tejina you can reach two resorts by the sea, which are mostly frequented by Germans. **Bajamar** with its large seawater swimming pool is a popular meeting place for the young people from nearby La Laguna. Not far away you can sit and watch the fishermen bringing in

their catch. Otherwise there's not a lot going on here – but it appears to be just what the regular visitors here from Europe seem to like.

Punta del Hidalgo, at the foot of the Anaga Mountains, looks more touristy because of its high-rises on the coast, but that doesn't make it any more attractive. Here, too, things are amazingly quiet: all you can hear is the sound of the surf and the occasional shriek of a seagull. Two seawater swimming pools and a beach promenade form the center of the holiday action here. The main road leads to a raised round tower, from which there is a good view of the jagged coastline, and also of a valley in the Anaga Mountains with the double rock formation of **Roque Dos Hermanos** at its eastern end. A well-marked hiking route leads from here to the still-inhabited cave dwellings at Chinamada, where the houses and apartment blocks peering over the top of the mountain ridge are actually set into the rockface behind. The ascent takes two and half hours or so, but provides great

views of the steep coastline and the bays below. To continue the journey you have to go back to Tejina and then turn off southeastwards in the direction of **Tegueste**, which has one of the best wrestling teams in the Canaries for the local sport of *lucha canaria*. The large arena says it all.

Along the Ridges of the Anaga Mountains

A left turn near Lass Canteras leads into the green heart of the Anaga Mountains, with their wild, jagged peaks and deep valleys. A small village is followed by the forest of the same name, **Las Mercedes**, one of the densest laurel forests (*laurisilva*) in the Canaries. It blends into a bush-like plant formation known as *Fayal-Brezal*, the characteristic plants of which are the Dutch myrtle (*faya*) and the brier (*brezo*).

Above: Lucha canaria in Tegueste. Right: The Playa de las Teresitas.

A series of observation points now follow along the winding road: the **Miradores Jardín** and **Cruz del Carmen** provide very good views across the plain of La Laguna and Teide in fine weather.

The panoramic view from the **★Pico del Inglés ㉒**, however, is unbeatable: from here, at an altitude of around 1,000 meters, you can look in every direction, across the green valleys and rough coastline around the Anaga Mountains – that is assuming there are no trade-wind clouds shrouding the scenery, which often happens after 11 a.m. There's a slightly more limited view from the drafty ridge of the **Bailadero**: to the south you can see part of the harbor installations at Santa Cruz de Tenerife, to the north you'll see **Taganana**, a picturesque village, with thin rows of white houses against the green of the valley. The heavy *Mavasía* grape is still grown here – the high altitude saved the vines from destruction during the phylloxera epidemic.

Down by the sea, on a weird-looking rocky outcrop, is the hamlet of **Roque de**

Tenerife

las Bodegas, which consists almost exclusively of seafood restaurants. It's best not to go swimming on the sand-and-pebble beach here with the rocks in between, though some surfers are actually attracted by the big waves.

If you want to explore the eastern Anaga Mountains, travel back to El Bailadero and go to the end of the road from there to **Chamorga** ㉓. This town is the starting point for an extremely varied, day-long hike around the northeastern tip of Tenerife, which will take you through El Draguillo, Las Palmas and Roque Bermejo.

In good weather, walking among the great variety of plant and rock formations, you'll be able to see the entire Anaga coastline. Apart from a long, slow climb at the end, this hike is well-marked and can easily be undertaken by the reasonably fit. Bring food and drink along, however, because there are no places to buy anything along the way.

You can reach the capital, Santa Cruz de Tenerife, by taking the coast road via

San Andrés ㉔. This small fishing village with its simple white houses is visited either for its excellent seafood or for a swim. Situated at the end of the 10-kilometer-long harbor installation of Santa Cruz, San Andrés formerly had the job of securing the northeastern flank of the capital in times of trouble. A collapsed watchtower stands as a reminder of that time.

On weekends or after work the *chicharreros*, as the people of the capital call themselves, come and have fun on the long, palm-lined **★Playa de las Teresitas**. A breakwater made of moss-covered stones allows people to bathe in peace, and protects the beach with its yellow sand which was imported here from the Sahara Desert. Showers are placed at regular intervals along the beach. Restaurants behind the beach area provide tapas and fresh drinks, and in the evenings the seafood restaurants along the Avenida Marítima in San Andrés are very popular. The fish is usually fresh, but to make absolutely sure it's best to eat at restaurants that keep live fish swimming outside their doors in aquariums.

*SANTA CRUZ DE TENERIFE
The New Metropolis

Santa Cruz de Tenerife ㉕, with its population of 200,000, is the largest town on the island and the second largest on the archipelago. It jointly runs the autonomous region of the Canary Islands together with the larger Las Palmas de Gran Canaria. Unlike Las Palmas, Santa Cruz de Tenerife has a far more harmonious appearance. This is largely because of its amphitheater-like location, framed as it is against the towering peaks of the Anaga Mountains.

At the heart of this semicircular city panorama is the **Plaza de España ❶**. If a large social event is about to occur – whether it's an open-air concert or a carnival – you can be sure it will take place here in this partly traffic-free square by the sea.

The Historic City Center

In the middle of the Plaza de España is the cruciform **Monumento a los Caídos**, in memory of all the Civil War dead of the island who fell fighting on the side of Franco. It was designed as an observation tower, and the plinth contains a small remembrance chapel. The tower has been closed ever since it became a May Day target for Canarian separatists in the 1970s so that, unfortunately, it cannot be climbed. Southwest of the monument is the **Palacio Insular** with its clock tower. Built in the eclectic style of the 1930s, it contains the island council (*Cabildo Insular*) and the tourist information office. The post and telegraph office to the right of it is housed inside a similarly monumental structure.

Beyond the Plaza de España, towards the center of the city, is a gently sloping square dedicated to the patron saint of the

archipelago, the light-giving Madonna of the Candelaria. In the representative **Plaza de la Candelaria ❷**, with its fountain and numerous palm trees, there are several attractive street cafés. The lower part of the plaza is dominated by the **Triunfo de la Candelaria**, a monument in white Italian marble portraying four Guanche princes (*menceyes*) who collaborated with the Spanish worshiping the Madonna. On the northeastern side of the square is the **Casino de Tenerife**, an exclusive gentlemen's club where the most high-ranking members of the civic administration meet up. To the left of the modern Plaza Hotel is the **Palacio de los Rodríguez Carta**. This former townhouse, built in 1742, is now occupied by a

bank. The noble patio, with its verandas and staircases of dark Canary pine, can be admired during opening hours.

On **Calle del Castillo** a little farther on, there is one store after the next. As you stroll through this narrow pedestrian precinct with its attractive window displays, keep in mind that the stores (not the cafés) close between 1 and 4:30 p.m. The same applies to **Calle de Béthencourt Alfonso**, which runs parallel and also leads to the shadiest square in the capital, the **Plaza del Príncipe de Asturias 3**. Under the impressive roof of mighty Indian laurels, the Café del Pricipe inside a fin-de-siècle-style glasshouse serves Canarian cakes, and concerts also take place here quite often.

The most striking-looking of the buildings around here is the clubhouse of the **Círculo de Amistad XII de Enero**, a private cultural association. Since it is not open to visitors you will have to content yourself with the sight of its eclectic early 20th-century facade with its dragons and female statues up on the gables. The **Museo Municipal** on the southeastern side of the square mainly contains works by local artists.

At the top end of Calle del Castillo you'll reach the **Plaza del General Weyler 4**, with its noisy traffic and a marble fountain in the center called "The Well of Love" (*Fuente del Amor*) by the Genoese sculptor Achille Caresse. A more romantic place is the smaller **Plaza**

de los Patos ⑤ on Avenida del 25 de Julio. Located at the center of an attractive villa area, this square – with its frog fountain and its Seville-tiled benches complete with nostalgic advertisements – is a very comfortable, quiet place to relax. South of it there is a row of government buildings that includes the seat of the Canarian president, the Bank of Spain, the Town Hall and the palazzo of the governor. The lime-green **Casa Quintero** ⑥ at Calle Jesús y María 15, with its Art Nouveau stucco, is the most eye-catching building in this neighborhood.

It's not far now to the botanical gardens, also known as the ***Parque Municipal García Sanabria**. This six-hectare-large municipal park contains a vast number of plants, both endemic and imported. There are also leafy promenades, romantic trellises and splashing fountains, plus some bizarre items of

Above: The Plaza de España – the heart of Santa Cruz. Right: The idyllic Plaza de los Patos on Avenida del 25 de Julio.

modern sculpture – the relics of a public exhibition during the 1970s.

At the top end of the park you should walk a short way down the **Rambla del General Franco**. This avenue is where the locals meet up for their *paseo* after the siesta. As in the park, there are sculptures here dating from the 1970s, including a *Reclining Warrior* by Henry Moore.

Near the **floral clock** beside the lower entrance to the park you can recover nicely from your stroll in a café. The best way back to the Plaza de España is along **Calle de Pilar**, a shopping street with shops for elevated tastes.

Southwest of the City Center

If you take Avenida de Bravo Murillo southwestwards from the Plaza de España, you'll arrive at the freshly renovated **Iglesia de la Concepción** ⑦. It was built in 1652 and is the successor of the town's first-ever church, built in 1502, which was destroyed in a fire. Its bell tower was also used as a lookout post, to

check whether pirates were around or anything was on fire. Typical features of Canarian architecture are the dark basalt stones on the tower and in the nave, and the balcony above the entrance. The octagonal tower served as a lookout post. Inside the low, five-aisled church the most noticeable features are the finely-carved Canary wood choir stalls and the various *mudéjar*-style ceilings. The Chapel of the Holy Heart, to the left of the altar, contains the cross carried by Alonso Fernández de Lugo when he claimed the islands. A further chapel contains the tombs of the islands' most famous classical composer, Teobaldo Power ("Cantos Canarios"), and General Gutiérrez, Lord Nelson's successful opponent.

On the other side of the Barranco de Santos is the building that housed the former hospital, and which today contains the *Museo de la Naturaleza y el Hombre* ⑧. This well-organized double museum has an archeological section displaying finds dating from the Guanche period, including some well-preserved

mummies, and a natural history section with fossils, stones, and Canarian flora and fauna.

If you take a detour away from the city center, to the other side of Avenida 3 de Mayo, you can visit the **Parque Marítima** ⑨: open-air swimming baths with a seawater pool and a South Seas atmosphere. Rather unfortunately, the park, designed according to plans by César Manrique, is located right next to a large oil refinery.

From the museum, go up Avenida de San Sebastián to the **Mercado de Nuestra Señora de África** ⑩. In the mornings this place is a colorful jumble of stalls selling fish, fruit and vegetables, and is more akin to an Oriental bazaar than anything else. Outside the hall, food stands provide drinks and snacks. The market hall dates from the Franco period, and is supposed to have a stylized "Canarian village" look to it. On Sundays there's a large flea market all around the hall, which draws quite a few locals from round about. Handmade jewelry, mass-

produced junk and exotic imports all lie outside in the hot Canarian sunshine waiting for buyers. Beer and *café con leche* are served in the market halls.

On the way back into the center, just beyond the bridge over the Barranco de Santos, is the **Teatro Guimerá** ⑰, home of the Tenerife Symphony Orchestra. Numerous foreign artists perform here during the winter festival. The theater is named after the Catalan dramatist Ángel Guimerá, who was born here, and is used for theater, opera and ballet performances. Rather simple-looking on the outside, it has a great deal of Art Nouveau decoration inside.

Next door, in the **Centro de Fotografía**, housed inside a former market hall, there are alternating art and photographic exhibitions.

Above: A quick swig from a goatskin during a fiesta. Right: The pilgrimage destination of Santuario del Cristo on the northern edge of La Laguna contains a statue of Christ revered throughout the Canaries.

Calle Valentín Sanz will take you back to the city's pedestrian precinct for a well-earned rest at the Plaza del Príncipe.

*LA LAGUNA
The Old Capital

The island's former capital of San Cristóbal de La Laguna, now known as **La Laguna** ㉖, is perched in a commanding position on the Aguere plateau, 500 meters above sea level. This sister city of Santa Cruz, with its cooler climate, has grown together with it. In 1496, immediately after the *Conquista*, the conqueror Alonso Fernández de Lugo had La Laguna built beside a lake as the capital of the island. In 1723, it lost this status (the lake dried up long beforehand), but to this day has remained the intellectual and religious center of the Canary Islands. The clearest sign of this is the university, which has been here since 1816 and was the only one on the entire archipelago until the end of the 1980s. Shortly after the university was founded in 1818,

Tenerife

the town became a bishopric. The church and the university have controlled social and cultural life here ever since. The historic center is definitely worth a visit, and looks almost medieval with its narrow streets and numerous historic houses. Some of the ancient structures have been affectionately restored and are open to the public as museums.

The best starting point for a tour of La Laguna is the leafy ★**Plaza del Adelantado** in the eastern part of the Old Town. This magnificent square is surrounded on all sides by historic buildings. To the east are the market and the law courts, and in between is the **Ermita San Miguel**, a monastery commissioned by the city's founders. Today it houses an art gallery.

At the southeastern corner of the square is the **Birthplace of Father Anchieta**, who went to Brazil as a missionary and founded the city of São Paulo. The neoclassical **Town Hall**, built in 1822, is to the right of it. To the left, on Calle Nava y Grimón, is the neo-Gothic

Consistory with its finials and foliage decoration, and across to the right of the square is the **Convento de Santa Catalina**. A wrought-iron balcony on one corner of the rather forbiddingly high wall is the most striking feature of this monastery, which dates from the early 17th century. The next building along is the baroque **Palacio de Nava y Grimón**, a dark-gray palazzo dating from 1590 with a portico flanked by double columns. This was the home of an influential family of Canarian nobles during the Enlightenment.

If you carry on northeastwards along Calle de Nava y Grimón and then turn onto Calle San Agustín, you'll arrive at the ★**Museo de Historia de Tenerife** in the **Casa Lercano**, another late-16th-century townhouse. The exhibition here is very good and centers around the history of the island since it was conquered.

Next, on the right, is a palazzo very similar in style to the Palacio de Nava y Grimón. It's the **Palacio Episcopal**, which was actually built half a century

later. The building, with its baroque, gray basalt facade was a casino for the town's prominent citizens before it became the episcopal palace. It was here that Canarian composer Teobaldo Power wrote his "Cantos Canarios."

Passing the mighty ruins of the late-15th-century **Convento de San Augustín**, take a narrow street to the left and you'll arrive at the oldest church in the city, the ***Iglesia de Nuestra Señora de la Concepción**. It dates from 1497, and owes its present appearance to various different late Gothic, Renaissance and baroque alterations. The first subjugated Guanches were baptized in its glazed font, which was brought here from Seville. In the 16th century the church received its colorfully-painted Artesonado ceiling in the *mudéjar* style, part of which collapsed in 1972 and has since been re-

Above: The Virgin of Candelaria, harbinger of Christianity and the patron saint of the archipelago. Right: Nine Menceyes, cast-bronze chieftains of the Guanches (Candelaria).

placed by a vaulted ceiling. The numerous impressive examples of Canarian woodcarving here include late baroque statues of the Virgin by José Luján Pérez and Fernando Estévez, and also some fine carving on the pulpit and the choir stalls at the back.

Take the main shopping street, Calle Obispo Rey Redondo, to get back to your starting point. On the way you'll pass the **Teatro Leal**, with a facade in the eclectic style of its architect Antonio Pintor (see also pp. 183-184).

The ***Catedral de los Remedios** stands on a small plaza behind high palm trees. It was built in 1511, while its neoclassical facade dates from 1820. Highlights inside include the gilt retable with paintings from the Flemish school, and the marble pulpit by Genoese sculptor Pasquale Bocciardo. Behind the altar is the tomb of the man who conquered Tenerife, Alonso Fernández de Lugo.

Before completing this stroll at the Town Hall on the Plaza del Adelantado, take a quick look at the **Casa de los Capitanes**. This former regent's palazzo contains some good exhibitions on the cultural history of the archipelago.

One of the most popular attractions of La Laguna is outside the city center in the direction of Santa Cruz: the ***Museo de la Ciencia y el Cosmos** belongs to the university, and is designed interactively so that it will appeal to children in particular. There are all kinds of buttons to press, computers, film rooms, and even a planetarium.

THE ARID SOUTH

The stretch of road that runs south from Santa Cruz is rather tedious at first glance: the landscape is often barren, and the monotony of earth colors is not even broken up by the odd green field. Nevertheless, this stretch does have its attractions, because this is a largely unknown side of Tenerife.

Tenerife

The highway south travels through the uninteresting suburbs of the capital as far as **Candelaria ㉗**. The main sight to see in this coastal town is the neo-Canarian **Basílica de Nuestra Señora de Candelaria**, located right next to the sea. It contains the *Black Madonna of Candelaria*, a statue of the Virgin who is regarded as the patron saint of the archipelago. According to legend, the carved statue was washed up on the beach, and was worshiped for its miraculous powers by the Guanches who lived here long before they had contact with Christianity. The Spanish conquerors took advantage of this and won the Guanches of Güímar as allies against the Mencey of Taoro. The original statue, which could have come from the altar of a Portuguese ship, was washed into the sea after a tidal wave in the 19th century and never found again. The statue you see today is a copy of a copy that stands in the Pilar church in Santa Cruz.

On the side of the huge square outside the basilica that faces the sea, you can see realistically rendered ***bronze statues** depicting the nine Menceyes from the time of the *Conquista*. These figures are present at the celebrations marking the end of a pilgrimage right across the island that takes place in mid-August each year, and in which the conversion of the so-called heathen Guanches to Christianity plays a central and symbolic role. The dark pebble beach just beyond the Guanche statues is not a good place for swimming, by the way; bathing here is okay if the water is calm, but don't venture out too far.

The road inland from Candelaria passes several partially cultivated fields on its way to **Arafo**. This small peaceful village on the eastern slopes of the Cumbre Dorsal has won several "best-kept village" awards. Its church square, in the shade of an old Indian laurel, has a coffee pavilion that is an excellent place to stop for a refreshing drink or a snack. Alternatively you can visit one of the village bakeries to try some delicious *truchas*, a form of ravioli.

The next village to the south, **Güímar** ㉘, has made quite a name for itself because of its delicious wines. It was in the early 1990s, however, that it really hit the headlines when several carefully terraced pyramids made from uncut stone were unearthed in the suburb of Chacona. The Norwegian Thor Heyerdahl managed to have the area sealed off and began a systematic scientific investigation. His friend, shipowner Fred Olsen, was delighted by the idea of an ethnographic park and bought the land. Open since the end of 1997, the **Museo Casa Chacona** contains fascinating information about Heyerdahl's theories about ancient cultures being interconnected.

The almost forgotten part of Tenerife begins near the **Mirador de Don Martín**. Piles of volcanic ash and lava border carefully terraced fields, and narrow little

Above: Rural peace and quiet in Arico el Nuevo. Right: In May the normally barren landscape of the Cañadas becomes a majestic carpet of colorful flowers.

bridges bravely span eroded barrancos. For a while little canals run parallel to the road, carrying drinking water from the heights of Güímar to Las Américas.

The village of **Arico** ㉙ consists of several sections spread out along the main road, and the middle one, Arico el Nuevo, is worthy of note. This tiny jewel of a village, with its houses and cobbled streets, is situated incredibly picturesquely against a barranco. The pilgrimage church in the main village of Lomo de Arico was based on the one in Granadilla, and contains a Gothic statue of the Virgin which, legend has it, was once washed up on the beach near Porís de Abona.

After several more tiny hamlets and hairpin bends you'll arrive at **Granadilla de Abona** ㉚, which greets its visitors with the **Iglesia San Antonio de Padua** (1711). This ambitious village is playing its part in the tourist boom by delivering produce to the tourist centers along the coast. The area produces wine, tomatoes, peppers, potatoes and maize. Beyond San Miguel is the **Mirador de la Centinela**,

Tenerife

with more bizarre landscape to round off this route through the interior. The coastal strip is lined with what look like enormous molehills: volcanic cones, as far as the eye can see. The best time to look at this weird scene is at sunset, when the hills throw long shadows.

From the observation point you can also see the much-cultivated **Valle de San Lorenzo** in the west. Its fertile volcanic soil, sheltered location and plentiful supply of water from the mountains create ideal conditions for agriculture. The modern town of the same name is located on one of the oldest parts of the island, geologically speaking; far older than the central massif behind it to the north.

★★LAS CAÑADAS AND ★★TEIDE
Top of the World

This tour to the top of Tenerife is the true "highlight" of any trip round the island. The sight of majestic Mount Teide, and of the seemingly infinite lava fields of the Cañadas, is quite unforgettable, and more varied and monumental than anywhere else in the Canary Islands.

Even when seen from the road, the lava has its own story to tell. Particularly rough and bizarrely shaped surfaces have been produced by lava with a higher gas content, while the shiny black glassy surfaces mark the areas that cooled down rapidly without having the time to crystallize. This black substance is known as obsidian, and the Guanches used it to make axe blades.

This is a superb hiking area. The massive, elliptical Caldera (sunken crater) is 17 kilometers long and 11 kilometers across, and is worth visiting at any time of the year. If the rather dry and barren landscape here in the fall doesn't appeal, come back in May when the lava fields are covered with pink, white and yellow flowers, and the air is full of the sound of honey bees. The experience is quite unforgettable. By the way, anyone who wants to spot a *moufflon* (it's a famously shaggy sheep) will need a pair of binoculars and a great deal of patience!

Reaching Teide by Car

Just outside Arona the people in charge of the ***Parque Ecológico Las Águilas del Teide** have turned the stony desert into an artistic oasis most effectively. The crocodile pool, floodlit with various colors at night, is especially impressive. There are several feedings and shows every day, and highlights also include condors in flight. Variety shows in the evenings are also a regular attraction.

Anyone who reaches **Arona ㉛**, a village that was probably founded by an Italian, has well and truly escaped the tourist bustle of Tenerife. In front of the neo-Canarian Town Hall is a shady and idyllic plaza, which suits the little village perfectly. The **Iglesia San Antonio** was built in the Spanish colonial style in 1627. Its retable is one of the finest in Spain and

Above: Vilafor lace is homemade, and takes a long time to create. Right: The Teide echium, which can flower up to 80,000 times, is endemic to Tenerife.

was brought here on mules from Adeje, when church property there was threatened with secularization. Arona lies at the eastern edge of the most striking mountain in the south, the 1,003-meter-high **Roque del Conde**. This sloping table mountain, popular as a starting point for paragliders, can easily be distinguished among the other volcanoes.

A well-surfaced but winding road leads up to **Vilaflor ㉜**, often praised in old travel reports as a health resort for those with respiratory problems because of the many pine forests surrounding it. Located at an elevation of 1,400 meters it is not only the highest village in the Canaries but in all of Spain! A Mirador upon a steep hill to the west will help you get your bearings.

In the slightly sloping plaza in the upper part of the village you will see the small historic section, with the **Iglesia San Pedro** (1550), a ruined monastery and a former mill. On the hill behind the monastery, the people in charge of *Las Águilas del Teide* have set up a small **ad-**

venture park with a Guanche history museum. This village became famous for the fine lace produced by its women: Vilaflor Lace has been exported to Spain and overseas since the 19th century. Several old women in Vilaflor still know the technique, and their work is on sale.

Many hikers come to Vilaflor and the surrounding region each year. One very good tour from here leads across the so-called ★**Paisaje Lunar** ("Lunar Landscape"), an eroded section of landscape that resembles Turkey's Cappadocia in miniature, and on into the Cañadas. If you want to see the lunar landscape without venturing any farther, follow a broad forest road six kilometers above Vilaflor as far as the start of a signposted hiking route. It's just half an hour's walk to the first weird rock formations.

If you continue farther into the Cañadas by car you'll pass through airy pine forests, and then get one of the most spectacular views of neighboring islands that Tenerife has to offer. At first, Gran Canaria to the east will be all you can see, but later on both La Gomera and El Hierro will appear in the southwest. Near the Boca del Tauce you'll finally arrive at the crater arena of the Cañadas, and at the 136-square-kilometer **Teide National Park ㉝**.

Tenerife

★★Teide National Park

★★**Las Cañadas**, made up of two levels of differing heights, is oval in shape, almost 17 kilometers long and 10 kilometers across. At some locations the crater walls reach elevations of 700 meters or more above the crater floor. From the very highest point, the **Guajara** (2,717 meters), there is an absolutely stunning view of the Cañadas and Teide. The stone desert of solidified lava, volcanic cones, pumice stone and bizarre rock formations has very distinctive vegetation, which has adapted to the very dry summers. It starts flowering in spring and

makes the Cañadas glow with all kinds of different colors for three months. In the winter snow falls, covering Teide and also the Cañadas with a white blanket for weeks on end.

On the right, beyond the Boca del Tauce and on the crater floor of the **Zapato de la Reina** ("Queen's Shoe"), there's a rock formation that is reminiscent of a high-heeled shoe. On the left is the **Llano de Ucanca**, an alluvial landscape that has been used in several science fiction movies. In the background you can see the Roques de García, reached via **Los Azulejos**; the turquoise colors on them are caused by iron.

The ★**Roques de García** are among the strangest rock formations in the Cañadas; some of these are frozen rivers of volcanic vents, others are eroded structures with several layers. Nearby there's a **Parador Nacional** with a restaurant and a small museum documenting the national park.

Towering above all this, however, is the cone-shaped summit of ★★**Pico del**

Teide. The highest mountain in Spain (3,717 meters) has destroyed the north wall of the Caldera in its various eruptions, and completely buried it. Its older neighbor, **★Pico Viejo**, is 3,135 meters high and actually has a more impressive crater than Teide itself. The **Centro de Visitantes** 🆔 on the northeastern edge of the Cañadas provides video presentations (in English, Spanish and German) about the National Park. You can also obtain information here on hiking routes, guided tours and accommodation at the *Altavista* mountain hut.

Teide can be ascended on foot, but to get to the actual summit via the Rambleta you'll need a permit (available from the *Patronato del Parque Nacional de las Cañadas del Teide* in Santa Cruz). The most popular route (five hours) starts at **Montaña Blanca** (2,750 meters) and first leads along a dirt track, passing pumice

Above: The oval crater arena in the Cañadas at the foot of Teide has a diameter of between 10 and 17 kilometers.

fields with the famous "Teide eggs," volcanic boulders as large as automobiles. A steep and winding path leads up to the newly-renovated *Altavista* mountain hut, almost 3,300 meters up, from which it takes around one more hour on foot to reach the Rambleta (3,560 meters). That's where the **Teleférico del Teide** cable railway comes in – its two gondolas arrive up here from a station located at an altitude of 2,356 meters, but only if there's no wind. For environmental reasons, only 150 people are allowed on the Rambleta at any one time, so if the weather is nice you can expect lengthy waits for the cable car.

In **El Portillo** at the eastern end of the National Parks, at 2,000 meters above sea level, there are several restaurants. Beyond them you can drive down northwards into the Valle de la Orotava, where the pine and laurel forests in the upper section of the valley, with its moderate climate, are a very attractive place to go hiking (see pp. 140-141). If you turn east near El Portillo, you'll arrive at the

Cumbre Dorsal, a mountain ridge consisting of a chain of volcanoes that all merged into each other long ago. Near **Izaña** there are several white observatories keeping a regular eye on the universe.

Now you're on a pass road with views of the coastal strip on either side. Depending on the trade-wind cloud situation, you'll plunge from the sunny heights into a weird world of fog between 1,500 meters and 800 meters above sea level, and it often only dissipates once you get down to **La Esperanza ㉟**. This village is the main one in the scattered community of **El Rosario**, whose hamlets extend from the La Laguna plateau as far as the largely pine-filled **Bosque de la Esperanza**.

Ecologically, this forest is very important to the island. The long pine needles collect water from the clouds and the soil in the forest here therefore has three times the water content of other areas. Canary pine is more resistant to forest fires than other trees because of its thick, nearly impenetrable bark, and is also relatively impervious to extended periods of winter cold or summer drought. These advantages have been realized, and much reforestation is now under way using the endemic variety, rather than other faster-growing species which have proven unsuitable.

This area is famous for restaurants that serve large quantities of very filling food. Pork, veal and rabbit dishes are especially popular, but things tend to get crowded on weekends so make sure you book in advance. Apart from the restaurants along the access route to the Cañadas, however, this region has almost remained untouched by tourism: this is the true, unadulterated Tenerife. Popular spare-time activities up here include hikes through the Esperanza Forest, and barbecues and picnics at the special sites (but beware of forest fires!). Near La Laguna, down in the valley, a highway junction takes you back to the outside world.

TENERIFE

🛫 *ARRIVAL:* **By Plane:** International air traffic arrives at the *Aeropuerto Reina Sofía* in the south, and national flights arrive at *Tenerife Norte* (Los Rodeos near La Laguna). Charter flights are available from the UK the whole year round. **By Ship:** From *Los Cristianos* habor in the south there are daily ferry connections to La Gomera (90 mins.; hydrofoil 35 mins.), La Palma (4 hours) and El Hierro (5 hours). From the capital, *Santa Cruz* ships travel to Lanzarote (10 hours), Gran Canaria (3.5 hours; jetfoil 80 mins.), Fuerteventura (14 hours), La Palma (8 hours) and – once a week – to Cádiz on the Spanish mainland. Info: Lineas Fred Olsen, tel. 922-628200, and Trasmediterránea, tel. 902-454645. Internet: www.fredolsen.es / www.trasmediterranea.es.

THE SOUTHWEST

EL MÉDANO

🏨 😊😊😊 **Playa Sur Tenerife**, tel. 922-176120, 922-176180, fax. 922-176337. On windsurfing beach, 70 rooms, restaurant, bar, pool, billiards, table tennis, library. Winsurf boards can be rented next door (courses also provided).

😊😊 **El Médano**, Playa del Médano 2, tel. 922-177000, fax. 922-176048. Oldest hotel in El Médano, by the sea. Renovated rooms, not all with sea view; **Carel**, Avda. de los Príncipes 22, tel. 922-176066, fax. 922-176828. Simple boarding house on the way into the center, 20 rooms.

😊 **Camping Nauta**, Cañada Blanca, near Las Galllettas, tel. 922-785118, 922-785027, fax. 922-795016. Small wooden bungalows, pool and sports facilities; also for caravans; open all year round.

🍽 **Alabama's**, between San Isidro and Granadilla, tel. 922-770608. Live music, American cooking. Popular with package tour groups, Sun-Thu 10 pm to midnight, Fri-Sat 10 pm to 2 am.

ℹ️ Plaza del Príncipe, tel. 922-176002, Mon-Fri 10 am to 1 pm (in peak season also 4 to 7 pm), Sat 9 am to 2 pm.

LAS GALLETAS

⛳ *GOLF:* **Amarillo Golf Country Club**, near Costa del Silencio, tel. 922-730295; **Golf del Sur**, between Las Galletas and Los Abrigos, tel. 922-731070, fax. 922-785272. 27-hole course; **Los Palos**, on the Carretera near Guaza, tel. 922-730080, fax. 922-731898. 9-hole course and golfing school.

GO-CARTS: **Karting Club Tenerife**, between Guaza & Las Chafiras, tel. 922-730703, daily from 10 am.

Tenerife

DIVING: Courses and excursions at **Buceo Tenerife Diving Center**, Calle María del Carmen García 22, tel. 922-731015; **Island Divers**, Urbanización Tamaide J42, Costa del Silencio, tel./fax. 922-730815.

Centro Médico, Calle Galván Bello 23, tel. 922-785092.

POST OFFICE: Calle Luís A. Cruz.

Entrada al Muelle, tel. 922-730133, Mon-Fri morn.

LOS ABRIGOS

SEAFOOD RESTAURANTS: **Perlas del Mar**, tel. 922-176414. Situated on a rocky outcrop on the eastern edge of the harbor; **La Langostera**, tel. 922-176319; **Vista Mar**, tel. 922-176156; **La Dorada**, tel. 922-176584, delicious paella; **Colibrí**, Las Galletas, Paseo Marítimo 9, tel. 922-730205. Terrace with sea view, fresh fish daily.

LOS CRISTIANOS

Gran Hotel Arona, Avda. de los Cristianos, tel. 922-750678, fax. 922-750243. At the end of the beach promenade, view of bay and harbor, restaurants and bars, pools, sauna, squash, fitness center; **Oasis Moreque**, Avda. Penetración, tel. 922-790366, fax. 922-792260. On the beach promenade, 170 rooms, swimming pool, tennis courts, playground.

Casa del Mar, Explanada del Muelle, tel. 922-793275 and 922-791323. Good seafood restaurant, awarded the Spanish Gastronomy Gold Medal in 1994 and 1995, Tue-Sun 1 to 11:30 pm; **El Cine**, Calle Juan Boriajo 8, tel. 909-044804. Small tapas bar with tables outside, Tue-Sun 7 am to 10:30 pm.

Parque Ecológico Las Águilas del Teide, on the road from Los Cristianos to Arona, tel. 922-753001, fax. 922-753062. Artistically arranged tropical landscape with kangaroos, crocodiles, hippopotami and penguins, parrot shows on open-air stage, restaurant. Flight displays with birds of prey, daily 9 am to 9 pm, variety performances in the evenings; **Centro Alfarero**, Arguayo, tel. 922-863485. Pottery museum, Tue-Sun 10 am to 1 pm and 4 to 7 pm, admission free.

Pirámide de Arona, Avda. de las Américas, tel. 922-796360. Shows daily.

DISCOS: **El Templo**, north of the Autopista del Sur near Los Cristianos. Ancient Egyptian decor, dancing for young and old, daily 10:30 pm to 6 am.

PARASAILING: For info tel. 922-793824 or ask at the kiosk at the dry dock (Los Cristianos harbor).

WHALE AND DOLPHIN SPOTTING / DEEP SEA FISHING: See Los Gigantes / Puerto de Santiago.

Librería Barbara, Calle Generalísimo Franco/Juan Pablo Abril, tel./fax. 922-792301. From hiking maps to beach books (in various languages).

Centro Médico del Sur, Avda. de los Cristianos, tel. 922-790486.

POST OFFICE: Calle Los Sabandeños.

Centro Cultural, Calle General Franco, tel. 922-752492, Mon-Fri 9 am to 1 pm.

LOS GIGANTES / PUERTO DE SANTIAGO

Los Gigantes, Flor de Pascua 12, tel. 922-101020, fax. 922-100475. 225 rooms with balcony, bath, pool, sauna, tennis, squash, fitness center.

Barceló Santiago, Puerto Santiago, Calle La Hondura, tel. 922-860912/925, fax. 922-861808 and 922-863036. Comfortable. Pools, sauna, massage, tennis, squash.

DIVING: **Baracuda Tauch Club** Heinz Scheffler, Paraíso Floral Hotel, tel. 922-740726, tel./fax. 922-741881; **San Borondon** Dan Mihajlivic, Playa San Juan, Marina 10, tel. 922-865614, fax. 922-865100; **Los Gigantes Diving Center** John Punton, Puerto de los Gigantes, P41, tel./fax. 922-860431.

WHALE AND DOLPHIN SPOTTING / DEEP SEA FISHING: Several places do this in the harbors of Los Cristianos, Playa San Juan, Los Gigantes and in the Puerto Colón of Las Américas.

Medical Center, Puerto Santiago, Calle Manuel Ravelo, tel. 922-861462.

POST OFFICE: Puerto de Santiago, Carretera General.

Avenida Marítima (behind the beach of La Arena), tel. 922-860348, Mon-Fri 9 am to 1 pm.

PLAYA DE LAS AMÉRICAS

Gran Hotel Bahia del Duque, tel. 922-713000, fax. 922-746916. Luxury first-class hotel by the sea, 362 rooms in several different buildings (some resembling historic structures on the island). Conference rooms, restaurants, bars, pools, tennis, squash, putting green, fitness center; **Jardín Tropical**, on the beach promenade, tel. 922-750100, fax. 922-752844. Quiet, luxurious, excellent restaurants, pool by the sea.

Las Rocas, hotel restaurant in the *Jardín Tropical*, Urbanización San Eugenio, tel. 922-750100. Terrace by the sea with a South Seas touch; fish, seafood, paella; **El Patio**, Hotel restaurant in the *Jardín Tropical*, tel. see *Las Rocas*. Has been awarded several prizes; **Harley's American Restaurant**, behind the Puerto Colón, Club Flamingo, tel. 922-796260. American style, cocktails, Mexican snacks, vegetarian food, open daily; **Otelo**, at entrance to the Barranco del Infierno, tel. 922-780374. Delicious Canarian cuisine, view of Adeje, Wed-Mon noon to 4 pm and 6 to 10 pm; **El Pescador de Alcalá**, harbor of Alcalá, tel. 922-865080.

Big fish restaurant; moderate prices; Wed-Mon noon to 3:30 pm and 7 to 11 pm; **Pancho**, Puerto Santiago, behind Playa de la Arena, tel. 922-101323. Specialties: fresh fish, pigeon in Malvasia wine. Large terrace, closed Mon; **Dieta Mediterránea**, at yacht harbor of Los Gigantes, Poblado Marinero 4, tel. 922-101134. Italian food, homemade pasta and good pizza, Tue-Sun 12:30 to 3:30 pm and 6:30 to 10:30 pm.

Verónica 1, 2 and **3**. Several discos for young people, latest hits; **Prisma's**, Avda. Litoral, international pop music, daily from midnight; **Macarena**, to the north of the Barranco del Rey. Music for the 25-45 age group, daily 10 pm to 5 am.

Casino, under the *Hotel Gran Tinerfe*, tel. 922-793712. Roulette, blackjack, slot machines. Identification required for the casino, admission to the machine hall is free.

HIKING: **Timah**, Adeje, Calle Tinerfe el Grande 1, tel. 922-710421 and 922-710242, fax. 922-710708. Helmuth Scheiber organizes mountain hiking groups for hikes on Tenerife and also other islands in the archipelago.

DIVING: Gruber's Diving Center Petra and Kurt Gruber, Park Club Europe, tel. 922-752708, fax. 922-796424, office hours daily 9:30 am to 6 pm. More offers in the Puerto Colón.

WHALE AND DOLPHIN SPOTTING / DEEP SEA FISHING: See Los Gigantes / Playa de Santiago.

WATER PARK: **Aguapark Octopus**, Playa de las Américas, San Eugenio, Exit 29 on the Autopista del Sur, tel. 922-792266. Fun waterpark with plenty of pools and slides, daily 10 am to 6 pm.

Kiosko Artenerife, Avda. Litoral to the north of Las Verónicas. Canarian crafts, Mon-Sat 9:30 am to 2 pm and 3 to 7:30 pm; **Flea Market**, every evening on the Barranco del Rey, Thu and Sat mornings above the beach of Torviscas.

Salus Medical Center, Calle Panamá 3, tel. 922-796161.

POST OFFICE: Pueblo Canario.

i Plaza del City Center, tel. 922-797668, Mon-Fri 9 am to 1 pm.

THE NORTH

BAJAMAR

Delfin, Avda. del Sol, tel./fax. 922-540200. 66 rooms, mostly with balcony, restaurant, pool, tennis; **Neptuno**, Carretera General, tel. 922-542562, fax. 922-150402. Inexpensive.

Café Melita, Carretera General Punta del Hidalgo 171, tel. 922-540814. Terrace café, good filter coffee, cakes. Daily 9 am to 9:30 pm; **Olga**, Roque de las Bo-

degas, tel. 922-590220. Good rice and fish dishes, medium price category. Daily 11 am to 9 pm.

POST OFFICE: Calle Castillo.

GARACHICO

Hotel San Roque, C. Esteban de Ponte 32, tel. 922-133435, fax. 922-133406. In restored manor house (18th century), designer furniture and objets d'art in every room. 20 double rooms and apartments. Restaurant, sauna, heated pool.

Il Giardino di Garachico, Calle Esteban Ponte 8, tel./fax. 922-830245. Centrally located boarding house in the Canarian style with up to 20 beds.

Further accommodation possibilities in unrented **private apartments** are available at the sea promenade.

Il Giardino, Calle Esteban de Ponte 8, tel. 922-830245. Pizza and pasta on the patio of a Canarian house, moderate prices, closed Thu; **Rivamar**, between Los Silos and Garachico, Carretera General, tel. 922-831311. Fresh fish, seafood, meat à la canarienne, closed Tue; **Monteverde**, east of El Tanque on the Carretera General 2, tel. 922-830902. Simple Canarian restaurant, poultry, fresh fish, moderate prices, closed Mon.

Museo de Arte, Plaza de Santo Domingo, tel. 922-830000. Modern canarian art in the side-chapels of a monastery church. Mon-Sat 9 am to 1 pm; **Casa de Cultura**, Gloriéta de San Francisco. Art exhibitions, photos and documents relating to municipal history, stuffed marine animals, birds, butterflies and religious artefacts, Mon-Sat 9 am to 6 pm, Sun 9 am to 1 pm; **Castillo de San Miguel**. Exhibition of minerals, fossils, mussels and snails. Daily 9 am to 6 pm.

CAMEL RIDES: Camello Center, southwest of El Tanque, Carretera General, tel. 922-831191 and 922-133393.

DIVING: **Argonautes**, Calle Esteban Ponte 8, tel./fax. 922-830245.

SOUVENIRS: **Patio El Limonero**, directly opposite the Castillo de San Miguel. Also local crafts, Tue-Sat 10 amto 6 pm, Sun 10 am to 3 pm; **La Paredita**, El Tanque, tel. 922-136033. Studio of the painter Antoine Manfredi, paintings and sculptures.

POST OFFICE: Calle Martín de Andujar 1.

ICOD DE LOS VINOS

Carmen, Calle Hércules 2, tel. 922-810631. At the *Drago Milenario*, Canarian specialties, closed Sun evening and Mon from afternoon onwards.

Iglesia San Marcos. Liturgical equipment, religious raiment and a large filigree silver cross, mornings until 12:30; **El Mariposario del Drago**, tel. 922-815167. Exotic butterflies from all over the world in the glass-

TENERIFE

covered butterfly garden beneath the famous dragon tree, daily 9:30 am to 6 pm; **Biblioteca Expresión Contemporanea Antonín Artaud**, San Juan de la Rambla, Calle Estrecha 5, tel. 922-350484, fax. 922-350376. Artists' meeting place, library, studio, exhibition rooms, Thu 5 to 9 pm, Sat-Sun 10 am to 2 pm and 3 to 9 pm.

SOUVENIRS: **Arte Ycodem**, Calle Sebastían 4. Crafts (textiles, ceramics, souvenirs), Canarian wine. *WINE:* **Salón Canario del Vino**, Plaza de la Pila 5. Wine-tasting center with sales of Canarian wine, liqueurs and cheeses.

POST OFFICE: Calle de San Sebastián 11.

LA OROTAVA

Hotel Victoria, Calle Hermano Apolinar 8, tel. 922-331683, fax. 922-320519. Splendid interior design, 13 double rooms and a suite inside a 300-year-old renovated manor house in the heart of the Old Town. Terrace with view of the Old Town, Orotava Valley and Teide. Good Canarian restaurant.

Silene, Calle Tómas Zerolo 9, tel. 922-330199. Simple boarding house, three rooms.

Hijuela, Calle Tomás Pérez 1, part of the botanical gardens of Puerto de la Cruz; Mon-Sat 9 am to 2 pm; **Museo de Artesanía Iberoamericana**, Calle Tomás Zerolo 34, tel. 922-323376, fax. 922-335811. Musical instruments, ceramics, basket weaving, textiles, award-winning furniture, Mon-Fri 9 am to 6 pm, Sat 9 am to 2 pm; **El Pueblo Guanche – Museo Etnográfico**, Carrera del Escultor Estévez 17, tel. 922-322725, fax. 922-333488. Finds from the pre-Hispanic era. Kitchen from the former house is in original condition. The *Sabor Canario* restaurant has good Canarian cuisine, Mon-Sat 9:30 am to 7:30 pm (museum), restaurant open until late.

CRAFTS: **Casa Torrehermosa**, Calle Tomás Zerolo 27, tel. 922-304013. Products from the province of Santa Cruz de Tenerife in a renovated historic building dating from the 16th century, Mon-Fri 9:30 am to 6.30 pm, Sat 9:30 am to 2 pm; **Casa de los Balcones**, Calle San Francisco 3, tel. 922-330629. Calado embroidery and traditional work, in a historic building; **Casa del Turista** (also: **de la Alfombra**), opposite the Casa de los Balcones. In a historic building.

POST OFFICE: Plaza Patricio García.

Carrera del Escultor Estévez 2, tel. 922-323041.

LOS REALEJOS

Maritim, El Burgado 1, tel. 922-379000, fax. 922-379037. On the coast to the west of Puerto de la Cruz, 450 rooms, small botanical garden, baths, sports facilities; **Tierra de Oro**, Realejo Alto, tel. 922-

341000 and 922-341213, fax. 922-344318. Spa hotel with 80 beds, German-run. Healthy food, fitness center, sauna, mineral water pool and outdoor swimming pool. Topless sunbathing terrace with view of the Orotava Valley. Can only be booked directly.

Gaiatours, Calle San Agustín 48, tel./fax. 922-355272. Tours of the Patronato de Turismo, including transportation, insurance and guides.

DIVING: **Atlantik**, to the west of Puerto de la Cruz, El Burgado 1, tel. 922-362801, fax. 922-344501. Hotel Maritim (behind the swimming pool), office hours: Mon-Fri 9 to 9:30 am, 12 to 1 and 5 to 5:30 pm, Sat 12:30 to 1 pm.

MASCA

The **El Guanche** restaurant, tel. 922-863424, organizes simple accommodation, half-board possible. **La Pimentera**, tel. 922-863438. Quiet, with terrace, panoramic view. Good international cooking with Canarian touch, Wed-Mon 12 to 6 pm; **Casa Enrique – Chez Arlette**, tel. 922-863459. Surrounded by luxuriant foliage. Specialty: grilled lamb. Sun-Fri 11:30 am to 6:30 pm; **El Guanche**, tel. 922-863424. In a former village school, leafy terraces, Canarian-inspired cooking, daily 11 am to 6 pm.

PUERTO DE LA CRUZ

Semiramis, La Paz, Calle L. Cólogan Zulueta 27, tel. 922-373200, fax. 922-373193. All rooms with balcony. Garden, heated pools; **Tigaiga**, Parque del Taoro 28, tel. 922-383500, fax. 922-384055. In a palm park near the *Taoro* casino, restaurant, pool, tennis; **Marquesa**, C. Quintana 11, tel. 922-383151, fax. 922-386950. Historic building in the center, 92 rooms with bath, most with balcony. Pool, bars, good restaurant with terrace above pedestrian precinct.

Finca Ventoso, Las Dehesas 73, tel./fax. 922-383820. Apartments for self-caterers, in a banana plantation.

Los Geranios, Ortsteil La Ranilla, Lomo 14, tel. 922-382810. Quiet boarding house in the harbor quarter with 10 rooms.

Magnolia, Avda. Marqués Villanueva del Prado 5, tel. 922-385614. Excellent restaurant for Catalan specialties. High prices; **Casa de Miranda**, Calle Santo Domingo 13, tel. 922-373871. In an 18th-century building. Comfortable atmosphere, good fish dishes, daily 1 to 11:30 pm; **Régulo**, Calle Pérez Zamora 16, tel. 922-384506. Fresh fish, international cuisine, Canarian dishes, Mon-Fri 12 to 3 pm and 6 to 11 pm; **El Monasterio**, above La Vera in La Montaña, Calle General de la Montaña, tel. 922-340707. In former monastery rooms. Specialty: meat grilled over charcoal, strong country wine, daily am to 1 pm; **Mi Vaca y Yo**, Calle Cruz Verde 3, tel. 922-385247 and 922-382086. Fish restaurant in the old fishing quarter, daily 1 to 3:30 pm and 7 to 11:30 pm.

Loro Parque, in the suburb of Punta Brava, tel. 922-374081 and 922-373841, fax. 922-375021. Biggest collection of parrots in the world. Shows with loros, sea lions and dolphins. Shark tunnel, bat caves, orchid house, daily 8:30 am to 5 pm; **Jardín de Aclimatación de La Orotava**, Calle Retama 2, tel. 922-383572. Botanical garden with many plants endemic to the Canaries, daily 9 am to 6 pm, in summer until 7 pm; **Bananera El Guanche**, 2 km east of Puerto, tel. 922-331853 and 922-330017. Plantation with video guide, sales of spirits and cut flowers. Free bus service from Playa Martiánez, daily 9 am to 6 pm; **Museo Arqueológico**, Calle del Lomo 9a, tel. 922-371465. Guanche pottery.

LIVE MUSIC: **Abaco**, El Durazno, Calle Casa Grande, tel. 922-370107. Nice cocktail bar in Canarian manor house (17th century), piano music (Thu-Sat after 10 pm) and chamber concerts, daily 8 pm to 2 am; **Bodega Mario's**, Calle Corales, tel. 922-375192. Basement restaurant with music from the Spanish mainland; **Otto's Piano Bar "Blue Note,"** Calle Zamora, 15. tel. 922-380943. Jazz cellar, Mon-Sat 10 pm to 3 am; **Andromeda**, Avda. Colón, tel. 922-383852 and 922-383899. Nightclub of the Lago Martiánez with Varieté and dancing, closed Mon.

CASINO: **Casino de Taoro**. Roulette, blackjack, slot machines. Minimum age 18, admission fee.

TENNIS: **Tennis Center Miramar**, La Romantica II (west of Puerto de la Cruz), Urbanización Valparaiso, Calle Los Tulipanes 2, tel. 922-340408, fax. 922-353046. Multilingual trainers, three courts. Badminton, swimming pool, bistro, sauna, qualified masseur.

Hiking with Gregorio: Apply for this in the Hotel *Tigaiga*, tel. 922-383500 (from 4 pm), fax. 922-330910. Organized tours with bus transfers. Internet: http://members.aol.com/gregorio2.

SOUVENIRS: **Karinia**, Calle Aceviño 45, tel. 922-371372. A woman designer creates blouses, jackets, pants, cloths, pictures and hiking clothing. Sat and Sun 10 am to 1 pm or by prior arrangement.

CRAFTS: **Artenerife**, Explanada del Muelle, tel. 922-388202. Kiosk at the harbor; **Casa Tafuriaste**, above Puerto de la Cruz, Carretera de la Luz – Las Candias 29, tel. 922-333396. Museum and ceramic shop in building dating from the 17th century, Mon-Sat 10 am to 6 pm, admission fee. *MUSIC:* Canarian music productions in all styles at **Manzanas** on Calle San Telmo.

FLEA MARKET: Sat mornings, market building El Tejar, San Felipe district 9 am to 2 pm.

Ambulatorio, Calle El Pozo, tel. 922-372287.

POST OFFICE: Calle El Pozo (bus station).

Plaza de Europa, tel. 922-386000, Mon-Fri 9 am to 8 pm, Sat 9 am to 1 pm.

SANTA ÚRSULA

La Quinta Park, highway exit to the west of Santa Úrsula, La Quinta 21, tel. 922-300266, fax. 922-300513. 200 apartments and studios with balconies. Garden with pools, restaurant, bar, supermarket, tennis, squash, spa center with doctor, fitness center, cosmetic salon, hydrotherapy.

Los Corales, Calle Cuesta de la Villa 30, tel. 922-301918. Good international and Canarian dishes, Tue-Sun 12:30 to 4 pm and 7 to 11 pm; **Faisan Azul**, La Matanza, Calle Acentejo 68, tel. 922-577782. French and German cuisine.

TACORONTE

Camping Playa La Arena, Mesa del Mar, tel. 922-572555. Bungalows for two people.

Casa del Vino, country house in the *La Baranda* area with wine museum, tasting cellar, bar, restaurant, shop. Autopista del Norte, "El Sauzal" exit, tel. 922-572535/42 (museum), 922-563388 (restaurant), fax. 922-572744. Museum: Tue-Sat 11 am to 8 pm, Sun 11 am to 6 pm. Bar: 11 am to 10:30 pm. Restaurant: 1 to 4 pm and 7:30 to 10:30 pm; **Museo Etnográfico de Tenerife**, Carretera Tacoronte-Valle de Guerra 44, tel. 922-543053, fax. 922-544498. Farming implements in the De Carta country house (17th century); Tue-Sat 10 am to 5 pm, Sun 10 am to 2 pm.

WINE: **Bodegas Álvaro**, Tacoronte, Calle Waque 4, tel. 922-572331, closed Sun.

POST OFFICE: Punta del Hidalgo, Carretera General 128.

THE TWO METROPOLISES

LA LAGUNA

Aguere, Calle Obispo Rey Redondo 55, tel. 922-259490, fax. 922-631633. Has seen batter days. 22 rooms in an 18th-century building, various conference rooms, large lobby, boutiques; **Nivaria**, Plaza del Adelantado 11, tel. 922-264298, fax. 922-259634. Best hotel in La Laguna, mainly apartments. Café bar, salon, squash.

Tasca Lagunera, Plaza Doctor Juan Régulo Pérez 6, tel. 922-256653. Elegant and busy restaurant, good wine list; **La Gotera**, Calle San Agustín 9, tel. 922-255666. Comfortable, in the Old Town, medium price category, Mon-Sat 1 to 4 pm and 8 pm to 2 am; **Los Limoneros**, expensive restaurant for big city people in

Los Naranjeros, tel. 922-636637 and 922-636144, closed Sun.

🏛 **Museo de Historia de Tenerife**, Calle San Agustín 22, tel. 922-630103 and 922-630121. Museum in the Casa Lercano (built 1593) documenting history of the island in Spanish times, Tue-Sat 10 am to 5 pm, Sun 10 am to 2 pm; **Museo de la Ciencia y el Cosmos**, road from Santa Cruz to La Laguna (via La Cuesta), Via Lactea, tel. 922-263454/494. Modern interactive museum, planetarium and film room, Tue-Sun 10 am to 8 pm; **Casa de los Capitanes**, Calle Obispo Rey Redondo 5. Exhibitions on the cultural history of the Canary Islands, Mon 5 to 8 pm, Tue-Sat 11 am to 1 pm and 5 to 8 pm, Sun 11 am to 1 pm; **Ermita San Miguel**, Plaza del Adelantado. Modern art, Mon 5 to 8 pm, Tue-Sat 11 am to 1 pm and 5 to 8 pm, Sun 11 am to 1 pm.

🍷 **El Tocuyo**, Calle Juan de Viana. Wine bar.

DISCOS: **O'Clock Disco Pub**, Calle Barcelona 6, tel. 922-633561, bar opens at 7 pm, then a DJ or live band; **Discoteca NOOCTUA**, near the airport, "Los Rodeos" exit northbound, Fri and Sat from 11:30 pm.

PUBS: On weekends the action starts from midnight onwards, e.g., in the **Nueva Visión** (C. Elias Serra Rafols) with its video wall, in the **Bar de Blues** (C. Doctor Zamenhof 9; occasional live music or poetry readings), and in the **Buho Jazz Bar** (Calle Catedral 3).

Main shopping street in La Laguna: *Calle Obispo Rey Redondo* (fashion and shoe stores). *BOOKS:* **Lemus**, Calle Heraclio Sánchez 64, tel. 922-253244. *MARKETS:* **Mercado** on the Plaza del Adelantado; also with biological and herbal stalls.

WINE: **La Vinoteca**, Plaza de la Concepción 24, tel. 922-261602. Spanish and Canarian wines.

GOLF: **Campo de Golf**, Los Rodeos, tel. 922-630115. Signposted on the Autopista del Norte at the "Los Rodeos" exit. 18 holes.

➕ **Hospital Universitario de Canarias**, Carretera Cuesta-Taco, tel. 922-678000.

☎ *POST OFFICE:* Calle Santo Domingo.

ℹ Pavilion on the Plaza del Adelantado.

SANTA CRUZ DE TENERIFE

AECAN, Calle Villalba Hervás 4, tel. 922-240816, fax. 922-244003. Agency with "turismo rural" program, renovated country houses on Tenerife, La Palma, La Gomera and El Hierro.

😊😊😊 **Mencey**, Calle Dr. José Naveiras 38, tel. 922-276700, fax. 922-280017. For VIPs and the jet set, 300 rooms and suites, elegant restaurant, bar, gardens.

😊😊 **Atlántico**, Calle del Castillo 12, tel. 922-246375, fax. 922-246378. In the pedestrian precinct, 60 rooms; **Horizonte**, Calle Santa Rosa de Lima 11, tel. 922-275359. In the town center, 45 small rooms; **Plaza**,

Plaza de la Candelaria 10, tel. 922-272453, fax. 922-275160. Centrally located, bar on the rooftop terrace.

😊 **Mova**, Calle San Martín 33, tel. 922-283261. Family-run boarding house in town center, 20 small rooms.

✖ *SEAFOOD RESTAURANTS IN SAN ANDRÉS* (all by the sea with the exception of Pinchitos): **El Rubí**, tel. 922-549673, rice specialties; **Ramón**, tel. 922549308. Specialty: perch in red fish sauce; **La Costera**, tel. 922549006, closed Sun evenings; **Los Pinchitos**, Calle Guillén 14, tel. 922-549283. Good grilled fish.

OTHER RESTAURANTS: **Los Menceyes**, elegant restaurant in the Hotel Mencey; **Café del Príncipe**, Plaza del Príncipe, tel. 922-278810. Fish, Canarian cuisine, medium prices, closed Mon; **Cervecería Central**, Calle La Luna/San Clemente, tel. 922-291114. Tapas, Canarian dishes, tables also out of doors, daily 8 am to 2 am; **Montecarlo**, Avda. de Anaga 43, tel. 922-289841. On the harbor promenade. French-influenced cuisine, closed Sun; **Harley's**, Calle Mendez Nuñez 5, tel. 922-293000. Mexican, Italian and Asian dishes, video wall and bowling alley, daily noon to midnight.

🏛 **Museo de la Naturaleza y el Hombre**, Calle Fuente Morales, tel. 922-209314-5. Double museum in former hospital, archeological and natural history department, Tue-Sun 10 am to 8 pm; **Museo Municipal**, Calle José Murphy 4, tel. 922-244358. Municipal art gallery, in summer Mon-Fri 10 am to 1:30 pm and 12:30 to 6:30 pm, winter Mon-Fri 10 am to 8 pm, admission free; **Centro de Fotografía**, Plaza Isla de la Madera, tel. 922-290735. Alternating exhibition of photographs and paintings, Tue-Sat 10 am to 1 pm and 5 to 8 pm, Sun 11 am to 1 pm, admission free.

🎭 **Teatro Guimerá**, large theater for plays, opera, ballet, concerts and festival events.

DISCOS: **KU**, Santa Cruz, La Granja Park, Avda. Madrid, tel. 922-203636. Shows and good Mexican restaurant; **Ñoh!**, Santa Cruz, Avda. de Anaga 32, tel. 922281453. Trendy cocktail bar with tables out on the boulevard and a dance floor, daily 10:30 pm to 3 am.

PUBS: Around the Plaza de la Paz and on the Avenida de Anaga. *TRENDY BARS:* **Parra**, Pasaje Sitja 19; **El Desván**, Pasaje Sitja 17. Sometimes with live music at weekends.

Long Way, Calle Castillo 41, office 221, tel./fax. 922-292061. Also mountain-biking, paragliding and diving; **Canarias Trekking**, Calle Quevedo 4, Edifício Gran Vía, intermediate floor, office 2, tel./fax. 922-201051. Tour organization.

BINGO: Hall for 400 players on Calle Imeldo Serís.

Main shopping streets in Santa Cruz: *Calle del Castillo* with fashion boutiques, drugstores and electronic stores and *Calle Béthencourt Alfonso*. More expensive boutiques between *Calle del Castillo* and *Calle del Pilar Señora de África*, daily market in the mornings, flea market on Sun.

🔲 *DIPLOMATIC REPRESENTATION:* British Consulate: Plaza de Weyler, Santa Cruz de Tenerife, tel. 922-286863 (if you phone outside of office hours a recording will give you a number), Mon-Fri 9 am to noon. American Embassy: Call Cerrano 75, 28006 Madrid, tel. 091-5774000, Mon-Fri 10 am to noon.

📱 *POST OFFICE:* Plaza de España.

ℹ️ Plaza de España (in the Palacio Insular), tel. 922-239592 and 922-239500, fax. 922-605781, daily 8 am to 6 pm.

THE SOUTH AND THE CENTER

ARONA / LA ESCALONA

🔲 😊😊 **Tenerife Tracks & Trails**, La Escalona, Mountain Lodge, Los Quemados 2, tel. 922-725358. Apartments for self-caterers and hikers in rural environment. Guided group tours and hikes (English and Spanish; from 8 participants up). Bar, pool, billiards, table tennis and darts.

❌ **Patio Canario**, Arona, Calle Domínguez Alfonso 4, tel. 922-725503. Belgian and Canarian cuisine. Reservation recommended, Tue-Sat 1 to 3 pm and 7 to 11 pm (winter; 8 to 11 pm in summer); **El Refugio**, near Arona, El Topo 34 (access signposted), tel. 922-725894. International cuisine, Tue-Thu 12 to 9 pm, Thu from 6 pm.

🔺 **Tenerife Tracks & Trails** (see "Accommodation").

CANDELARIA

🔲 😊😊 **Tenerife Tour**, Caletillas district, Avda. Generalísimo 170, tel. 922-500200/4, fax. 922-502363. 90 rooms in bungalow style by the sea, garden, pools, tennis, boules, conference rooms, disco.

🏛️ **Basílica**, consecrated to the patron saint of the Canary Islands, daily 7:30 am to 1 pm and 3 to 7:30 pm.

➕ **Centro Médico de Candelaria**, Calle José Antonio near the harbor.

📱 *POST OFFICE:* Calle José Antonio.

ℹ️ **Centro de Información Turística:** Caletillas, Plaza de la Constitución.

GÜÍMAR

❌ **La Cuevita de Nemesio**, Arafo, Carretera La Cumbre near km 2, tel. 922-513402. Cave restaurant with Canarian cuisine, delicious specialties. Wed-Mon 1 pm to midnight.

📘 **Parque Etnográfico Pirámides de Güímar**, Calle Chacona, tel. 922-514510, fax. 922-514511. With Museo Casa Charcona. Internet: http://www.fredolsen.es/piramides.

LA ESPERANZA

❌ **Las Cañadas**, Carretera General 73 (access road to the Cañadas), tel. 922-548030. Large dining room, bar, café and souvenir shop. Specialties: rabbit, suckling pig and chicken baked in a wood oven.

TEIDE

🔲 😊😊 **Parador de Turismo Las Cañadas del Teide**, tel. 922-386415, fax. 922-382352. Located 2,100 meters above sea level, pool, sauna, fitness center, restaurant, small museum.

😊 **Refugio de Altavista**, mountain hut 3,300 meters up, limited to 50 people, apply by phone at tel. 922-239811 or 922-239592.

Group accommodation in log cabins: In the Teide National Park near Arenas Negras. Information from the Ayuntamiento de Garachico, Plaza de la Libertad 1, E-38450 Garachico, tel. 922-830000/01, fax. 922-831301.

📘 *TEIDE CABLE CARS:* As far as the Rambleta (3,550 meters). No service if windy, and long waiting times in peak season, daily 9 am to 4 pm, tel. 922-287837.

🔺 Hiking information from the Centro de Visitantes.

ℹ️ **Centro de Visitantes**: Information center about Teide National Park near El Portillo. Bookstore, video show, various signboards and maps; **Patronato del Parque Nacional de las Cañadas del Teide**, Santa Cruz, Calle Emilio Calzadilla 5, tel. 922-290129. This is where you can get permission to ascend the summit. Guided hikes through the Cañadas, daily 9 am to 4 pm.

VILAFLOR

🔲 😊 **Alta Montaña**, Morro del Cano 1, tel. 922-709049, fax. 922-709000. Quiet, 25 beds, ideal for hikers. Rooms with bath and terrace, pool, healthy food. Double room with breakfast 6,000 Ptas.

❌ **El Mirador**, panoramic view of Vilaflor. Tel. 922-709135; Mon-Thu 10 am to 8 pm, Sat, Sun 12 to 8 pm.

📘 **Parque San Roque**, tel. 922-709124. Adventure park with museum, goat enclosure, Mexican hacienda, souvenir shop with restaurant, daily 10 am to 6 pm (museum) and 11 am to 10 pm (restaurant).

🖼️ *Rosetas* and *Calados*: In the store on Calle Hermano Pedro 28 and in the *Multivisión Parque Nacional del Teide* outside town in the direction of Arona, Camino Lomo Oreja 6. You can also get other craft items here, plus honey, rum, mojo and gofio.

VILLA DE ARICO

🔲 😊😊 **Aricotour**, Carretera General 11, tel./fax. 922-161133. Organizes accommodation in old farmhouses, info about hikes, visits to dairies, etc.

LA GOMERA
Wild and Romantic for Dreamers and Dropouts

SAN SEBASTIÁN DE LA GOMERA
THE SOUTH COAST
THE WEST
PARQUE NACIONAL DE
GARAJONAY
THE GREEN NORTH

Back to Nature!

The first tourists on La Gomera during the 1960s and 70s were mostly dropouts, but they were soon joined by hikers and nature lovers. The protected laurel forest at the center of the island is a very special place to hike, with its streams and waterfalls, and the odd trade-wind cloud hanging eerily above the various liana-covered trees and bushes. Swimming is possible, too, but the possibilities are rather more limited than on the larger islands. If small rocky, pebble and sand beaches don't bother you, you certainly won't mind; though Gomera certainly isn't a typical tourist island.

Like most of the Canary Islands, its most striking and attractive feature is its sometimes bizarre, sometimes gentle landscape. Traces of the volcanism that shook and transformed this little island over two million years ago are certainly in evidence, though hidden and softened by the profusion of foliage and also the large number of cultivated fields. The terraced fields here reach almost inaccessible heights, and are most impressive; the views from them, especially wherever

Previous Pages: Agulo (Tenerife) provides a breathtaking view across the sea. Left: Banana harvesting in Hermigua.

Canary palms have been planted, are gorgeous. These steep terraces cannot provide the local farmers with prosperity, however, which is why many young *Gomeros* earn their pesetas in the tourist industry on Tenerife, or in the growing tourist center of Valle Gran Rey.

One strange feature of this island, which should be saved as a UNESCO World Heritage Site before it vanishes altogether, is *silbo*, the special means of communication by whistling. This ancient "language" made up of short, long, low and high whistles has long been used for communicating across the barrancos.

Arrival

La Gomera is still considered the most "alternative" island to visit. It's certainly true that the people who come here, especially to Valle Gran Rey, are a far more colorful assortment than elsewhere in the Canaries. The place is not especially easy to reach, and this has prevented mass tourism from gaining a foothold: you have to fly to Tenerife, then take a ferry to the island from Los Cristianos, and then take a taxi to your final destination.

The controversial airport that was built near Playa de Santiago – but was still not in operation at the time of printing – is only supposed to be used for inter-island

La Gomera

flights. Despite all official reassurances to the contrary, the fears of environmentalists about it ushering in mass tourism do seem to be largely well-founded.

SAN SEBASTIÁN DE LA GOMERA

Even from the ferry boat you can tell that **San Sebastián de La Gomera ❶**, nestling among steep rocky cliffs, is little more than a small provincial town. From the northern barranco wall it is dominated by one of the finest state-run hotels in the Canary Islands, the Spanish-colonial style *Parador de Turismo Conde de la Gomera*.

In the harbor, in the street cafés of the **Plaza de las Américas** and in the laurel-shaded **Plaza de la Constitución** it becomes clear that this town, with its population of 2,500, only ever opens one sleepy eye briefly whenever ferries arrive from Tenerife, La Palma or El Hierro. Indeed, San Sebastián seems to be quite

Above: Silbo – a language of whistles.

happy with its role as a brief stopover for visitors, even though it does try to place its attractions in a favorable light.

The town's only ever real claim to fame was its immediate participation in the discovery of America: Christopher Columbus stopped on Gomera three times before crossing the Atlantic; in 1492, 1493 and 1498. Apparently he didn't only come here because the island was the last place to stock up on provisions, but also because he felt attracted to Beatriz de Bobadilla, wife of Hernán Peraza, the governor of Gomera.

Calle del Medio

At the beginning of the **Calle del Medio**, near the Plaza de la Constitución, you'll find the tourist information office inside a former customs building. The inner courtyard contains the **Pozo de Colón**, and according to the inscription it was with water from here that Columbus baptized America – *con esta agua se bautizó América*. Columbus is thought to

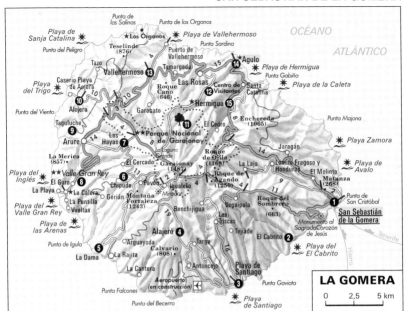

have taken water from this well on his voyages, and baptized the first of the "West Indian" islands in the name of Christianity.

Along Calle del Medio there are several attractively renovated townhouses that once belonged to merchants and nobles. Apart from the compulsory Canarian balconies, they also have fine interior courtyards and sometimes even wrought-iron decoration that betrays Moorish influence. The narrow shopping street leads to the main church of the island, the *Iglesia Nuestra Señora de la Asunción. This is where Columbus is supposed to have knelt down to ask God's blessing for his voyage. The three-aisled church, built in the 15th century and extended several times in the 17th and 18th centuries, has some noteworthy features.

After the **main portal**, with its stone carvings and ornamentation in the Manuelesque style, the entrance is flanked by a wooden **grille** made from Canary pine. Behind the grille on the left is a statue of Christ lying in an open cof-

fin. Inside the church there are several **retables** with some fine baroque ornamentation. The simpler ones, more influenced by the late Renaissance, mostly have realistically painted pictures in the panels around the central saints. The retables dating from the rococo period have sculptures in these panels rather than paintings.

A **fresco** by the local artist José Mesa in the left-hand side-chapel shows the attack carried out on the town in 1743 by the English pirate Windham. Above it is the oldest and most valuable **Artesonado ceiling** in the church, executed in the Moorish *mudéjar* style of Andalusia. The colors, a common feature in former days, are still in very good condition. Like everywhere else on the Canary Islands, the astonishingly prolific and also highly gifted architect and sculptor Luján Pérez from Gran Canaria left his traces here in the Asunción church as well: the late baroque altar and also the crucifix are both his work.

A little farther out of town, on the same side of the street, is the **Casa de Colón**.

The house dates from the 17th century, so the legend about Columbus having actually lived here cannot be true. It contains models of the great explorer's three ships, a model of the Asunción church made of sugar, and a relief map of the island. On the upper floor there are exhibitions on the themes of Gomera, Columbus and Latin America.

Late Medieval Features

Located just beyond the post office is the oldest building in town, the **Ermita de San Sebastián**, a simple chapel built at the start of the colonization period in around 1450, and consecrated to the town's patron saint. Like the Asunción church, it was burned to the ground every time pirates passed this way, and only the Late Gothic side entrance survives from the original structure. The **Torre del Conde** is the only late Medieval fortifica-

Above: Colorful retable in the town's main church. Right: The Torre del Conde.

tion on the entire island. Apart from a few additions by the Italian fortress builder Leonardo Torriani, it has largely retained its original appearance. The tower dates from the time of governor Hernán Perazas the Elder, and was built at around the same time as the Ermita de San Sebastián. The 18-meter-high cube on the northwestern side of the Plaza de las Américas, with its two-meter-thick walls, rises from a square ground plan, and is today surrounded by a park; inside it there is an interesting exhibition of historical maps of the Canary Islands.

The tower was originally built as a last refuge for the ruling noble family of the Perazas against Gomero rebels, and then as a defense against pirate attack. The Perazas, including the governor's wife Beatriz de Bobadilla, had total control of the island and mercilessly sold its entire original Guanche population into slavery, against all rules of the Spanish crown. When Beatriz's faithless husband Hernán Peraza the Younger arrived for a secret amorous rendezvous with Iballa, a native

La Gomera

princess, at a cave just outside San Sebastián, a Gomero ran him through with a lance.

This marked the start of an uprising in the town, and Beatriz hurried inside the Torre del Conde with her children. When Pedro de Vera, the ruler of Gran Canaria, rushed to the scene with 400 soldiers and smashed through the Gomeros' siege ring, Beatriz and her liberators avenged themselves on the local population by putting virtually every single male Guanche inhabitant of Gomera to death. The Gomeros who had not taken part in the uprising were lured by a phony promise of amnesty through the **Puerta del Perdón** ("Gate of Forgiveness") and into the main church before being mercilessly slaughtered. Even the Gomeros who had been sent away as slaves to Gran Canaria were butchered.

On a lighter note, north of San Sebastián you'll find the attractive beach of ***Playa Avalo** (with a freshwater spring), which is an ideal destination for swimmers and divers.

THE SOUTH COAST
Pretty – But for How Much Longer?

If you leave San Sebastián in the direction of Valle Gran Rey, after a few bends in the road you'll arrive at a turnoff that takes you to the **Monumento al Sagrado Corazón de Jesús** along a dirt track. From this seven-meter-high statue of Christ there's a very impressive view of the town, the sea and Tenerife.

At first the road is lined by plants that thrive in dry weather, such as cacti, euphorbia and agaves. Many of the terraced fields are barren, and their walls are slowly crumbling. Just before the **Degollada de Peraza** you'll get your first impression of the very special rock formations on Gomera. The peak across to the left, for instance, the so-called **Roque del Sombrero**, which looks like a stone yurt from the steppes of Central Asia.

At its feet, at the end of the barranco on the coast, lies **El Cabrito ❷**, which can be reached from the sea and which has its own organic farm. The controversial

Viennese artist Otto Mühl, famous for his shocking "happenings," used to live here. It was close to the pass here that Hernán Peraza the Younger is supposed to have been run through by Huatacuperche of the Agana tribe during his rendezvous with Iballa.

The quickest way to reach the Valle Gran Rey is to stay on the main road, which has two more observation points on it about three kilometers after the turn-off to Playa Santiago. From these you can admire four of the most impressive *roques* on Gomera, volcanic vents that hardened to stone over millions of years and have now been revealed by erosion of the softer outer material. To the left is the **Roque de Agando** (1,250 meters), and to the right the **Roques de Carmona** (1,103 meters), **La Zarcita** (1,234 meters) and – a little farther away from the road – the **Roque de Ojila** (1,168 meters). You'll also notice the unusual, jungle-like flora of the island interior: juniper, brier, sweet willow and laurel trees line the road from here to almost as far as Arure.

Playa de Santiago –
The Expanding Village

A well-surfaced road leads through two new tunnels and down an almost 12-percent gradient to **Playa de Santiago ❸**. From almost 1,000 meters up, it travels down through an almost desert-like landscape with deep valleys before finally arriving at the sea. If you're lucky, you may hear the famous *silbo*, the Gomeros' whistling language, for the first time as it echoes through the barrancos. In the higher elevations, freshly-planted pine trees have added a bit of sparse vegetation, and there are quite a few banana plantations near Playa de Santiago.

This small fishing village, which has a long-closed fish factory in its neighbor-

Right: Fisherman mooring his boat in Playa de Santiago.

ing bay, is still an intact community: young and old meet up in the village plaza, and there are some pleasant bars and restaurants along the quay. Tourism arrived here when the four-star Jardín Tecina Hotel was built high above Playa de Santiago by the Norwegian shipping company Fred Olsen Lines.

Romantic spots are becoming increasingly hard to find because of all the construction activity. The hotel complex is like a "village within a village," and is the nicest place here for many visitors because of its commanding view of the bay and the harbor. An elevator leads to the pebble beach of Playa de Santiago, which isn't all that attractive and is partly limited by the main road.

If you'd rather swim in the Atlantic than the hotel pool, just take a 15-minute walk eastwards from the Jardín Tecina to the wild and romantic **Playa del Medio**. You'll need something soft to lie on in the first bay because of the big rocks, but there's actually some sand in the next bay along. Both of these bays are nice, quiet and relatively deserted.

To the west of Playa de Santiago the shipping firm of Olsen – the largest private real estate owner on Gomera – has extended its interest in tourism by building an **airport**. It isn't in operation yet, and the runway is not meant to be suitable for large passenger jets – that's the official version at least. Environmentalists are complaining that construction of the place alone has frightened away several species of bird, and that the ecosystem has already been severely damaged.

The Hilly Hinterland

In the small hamlets you'll pass as you head for the 800-meter-high **Alajeró ❹**, many houses are empty because their owners grew tired of the meager existence here, or because not even that can be guaranteed any longer now. The vegetable patches, vineyards and pumpkin

La Gomera

fields largely serve to nourish the local inhabitants. From the square by the village church (16th century) there is a view of the barren southern part of the island. Up on Mount Calvary (807 meters) in the foreground you can see the simple **Ermita San Isidro**. A *tagoror*, or Guanche meeting place, was discovered near this monastery, and there are also several other ruined tumuli and burial mounds from the pre-Hispanic era. It is interesting that monasteries and other structures were almost always built above the ancient Guanche sacred sites, rather than at new locations of their own; it testifies to the former power of the old Guanche beliefs.

Around one kilometer above Alajeró, an elaborately cobbled road leads down sharply, covering 200 meters of altitude, to a very symmetrical-looking dragontree, the **Drago de Agalán**, which is 150 years old and is considered to be the most ancient on the island.

A left turn near Igualero leads to an observation point next to a chapel. From there you can see the **Montaña Fortaleza* (1,243 meters), a mighty plateau which was used by the aboriginal population as a cultic site and, finally, as their last bastion before the Spanish intruders. From Pavón, a hamlet at the foot of the mountain, a path leads up to the plateau, which also includes a 10-minute climb for people who aren't afraid of heights (the whole hike, including a tour of the plateau, takes around two hours).

Continuing the journey you will pass through a forest, much of which has been destroyed by a fire. Just before you get to Chipude there's a good detour you can take to **La Dama ⑤**. The road leads through a deserted, arid region, similar to the one around Playa de Santiago. In La Dama, however, artificial irrigation has created a large plantation area for bananas, avocados and pineapples. This contrast is a typical feature of much of La Gomera, where you can see barren and deserted regions with tiny villages followed by amazingly fertile oases watered by reservoirs.

THE WEST
More Than Just the "Valle"

Taking the route that is also driven by the local bus when it transports its back-pack-carrying passengers to the Valle Gran Rey, you'll pass a series of small mountain villages. Like the villages that follow it, **Chipude** ❻ is more than 1,000 meters above sea level, and temperatures here can fall even lower than 10°C if the weather is bad. The nearby forests have had to make way for fields (some of which are vineyards), and the center of the village consists of the large square in front of the church and a few bars. Hikers who want to make an early start from here into the national park, or to the Fortaleza, spend the night in the simple boarding house, Sonia, above the bar of the same name in the square.

El Cercado, the next village along the narrow road, is mainly visited because of its ceramic products, which are still made according to an age-old tradition. Like the Guanches, the women here form their pots without using a wheel. The tradition does not date back to Gomeran ancestors before the Spanish arrived, however, but to Galician influences, as has been discovered by Adam Reifenberger, one of the foremost experts on the Canary Islands. During the 19th century the people arrived here via a family of potters from Arguayo (Tenerife).

On the edge of the Garajonay National Park lies the tiny village of **Las Hayas** ❼, a favorite with vegetarian visitors to the island. Today numerous visitors come to see Efigenia in her **Bar Montaña** and indulge in her delicious food. Everyone sits at long tables and quite close together, too, because it can get rather cool up here; it's a communicative round table, very much in keeping with the image of the Valle Gran Rey. No one knows what will be on the menu – it's quite simply whatever Efigenia happens to serve, and it's always delicious.

Above: Old pottery production in El Cercado.
Right: A "dream finca" to retire to.

La Gomera

The direct, albeit winding, route to **Arure** often gets blocked by the odd herd of goats – something far less likely to happen on the larger islands with their efficient infrastructures. This village, with its population of 300, is worth a visit because of the view it provides of the neighboring village of Tagaluche (see pp. 181-182), which can be enjoyed from a Mirador on the other side of the aqueduct. After all those barren and deserted mountain villages, Arure is something of an oasis, and the profusion of vegetation here is due as much to the volcanic soil as to a couple of recently-built reservoirs.

★★Valle Gran Rey – Where the Tourists Meet Up

The palm-filled **Valle Gran Rey ❽**, the most popular tourist destination on the island, is similarly green. A well-surfaced mountain road leads you into the "Valley of the Great King." Dutch author Cees Nooteboom conveyed the euphoric feeling of arriving here: "You feel you're in the tropics, in a Balinese landscape with palm trees, in a world of magical beauty." At an exposed location on a long bend in the road, César Manrique (see p. 236) built one of his architectural specialties on the mountain ridge: a **natural stone restaurant**, which blends in smoothly with the landscape and affords a magnificent view of the wild rocks and luxuriant valley below through its massive picture window. As with all Manrique's architectural gems, this one has been placed at exactly the right location for the best view.

The Valle consists of several communities: the main town is ★**La Calera**, which rises above the northern end of the barranco, the banana plantations and the bay. It has an *Ayuntamiento* (Town Hall), a *Centro de Salud* (Health Center) and a gas station. The post office has meanwhile been transferred to **Borbalán**, a modern annexe between La Calera and **Vueltas**.

In the winding narrow streets of La Calera, most of which are inaccessible to

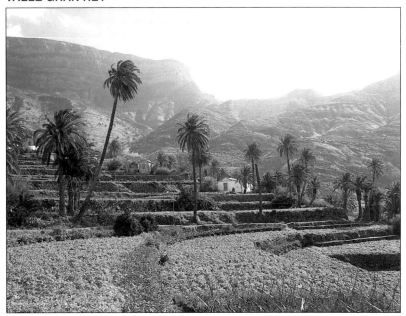

traffic, almost every family has a few guest rooms free, or has added annexes, so genuine accommodation is easy to find. Some foreigners have bought places here, too, to rent them out. Terraces with views have mostly become small restaurant – and the view at sunset here across the bananas plantations, dominated here and there by tall palms, of the sea and of El Hierro is quite unforgettable.

On the terrace of the *Zumería Carlos*, a juice bar that is the "in" place to meet, Valle guests with dark-brown suntans sit until the early evening observing the pink new arrivals to the island. Anyone who wants to get as brown as them has the choice between the absolutely safe *Baby Beach* near **La Puntilla**, the trusty local beach of **Playa de la Calera** (with gray sand and pebbles) and the **Playa del Inglés** with its black sand, which is rather dangerous if the sea is choppy. The sandy

harbor beach at **Vueltas** is also quite safe, something that cannot be said of the stony **Playa de Argada** slightly to the south. The **Playa de las Arenas**, slightly farther south still, is rather hard to reach. Nude sunbathing has become something of an institution here, and there are also some rock caves which are inhabited by a number of neo-hippies.

Popular La Playa as well as central, sterile La Puntilla are the unproud possessors of La Gomera's first boring hotels. Until now they have been built inconspicuously and haven't jarred with the general harmonious appearance of the landscape. The same goes for Borbalán, inland from La Puntilla. In Vueltas things are different: here the construction chaos is concealed by the busy harbor, with all its banana packing, and its various districts with names like the "Bermuda Triangle," the "Red-Light District" and the "Chinese Quarter."

The latter, a relatively harmless entertainment district with a few bars, has retained its charm despite all the new

Above: The Valle Gran Rey, reminiscent of Bali. Right: Bike and boat – the new trend? (La Puntilla, Valle Gran Rey).

buildings. Several of the bars have a pleasant, communicative atmosphere; here you often meet the same people you saw at the beach or on a hike the same day, and now you have the night ahead of you to listen to exotic anecdotes and share nostalgic memories of vacations in previous years.

Anyone who wants to go on hiking tours generally has to get up early, because the bus required, from Valle to the starting points on the plateaus in the interior, leaves at eight in the morning – and the next one doesn't leave until two-thirty in the afternoon (the stop is opposite the juice bar in La Calera). If you get up too late the only way to get to your starting point is by hitchhiking there (this usually works out well, because the people here are still more open and friendly than the rather hard-boiled denizens of the larger islands, and are still interested enough in people from other countries to give them a ride), or by taking a rental car or taxi.

There's one refreshing hike you can take on hot days which is quite independent of the bus timetable. Just before you reach the last houses in **El Guro** (on the main road into Valle before Calera) a small path, first marked by reddish-orange arrows and later by heaps of stones and blue and red dots, leads off westwards into the Barranco of Arure and up to a waterfall. Since you'll be mostly in the shade in the morning because of the high trees and there's a natural shower awaiting you under the waterfall when you get there, this makes a very pleasant hike on a hot day. Depending on where the water flows, you may have to leave the riverbed a few times and take the path up the side. The way back is the same as the way you came.

Unspoiled Coastline

From Valle Gran Rey there are two more places in the west of Gomera that can be reached along narrow and winding, but well-paved roads. On the way to **Taguluche ❾** you'll pass through a natural tunnel of trees and tree-like shrubs –

the mixed forest known as the *Monte-verde*, which consists of laurel (*lauri-silva*) and *Fayal-Brezal*. In the mornings, and in thick fog, enormous water droplets land on the car windshield as you go through here. From the road to Alojera, turn off after a few hairpin curves (beneath the Andenes de Alojera) towards the south and Taguluche.

This very tidy little village is an extremely quiet and peaceful place, day or night. Since the remaining inhabitants still subsist largely on agriculture, there isn't even a bar here. Regular irrigation of the tiny fields is a top priority. The road ends in the middle of the village in front of the **Ermita de San Salvador**, from which there is a good view of the rock formations on the coast. A footpath leads from the village to the sea, where there isn't much at all apart from a small pebble beach and an old mooring jetty.

Similarly well-tended terraces await visitors in **Alojera ⑩**, a slightly larger and busier place. Not only is there a bar here, named *Ossorio*, but (rather simple) accommodation, too. A dirt track leads to a tiny sand beach which is one of the best on the island because of the breakwaters sunk into the sea just offshore. In summer this quiet bay is packed with tourists, most of them from Tenerife and the Spanish mainland, and that's when all the small apartment buildings right beside the sea are fully booked.

PARQUE NACIONAL DE GARAJONAY

The landscape jewel possessed by Gomera is something the other islands can merely dream about: from the peak of the Garajonay and covering an area seven kilometers across is the largest intact area of rain forest on the entire archipelago, comprising laurel, forests of Fayal-

Right: The Parque Nacional de Garajonay – mysterious, magnificent and foggy forest.

Brezal, some bush, and even a few forests of pine. "There is often thick fog here during the day, and it's like driving through a Nibelungen land, accompanied by the sound of the windshield wipers," wrote Cees Nooteboom.

In 1981, the German botanist Günther Kunkel managed to have large expanses of the island's center protected. In 1986, the ****Parque Nacional de Garajonay ⑪** became the only Spanish national park to be placed on the World Cultural Heritage list by UNESCO. This is the reason why much of the forest is off-limits to visitors today. A hiking route through the center to El Cedro is, however, just as accessible as the paths that start at the picnic site near **La Laguna Grande**.

The **Visitor Center ⑫** near Las Rosas in the north gives those with a knowledge of Spanish a lot of interesting information on the special importance of this protected park landscape – from explanations of volcanism to background knowledge on the island's water reserves.

The best way to gain a practical idea is to take a short hike to the peak of Garajonay; the path begins at the parking lot on the main road. Bus travelers should get off near Pajarito and then go to the parking lot on the road leading to Valle Gran Rey. The tour there and back takes almost one hour and is well marked. If visibility is good (and it often is if you're up here before 11 a.m.) there is a great view of the entire island, and as far as Tenerife, El Hierro and La Palma.

From the same parking lot on the main road, a signposted path leads to **El Cedro** (two hours) and also to **Hermigua** (a further two hours). On this wonderful tour you'll be able to see almost all the flora this island has to offer, starting with low forest composed of sweet willow (*faya*) and brier (*brezo*), then laurel forest (*laurisilva*) and various juniper groves (*sabinar*), all the way to terraced fields dotted with palm trees. The entire hike is incredibly restful, the air sweet, and

La Gomera

there's just enough shade to keep you pleasantly cool on the hottest of days.

Around 45 minutes into the hike you'll hear the gentle splashing sound of the Arroyo de Cedro, which doesn't disappear until you get to the village. Perhaps it's the river that makes this hike so atmospheric – there's a magical quality to this part of the island.

Near the **Ermita Nuestra Señora de Lourdes** you can eat your packed lunch on a wooden bench, or go and relax in the *Vista-Bar* in El Cedro. They serve filling Canarian food here, and it's an excellent place for a break. The wines are good, and with your coffee you could try a shot of the popular local liqueur: made from herbs, it is called *Montañero* and is absolutely delicious.

Continuing on your way, you will now pass the highest waterfall on Gomera – a very impressive sight – before the route starts to descend steeply down into the valley of Hermigua. You can get back by bus (via San Sebastián), by cab or, of course, by hitchhiking.

THE GREEN NORTH
Gomera's Other Face

Not including the center of the island, the north of Gomera is its greenest and gentlest region. The Spanish conquerors must have felt much the same when they gave it its name of **Vallehermoso** ⑬ ("Beautiful Valley"). From far away you can see its landmark feature, the impressive 650-meter-high **Roque Cano**, a volcanic vent exposed by erosion. The name (*cano* = "white-haired") probably refers to the trade-wind clouds that often surround its summit.

In the center of the village is the **Iglesia San Juan Bautista**, a relatively large village church in the eclectic style, designed by the Tenerife architect Antonio Pintor, who was the most vehement exponent of eclecticism. This architectural style arrived on the Canaries around the same time as Art Nouveau, and looked for primarily ornamental elements from past stylistic epochs, rearranging them to form new compositions. It can also be de-

from the sea like organ pipes. These rock formations are best visited with one of the ships that travel there daily from Valle Gran Rey. In **Tamargada**, a section of Vallehermoso in the direction of Agulo, you'll still find houses built in the old traditional manner. Unfortunately, most of them are now neglected, dilapidated and abandoned. Another distinctive feature of this region: the protective terraced walls made of a yellowish stone. They, too, are crumbling away.

Continue now to the various small villages that make up **Las Rosas**, whose name is not derived from roses but from steady erosion. Here the islands offshore keep attracting one's gaze. At first you can see the hills on La Palma, and just before you get to Las Rosas the first outlines of Tenerife peek through the Gomeran rocks. This is an excellent place to do some photography.

From Las Rosas there's a steep downhill section to ★**Agulo** ⓮. This village with its Pintor-designed domed church, the Moorish style of which has earned it the ironical name *La Mezquita* (the name of the famous mosque in Córdoba), is the perfect place for a view of Mount Teide towering across the straits.

Hidden away behind a round red wall of rock facing the interior of the island, this narrow little place has extraordinary atmosphere. During a fiesta, when the hot rhythms of the salsa music echo from the rock walls here, an uncanny sound is produced that stays in your head for days.

scribed rather more succinctly as wedding-cake architecture! Pintor built two other churches on Gomera in the same style, those of Agulo and Hermigua.

A Gomera specialty is produced in Vallehermoso: palm honey. A juice flows from cut sections in the upper part of the tree trunk which, when thickened to one fifth of its original mass, gains a sticky consistency. The sweet, dark palm honey is often used for desserts and baby food because of its high mineral content. When fermented, the juice (*guarapa*) makes a strong palm wine.

At the time of going to press, the **Playa de Vallehermoso** was being turned into an elaborate *zona recreativa*. Plans include a seawater swimming pool, breakwaters, freshwater showers and even a sports harbor. To the northwest is ★**Los Órganos**, a steep section of coast consisting of a mass of basalt pillars that rise up

The most famous native son of this town was the painter José Aguiar (1895–1975), who was born of Gomeran parents and grew up in Cuba. His main works, monumental wall paintings on the rural life of the islands, can be seen in the Palacio Insular and the Casino of Santa Cruz de Tenerife (see p. 148). His work documents a style of life that is fast disappearing on these islands as tourism makes increasing inroads into traditional patterns of life.

Above: Los Órganos – basalt rock formations in the sea, northwest of Playa de Vallehermoso.

Agulo has duly included lessons in the weird whistling language known as *silbo* in its youth education program. A restaurant on the winding road to Hermigua also reminds passers-by of the whistling language, and just past it a fertile valley suddenly appears. From the heights you can look down on to the long pebble beach of **Playa de Hermigua**, with a sea-water swimming pool at its eastern end. In the bar above the pool, old pictures show the original function of the beach: it was once a freight-loading station. Swimming here is quite dangerous because of the powerful undertow. An attractive beach in the neighboring bay to the southeast, the **Playa de la Caleta**, is an hour's walk away, unless you happen to have a jeep.

*Hermigua ⓕ extends for many kilometers along the road and up into the valley, and almost seems to be bursting with fertility. Even after a seriously dry summer this valley is always a green oasis. The stream here – the Arroyo de Cedro, which has its source in the national park – is the only one on the island with water all year round. Around half of Gomera's banana production comes from the Hermigua region. The large amount of wealth all this is bringing in is reflected in the row of elegant country houses along the main road. Many are still in good condition today and have stuccoed facades. In the section of town called **El Convento**, named after a Dominican monastery here that was later dissolved, the **Los Telares** art exhibition contains a collection of historic looms.

To end the trip there are two rocks you can't help but notice on the right above the road, silhouetted against the magnificent panorama formed by the mountains around El Cedro. They're named after St. Peter (*San Pedro*) and are also commonly referred to as "Peter and Paul." After passing through the **Tunnel de la Cumbre**, you'll see San Sebastián once again in the distance.

LA GOMERA

ⓘ *ARRIVAL:* **By Plane:** The only way to get to La Gomera by plane is to fly to Tenerife first. La Gomera's airport is not open yet. **By Ship:** Several connections daily with *Lineas Fred Olsen*, tel. 922-628200, and *Trasmediterránea*, tel. 902-454654, from Los Cristianos / Tenerife to San Sebastián (90 mins.; hydrofoil 35 mins.). Further connections to El Hierro (daily; 3 hours) and La Palma (3 hours). Internet: www.fredolsen.es / www.trasmediterranea.es

SAN SEBASTIÁN DE LA GOMERA

🏨 😊😊😊 **Parador de Turismo Conde de La Gomera**, tel. 922-871100, fax. 922-871116. Finest parador on the Canaries. Rooms and salons in the style of the Columbus era. Pool, terraced garden.

😊😊 **Villa Gomera**, Calle Ruiz de Padrón 68, tel./fax. 922-870235. Bright, clean rooms, noisy on the road side.

😊 **Residencia Colombina**, Calle Ruiz de Padrón 83, tel. 922-871257. Remote but no more quiet than the others. Rooms with bath and small balconies.

❌ **Restaurante-Bar Marqués de Oristano**, Calle del Medio 26, tel. 922-870022. Gourmet restaurant in renovated historic building. Crayfish, rabbit, steaks. Expensive. Mon-Sat 12 to 4 pm and 7 to 11 pm.

🏛 Church of **Nuestra Señora de la Asunción**, **Ermita de San Sebastián**, **Casa de Colón** and **Torre del Conde**, open mornings and after siesta; **Galeria de Arte Luna**, Calle del Medio 28, tel. 922-870666. Exhibition of works by Guido Kolitscher, Vicki Penfold, et al.

🎵 *DISCOS:* **Fin Fan**, Calle Trasera, weekends; **Terraza-Disco Oh**, **Riviera**, open-air disco southwest of the Barranco de la Villa, almost on a level with the sports ground, and reached along a dirt road. Sometimes has live music.

🚤 *BOAT EXCURSIONS:* With the tuna fish cutter **Luz Mar**, tel. 922-141136, from the harbor of San Sebastián. Reservations must be made one day in advance.

⛵ *SAILING / HIKING:* **Green Explorer**, tel./fax. 922-871506, 908-413794 (cell phone). Agency for hiking, sailing, etc.

🚕 *TAXI:* Tel. 922-870524.

📮 *POST OFFICE:* Calle del Medio 60, tel. 922-871081, Mon-Fri 8:30 am to 2:30 pm, Sat 9:30 am to 1 pm.

➕ **Centro de Salud**, Calle Ruiz de Padrón 32, tel. 922-870256, outpatients daily 8 am to 3 pm.

ℹ Calle del Medio 4, tel. 922-140147, Mon-Sat 9 am to 1:30 pm and 3:30 to 6 pm, Sun 9 am to 1:30 pm.

La Gomera

THE SOUTH

PLAYA DE SANTIAGO

Hotel Jardín Tecina, tel. 922-895050, fax. 922-895188, Internet: www.fredolsen.es. Over 400 rooms, bungalows in the Canarian style, very elegantly furnished, 5 swimming pools, several restaurants, bars, shopping streets, tennis courts, fitness center, diving club, minigolf, conference rooms, group activities.

Apartamentos Bellavista, Laguna de Santiago, Calle Santa Ana, tel./fax. 922-895208. Newly built, attractively furnished, pool.

Apartamentos Tapahuga, Avda. Marítima, tel. 922-895195, fax. 922-895127. Newly built, very comfortable, pool on the rooftop terrace.

La Cuevita, Avda. Marítima, tel. 922-895568. Cave restaurant at the harbor. Fresh fish, high prices. Mon-Sat noon to midnight; **Jürgen's Infobar**,the in place to meet, with terrace on the beach, good cocktails and ice cream, daily 10 am to 7 pm; **Bar Peraza**, Degollada de Peraza, tel. 922-870390. Simple fare, view of the valley of Playa de Santiago, Wed-Mon 8 am to 8 pm.

Diving, tennis, minigolf, boat trips, etc. (via Hotel Jardín Tecina).

BOAT EXCURSIONS: With the **Luz Mar** (see San Sebastián de la Gomera).

Shopping center in the Hotel Jardín Tecina.

TAXI: Tel. 922-895022.

THE WEST

ALOJERA

Ossorio, tel. 922-800334, with simple restaurant; **Apartamentos Miguel Brito**, tel. 922-800217. Several houses on the beach, comfortable, with verandas.

CHIPUDE

Verode Senderismo SLL, Chipude, via the bar *Sonia* in the town center, tel /fax. 922-804088. Local officially-qualified guides (multilingual). Also offered: horseback riding, bike and kayak trips, sailing, diving, mountain-climbing tours in the Barranco, office hours 9:30 am to 1:30 pm and 4:30 to 6 pm daily.

VALLE GRAN REY

In the **VALLE GRAN REY** there are several places to stay in all price categories. You can find accommodation near the beach in La Playa or in La Puntilla; those who prefer water sports and evening entertainment might like Vueltas, and if you want a really cosmopolitan place with a good view, try La Calera.

LA CALERA: **Apartamentos Domínguez**, beside the La Orquidea restaurant, tel. 922-805030. Gen-erous, some with their own kitchen, also rooftop apartments with terrace, around 4,000 Ptas; **Pensión Concha**, pedestrian precinct, tel. 922-805007. Small, clean rooms, shared kitchen, rooftop terrace.

LA PLAYA: **Apartamentos Los Tarajales**, on the road to Playa del Inglés, tel. 922-805301, fax. 922-805653. By the sea, with pool and sun terrace; **Casa Rudolfo**, on the beach promenade, tel. 922-805195. Comfortable apartments, sea view, German-run.

LA PUNTILLA: **Hotel Gran Rey**, tel. 922-805859, fax. 922-805651, Internet: www.hotel-granrey.com. Around 100 double rooms, all with sea view, pool.

VUELTAS: **Pensión Candelaria**, last street on the slope, tel. 922-805402. Quiet rooms with views.

Restaurante Especial El Baifo, La Playa, Edifício Noramara, tel. 922-805775. Southeast Asian and French dishes for gourmets and vegetarians, Sat-Thu 7 to 11 pm; **Bar Las Jornadas**, at the entrance to town, tel. 922-805047/452. Also known as the *Casa María*. Sparsely furnished, trendy place to eat. Very filling Canarian food with good *Mojo*, Wed-Mon 12 to 4 pm and 7 to 11 pm; **Blaue Bar**, Vueltas, near the Plaza del Carmen, tel. 922-805192. Vegetarian food and nouvelle cuisine, high prices, daily 13:30 to 11 pm; **Restaurante Escuela Mirador César Manrique**, tel. 922-805868. Cooking school for prospective chefs, view across the Valle Gran Rey. Canarian specialties, excellent wines, moderate prices. Tue 6:30 to 10:30 pm, Wed-Sun 12 to 4 pm, 6:30 to 10:30 pm.

The most important information sheet for those looking for fun and nightlife is the *Valle-Bote*, a highly entertaining magazine.

LA CALERA: Cinema-bar **La Galeria**, upper section of town, tel. 922-805878. Films, lectures and concerts almost daily.

In *LA PLAYA* the nightlife centers around the disco **Con Gas** (on the beach promenade) and also in the Tasca **La Gomera**, tel. 922-805250 (Tue-Thu from 8 pm). This is the spot where a lot of people round off the night with a cocktail.

The nightlife in the harbor quarter of *VUELTAS* takes place in restaurants, bistros, cafés and the area's only disco. Popular places include **Cacatua**, **La Tasca** and **Pako's Disco**.

BOAT TOURS: **Capitano Claudio**, Vueltas, in the Club del Mar (near the harbor). Tours around the island. A trip around the island, with stops to swim and eat, lasts from 10:30 am to around 5 pm.

MOUNTAIN-BIKING / MOTORCYCLING: **Alofi Rentals**, La Playa, Edifício Noramara, tel./fax. 922-805554. Mountain bikes, motor scooters, enduros, motor cycles. For groups of mountain bikers of two or more there's an introductory tour to La Laguna Grande, office hours 9 am to 1 pm and 4 to 8 pm.

SAILING: **Barlovento**, Vueltas, tel. 922-805953. Sailing courses with catamarans and yachts.

DIVING: Diving school, **Fisch & Co**, La Playa, tel. 922-805688, fax. 922-805792. From beginner to professional.

Bioladen Ansiria, Vueltas. Natural and handmade products from creams to herbal teas, and from earrings to drums; **Zapatería**, between La Calera and La Playa in a banana plantation. Made-to-measure shoes, handmade leather bags, belts and accessoires (be sure you give them your measurements when you arrive!) In the mornings between 9 and 11 (except Sun) a fishdealer travels through all parts of town announcing his wares through a loudspeaker.

Centro de Salud, signposted at the upper exit to La Calera, tel. 922-805804.

TAXI: Tel. 922-805058.

Tel. 922-805458.

THE ISLAND CENTER

EL CEDRO

Casa El Refugio, El Cedro (located 800 meters up), tel. 922-880801, fax. 922-144101, Internet: www.canary-islands.com/gomera/refugio.htm. Remote and rural; three simple rooms for up to 8 people.

CAMPING: In El Cedro there's a terraced campsite below the *Vista Bar.* You can get official permission at the ICONA Office, San Sebastián, Carretera del Sur 6, tel. 922-870105.

Vista Bar, El Cedro. Hearty Canarian dishes with *mojo*, and cress soup (*sopa de berros*) with *gofio.*

Centro de Visitantes Juego de Bolas, to the north in the direction of Las Rosas, tel. 922-800993. Visitor center for the national park, museum, botanical gardens, crafts show, information center and tour office (Wed, Sat from La Laguna Grande, meet up between 10 and 10:30 am). Sales of crafts, books about Gomera and souvenirs, Tue-Sun 9:30 am to 4:30 pm.

Gomera Trekking and **Green Explorer** (see San Sebastián), **Verode Senderismo** (see West/Chipude).

THE NORTH

AGULO

Centro de Salud, Calle Nuevo, tel. 922-146014.

TAXI: Tel. 922-880931.

HERMIGUA

ROOM RESERVATIONS: **Centro de Iniciativas y Turismo Rural del Norte de La Gomera**, Callejón de

Ordaiz, tel./fax. 922-144101, Internet: www.canary-islands.com, e-mail: gomera@canary-islands.com. Rooms and apartments can be booked and reserved by the local tourist office, and not only in the north of Gomera.

La Casa Creativa, Carretera General 56, tel. 922-881023, fax. 922-144057. Creative center in Canarian country house. Attractive double rooms with full board and lodging (typical local dishes, healthy food). Pool, sun terrace, library, bicycles, sometimes also special events.

Los Telares, El Convento, tel. 922-880781, fax. 922-144107, Internet: www. canary-islands.com/gomera/telares.htm, e-mail: telares@canary-islands.com. Crafts and loom museum in country house, small pool. Apartments organized (also in the national park).

The café at the **Casa Creativa** in Hermigua serves its own homemade cakes, made using the choicest ingredients.

Guía Gomera, tel. 922-880232 (after 7 pm). Hikes in the region of Vallehermoso, Agulo, Hermigua and in the Valle Gran Rey, includes bus trip, packed lunch, insurance. Multilingual guides; The **Centro de Iniciativas** (see "Accommodation") offers guided hiking tours, bicycle tours and horseback-riding trips.

Gomera Art Center, Hermigua, opposite the Casa Creativa. Crafts, musical instruments, honey, palm honey, newspapers, etc., Mon-Sat 10 am to 3 pm to 7 pm. Store with geometrical textiles (*calados*) and souvenirs in the **Los Telares** (see "Accommodation").

TAXI: Tel. 922-880047.

Médico Seguridad Social, Carretera General, tel. 922-880727.

Tel. 922-144025.

LAS ROSAS

Las Rosas, tel. 922-800916. Large terrace restaurant with view of Teide. Gomera specialties, *silbo* performances, many tour buses, daily 12 to 3 pm.

VALLEHERMOSO

Asociación Roque Cano, Ayuntamiento, Plaza de la Constitución, tel. 922-800000. Renovated fincas available.

Hostal Vallehermoso, Calle Triana 9, tel. 922-800283. Quiet, simple, shared bathroom, shared kitchen; **Pensión Amaya II**, Plaza de la Constitución, tel. 922-800073, fax. 922-801138. Modern rooms, TV, centrally located.

Centro de Salud, Plaza de la Constitución, tel. 922-801186.

TAXI: Tel. 922-800279.

Tel. 922-800000.

La Gomera

LA PALMA
Shining Emerald in a Turquoise Sea

SANTA CRUZ DE LA PALMA
SMALL TOWNS IN THE NORTHEAST
THE LONELY NORTHWEST
THE WEST
CALDERA DE TABURIENTE

"La Isla Bonita"

La Palma is often referred to as the most beautiful of all the Canary Islands. To make sure things stay that way, the Palmeros have named it "The Beautiful Island," *La Isla Bonita*. A further title, *La Isla Verde*, reveals that La Palma is strikingly green all year round. The only exception here is the south, which is a wasteland of volcanic ash and dark streams of solidified lava.

La Palma's beauty consists of a garland of deep barrancos full of ferns and laurel forests, steep and craggy coasts, and the mighty Caldera de Taburiente, which dominates the northern half of the island. This enormous crater is absolutely ideal for hikes, from easy to strenuous, and is becoming tremendously popular with visitors to the island in search of vacations combining relaxation with a little exercise.

If simply lying on a beach is your idea of a good time, the tourist centers on the west and east coasts are good places to do so. Puerto Naos and Los Cancajos are

Previous Pages: The finest ensemble of Canarian wooden balconies is on the sea promenade at Santa Cruz de La Palma. Left: The family of Ramón y Vina makes pots without a wheel in El Molino (Hoyo de Mazo).

quite busy, but compared with the huge centers on the larger islands these two carbon-copy resorts are almost homely. Another advantage is that they can also easily be avoided by those who have no time for them. There are enough other places to swim around Puerto Naos and north of Santa Cruz.

Urban sightseeing is another must for any trip to La Palma: on the east coast, the capital of Santa Cruz de La Palma is well worth a visit for its historic center, and on the west coast there's the modern regional town of Los Llanos de Aridane.

Arrival

Arriving here by ship will take you straight to the heart of the capital, Santa Cruz de La Palma. Very few people arrive by sea, however. Even though the ferries from Los Cristianos (Tenerife) and El Hierro are cheaper, most vacationers fly in to the **Aeropuerto La Palma**.

The international airport is on the east coast just outside La Rosa, part of Mazo, and is connected with Santa Cruz de La Palma by an eight-kilometer-long highway. In the airport building you'll find the offices of all the major rental car companies, a cafeteria, a newsagent, souvenir stores and numerous products that are typical of the island. There isn't a bank,

La Palma

but you will find an automatic teller machine. Taxis are lined up outside waiting for fares, and there's also the public bus (No. 10).

Playa de los Cancajos

Traveling north from the airport, before you arrive at the capital, you'll see a turnoff towards the sea which leads to the largest tourist center on the eastern coast, the **Playa de los Cancajos ❶**. Its broad, dark beach is protected from the surf by large concrete blocks out in the sea, which makes it ideal for families. There aren't a lot of trees around to provide shade, however. Most hotels and facilities are geared towards package tourism, and therefore look very much the same. One refreshing exception is the *Hacienda San Jorge* (which is also booked by package tourists), with its Canarian-style apartments in the midst of a subtropical park. Even though the airport is close to here, there still aren't enough planes to disrupt people's holiday pleasure.

*SANTA CRUZ DE LA PALMA

La Palma's capital, the harbor town of **Santa Cruz de La Palma ❷**, is surrounded by a ring of apartment and hotel blocks. There are a few skyscrapers in the center, too, but they don't seriously interfere with the harmonious impression conveyed by the historic Old Town. Quite a bit of money has been spent on renovating the old buildings here. The two main streets run parallel to the coast: Avenida Marítima, with its heavy traffic, and Calle O'Daly, which has now been turned into a pedestrian precinct. The section of town most worth visiting is the roughly 200-meter-square area to the west of **Avenida Marítima**. If you're driving, it's best to find a parking space now on the seaward side of the coast road, or at the end of it, by the Barranco de las Nieves, near the Columbus caravel.

Despite all the traffic, the street cafés along the sea promenade are very popular with the local inhabitants. Along the section extending from the newly-built *Cabildo Insular* (Island Council) and the *Café Slogan* to the *Parador Nacional* (state-run hotel), the bars are very well patronized – especially after siesta time and on public holidays.

Also on the coast road, and north of the Parador, you'll see what is perhaps the most impressive ensemble of *★**Canarian balconies** anywhere on the archipelago. Colorfully painted and well-renovated, they mostly extend over two floors, and with their Portuguese-Moorish elements they have become one of the most-photographed sights of the capital. Most of the balconies were formerly barred over to protect the buildings from sunlight without interrupting ventilation; the glass wind protection on some of them is a more modern variation.

Just before the Barranco de las Nieves you'll reach the dark basalt **Castillo de Santa Catalina**, one of the fortifications that was meant to protect the town from pirate attack. It was built in response to the devastating pirate raid of 1553, during which many sections of the town were completely destroyed. On the other side of the Barranco a further bastion, the **Castillo de La Virgen**, towers above the Old Town and the northern coast.

Its cannon are partly trained at the reconstruction of Columbus's caravel, the **Santa María**. This stranded ship seems strangely out of place here, especially so since Columbus never actually visited La Palma at all. The apparently wooden hull (if you look more closely you'll see that the planks have been painted on to concrete) contains the **Museo Naval Santa María**, a small ship museum with nautical equipment and numerous old maps and charts.

On the nearby **Plaza de la Alameda** there's a small Moorish-style pavilion where you can take a break. A coffee un-

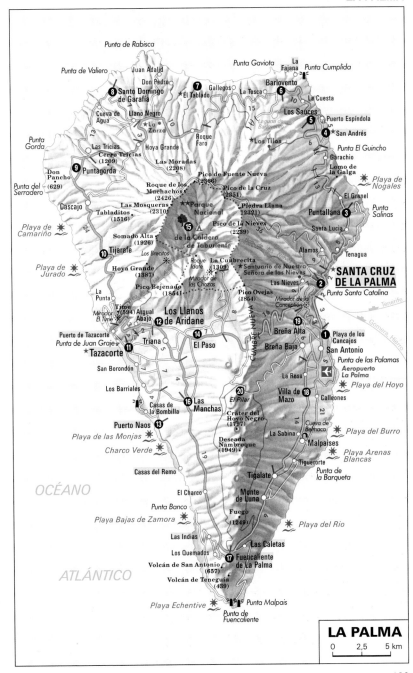

La Palma

OCÉANO

ATLÁNTICO

LA PALMA

0   2,5   5 km

der the Indian laurels here will give you added strength for your visit to the Island Museum (*Museo Insular*), housed inside a former Franciscan monastery on the **Plaza de San Francisco**. At the end of the Alameda, shortly before you reach this slightly elevated square, you'll pass the **cross** that was placed here by the conqueror of La Palma, Alonso de Lugo, in 1493, when he claimed the island for God and for Spain.

The **Museo Insular** is highly recommended to anyone interested in geology, stuffed animals, prehistoric finds, traditional crafts or the everyday Canarian life of long ago.The museum building is also worth a closer look: it is one of the largest monastery complexes on the island, with an inviting square in front of it and a large interior courtyard. At the time of going to press, this was being renovated and/or redesigned, and the retable in the monastery chapel was also being restored at the same time.

Walking towards the sea now, you'll arrive almost immediately at Calle Pérez de Brito, which leads southwards to one of the most restful and attractive squares in Santa Cruz, the **Placeta de Borrero**. There's a splashing fountain under some young coconut palms, and a small restaurant has set up some tables and chairs outside, creating a very comfortable place for strollers and shoppers to take a break. The atmosphere in general on La Palma is far less hectic than it is on the larger islands – people here still know how to take their time, and how to switch off when necessary.

The street goes up slightly now to the Avenida del Fuente and then, after a traffic light, turns into the **Calle O'Daly**. Before you continue walking up this street, which was named after a dynasty of Irish merchants, it's worth taking a quick look

Right: The Plaza de España, one of the most architecturally perfect squares anywhere in the Canaries.

inside the pharmacy with the stucco and crystal chandeliers.

The *Plaza de España

Calle O'Daly leads towards the finest architectural ensemble on La Palma, if not the entire archipelago: the **Plaza de España**. The Iglesia del Salvador, with its flight of steps, was placed here at an angle on the sloping terrain, and this has created a triangular area that rises above the street rather like a stage. In the background you can see the town's central **well**, which is no longer used. Children can often be seen running around the **monument** to the Humanist Manuel Hernández Díaz, or sometimes grown-ups engaged in deep conversation. The whole atmosphere is highly redolent of squares in mainland Spain, an impression strengthened even further by the black street lamps.

If you enter the ***Iglesia del Salvador** (assuming no Mass is being celebrated) through the Renaissance portal flanked by two pairs of pillars, you will find yourself inside one of the most impressive church interiors in the Canary Islands. High above the three aisles is a coffered ceiling in the *mudéjar* style, made of Canary pine. The paintwork on this magnificent ceiling was done during the 19th century and reveals a clear Portuguese influence.

In the right-hand side-aisle is one of the church's most striking sculptures, the *Cristo de los Mulatos* (early 16th century); in front the wall is covered by a monumental picture of St. Christopher. Artistically far more important, however, is the retable painting *The Transfiguration of Christ* by Antonio María Esquivel (1806-1857). Curtains have been painted in the trompe-l'oeil style on both side altars. Also worthy of note are the tomb slabs set in the floor, and the marble Renaissance-style font.

After the original structure was destroyed by fire in 1553 during an attack

by the French pirate Le Clerc, it was re-built almost immediately in today's form. The oldest section is the sacristy in the tower, with its Gothic vault.

If you leave the church through the portal on the Plaza de España and look half-right, on the street corner you'll see one of the finest buildings in the town, the 18th-century **Casa Kabanah** (also known as the *Casa Valcarcel*). This ancient and dignified building has some very impressive door-frames, artistically barred windows, and glassed-over wooden balconies.

Even more solemn-looking is the **Renaissance Town Hall** (1563) on the other side of the street. The facade of the *Ayuntamiento* still bears the Habsburg coat of arms, together with a medallion showing King Philip II, who was the reigning monarch when it was founded, and also the town's coat of arms. The arcades create a pleasant space in which to sit and relax. The staircase leading up to the **Sala Capitular**, or council chamber, has been given some very realistic paint-

ings representing rural life on La Palma – the work of artist Mariano de Cossio (1892-1960). The muted colors further emphasize the dignified character of this building.

If you continue along Calle O'Daly in the direction of the harbor, you'll pass a whole series of interesting historic buildings. The most striking of all of them is the **Palacio Salazar**, which also houses the island's tourist information office. This small 17th-century palazzo with its reddish, natural stone facade contains a small patio surrounded by a veranda supported on slender wooden pillars. Alternating exhibitions of art and crafts can be seen in the adjoining rooms.

In the street that runs parallel to O'Daly, above the Palacio Insular, there's a former **Dominican monastery** that dates from the 16th century, and which today houses the main secondary school. The large square in front of it is often used for open-air events of various kinds. The monastery complex also includes the **Iglesia Santo Domingo**, with its impres-

sive wooden ceiling in the *mudéjar* style, and several paintings of saints by the Flemish artist Pieter Pourbus (1523-1584).

Ecxcursion to Las Nieves

An excursion into the hills above Santa Cruz leads to the nearby ***Santuario de Nuestra Señora de las Nieves** (early 16th century). The artistically important side portal of this pilgrimage church dates from the 17th century, and is only opencd for very important occasions. On the walls of the richly decorated interior you can see maritime scenes praising the miraculous power of the Madonna on the high seas. The interior is vaulted by a typical *mudéjar* ceiling made of Canary pine. The central saint in the *Santuario* is a white, 82-centimeter-high **terra cotta**

Above: Nuestra Señora de las Nieves, perhaps the wealthiest madonna on La Palma. Right: The seawater swimming pool at Charco Azul.

Madonna, standing on a half-moon that symbolizes the victory of Christianity over the pagan goddess of the moon. The clothing on the statue, with all its precious stones, is impressively rendered. Some say that as much as two tons of Mexican silver were used to make the base of the altar at her feet. In fact, this Madonna is probably the most expensively dressed lady on La Palma.

SMALL TOWNS IN THE NORTHEAST

A generally well-surfaced asphalt road leads through various small villages to **Puntallana ❸**, up on its 400-meter-high hill. The most striking-looking building in this town is the **Iglesia San Juan Bautista** (built around 1730), with its belfry and church balcony above the main door. Below the church on the right is the **Casa Luján**, containing a small tourist information office for *Turismo Rural*. This former country house (19th century) has been turned into an ethnographical museum using EU funds, and provides a tastefully arranged exhibition of exhibits documenting daily life and culture in the Canary Islands during the 19th and early 20th centuries. On the top floor, the kitchen and the former council chamber are both open to visitors, and provide a fascinating insight into what life was once like here.

One still reasonably well-kept secret in this area is the ***Playa de Nogales**, beneath the steep coast. You can reach its picturesque dark sand beach after a 10-minute walk from the parking lot. It's ideal for people who like getting up early, because the cliffs plunge it into shadow after lunchtime.

From the footpath to Playa de Nogales you can see the white houses of ***San Andrés ❹** up on one of the mountain ridges to the north. This tiny, very homogeneous town was founded right after the *Conquista* and accorded municipal rights

La Palma

shortly afterwards. It was placed in charge of the *Municipio*, but had to surrender the job later on to its neighboring town of Los Sauces farther up. The former importance of this little gem is immortalized in the region's double name of *San Andrés y Los Sauces*.

A steep, cobbled road leads up to the center, where there's a nice restaurant near the church. Built as a fortified church in the 16th century, the **Iglesia San Andrés Apóstol** has a very fine retable (a shelf or frame enclosing decorated panels behind an altar). The Artesonado ceiling is also worthy of note. An unusual feature can be seen on the right-hand side wall: paintings of various human limbs, put here in thanks for the healing powers attributed to the patrons of the church.

A footpath leads between the numerous banana plantations of San Andrés to the sea, and past a renovated lime kiln to the seawater swimming pool of **Charco Azul** (it can also be reached by a signposted road). This pleasant and tastefully

designed pool has a terrace restaurant, a smaller pool for children, showers, changing rooms and access to the sea – assuming it's not too choppy, that is. There's no proper beach to speak of, however, nor even any sand.

In a bay further north lies the small fishing harbor of **Puerto Espíndola**, where moles and breakwaters effectively keep the big waves at bay, but aren't exactly attractive to the eye either. Far more enticing altogether is the harbor restaurant *Mesón del Mar*, with its airy verandas on two levels. This place is always well patronized because of its utterly delicious, albeit rather limited, menu.

There are several banana plantations and also a few sugar cane plantations in this area, but **Los Sauces** ❺ has largely lost its former rural character. The rather oversized **Iglesia Nuestra Señora de Montserrat** (16th century), with its polished copper domes gleaming in the sunshine, is typical of the urban look of the modern town. The most important treasure it contains is a painting on the right-hand side of the entrance by the Flemish master Pieter Pourbus, showing the *Virgin of Montserrat.*

Next to the church there is a generously-dimensioned area resembling a park, with a fountain, an ice-cream parlor and various benches. It's a good place to take a break and relax. If you feel like accompanying your coffee with something alcoholic, some of the stores here sell the regional variety of rum, made from sugar cane. You can also find a special kind of sugar cane syrup (*miel de caña*).

Hiking Tours from ★Los Tilos

Nature and hiking fans have a real treat here in the Los Sauces region: the laurel forest of ★**Los Tilos**. Named a biosphere reserve by UNESCO in 1983, this region can be reached by driving southwards down the main road from Los Sauces. Before you reach the southern turnoff to San Andrés there's a narrow road leading off to the right into the Barranco del Agua. Follow this to the forest lodge, where the road ends.

Los Tilos is one of the last intact areas of laurel forest anywhere in the world, and things are supposed to remain that way – but in the barranco and up on the walls of the ravine you'll see pipes and conduits everywhere, because the water from this region was canalized as far back as 1983 for a small hydroelectric power station. The rainfall here is double the average for the island, however, which is why the subtropical plants here are all as green and profuse as ever.

A brief hike (almost an hour there and back) with two brief sections where you have to climb leads directly to the bottom of the Barranco and gives you a very good impression of the reserve. The ravine sometimes narrows down to just a few meters' width, and tiny waterfalls over slippery stones make progress rather ar-

Right: In the biosphere reserve at Los Tilos.

duous now and then. The end point of this hike is a waterfall around 30 meters high, which often doesn't have that much water at all.

Another hike, not much longer, leads from the same starting point and weaves its way up northwards in a series of bends to the **Mirador de las Barrandas**. In clear weather there's a very good view from up here of the ravine below, and large sections of the northeast.

La Fajana and Barlovento

At the northeasternmost point of the island, the lighthouse on the **Punta Cumplida** shows ships the way. The sea is almost always rough here, and the trade wind is at its most powerful. One kilometer to the west, several restaurants have established themselves near the seawater swimming pool of **La Fajana**; tourist apartments can be rented there, too. La Fajana is larger than Charco Azul and less atractive, and is totally overrun by tourists and locals alike every summer. To get a good idea of just how powerful the sea can get round here, go and take a look at the eroded rocks and natural arches near the sheltered pool.

Barlovento ⑥ is mainly of interest because of its big *Fiesta de la Virgen del Rosario* in October, when the villagers re-enact the Battle of Lepanto. Not far from the village there's a rewarding hike to the **Laguna de Barlovento**, one of the largest reservoirs on the island, located inside a walled volcanic crater. Beside this lake there's a campsite with a restaurant, and accommodation for the night is also available.

The old, winding dirt road that leads straight on from Barlovento towards Santo Domingo de Garafía goes through several roughly-hewn tunnels and several barrancos. Hikers can walk along this route for a while: it leads through some magnificent forests and there are several good views along the way. If you're trav-

eling by rental car it's better to take the signposted, well-paved route to Santo Domingo, which has several fine views of the coast and of the central massif.

In the next village along, **La Tosca**, a particularly large collection of dragon trees can be admired at the edges of the terraced fields. This grove is actually the largest of its type in all the Canary Islands.

THE LONELY NORTHWEST

Beyond Barlovento, you'll reach the green and remote part of La Palma. There were only dirt tracks here for centuries, but now an ambitious highway construction program is in progress: two well-suraced roads now lead from Llano Negro to Puntagorda, one of them straight through the mountains, and the other along the coast via Santo Domingo de Garafía.

Long before you reach Llano Negro, however, you should certainly take a detour northwards into the depths, near **★El**

Tablado ❼ (because the roads are so narrow it's best to leave the car at the edge of the village). There are some magnificent views of the coast from this idyllically situated village, and of the barrancos on either side of it.

Around four kilometers before Llano Negro (at kilometer 29) you'll reach the petroglyphs (rock drawings) of **★La Zarza** and **★La Zarzita**, which are among the most fascinating archeological sights of the island. Park your car at the visitor center, and after a 10-minute walk through a pleasant green valley you'll reach the source of La Zarza. Weird patterns, most of them geometrical, have been carved into the rocks around here. The really mysterious part of this site is across to the right, however, around a small rise: La Zarzita, which has the most astonishing rock drawings. There's a strange-looking figure resembling a woman with the head of an insect, and right beside it is the engraved profile of a man. These drawings are very similar to others found in Aztec ruins in Mexico.

A drive to **Santo Domingo de Garafía** ❽ is worthwhile if only for the ruined windmills in the region, and also the spectacular coast. Following signs to Puerto, you'll arrive at a steep section of coastline with a rough and wild beauty to it. In the former harbor, where the cranes have stood idle for a long time now, the locals have built small weekend houses.

Near the cave dwellings of Buracas below **Las Tricias** there are also one or two rock drawings. The road there leads past a windmill on the right, up on a rocky outcrop; then you'll pass a group of dragon trees just outside a barranco.

A little more spruce and lively altogether than Santo Domingo is the regional town of **Puntagorda** ❾, located in the midst of numerous almond plantations. At the center of the town there's a massive pine tree, with a kind of altar inside it. The boulevard-like streets only

Above: Farm with old mill near Santo Domingo de Garafía. Right: "Looks like taxes are going up again!"

really fill up once a year, in early February, when the *Fiesta del Almendro* ("Almond Blossom Festival") is celebrated. The rocks and the breakers down in the old harbor are an impressive sight; the only place to go if you feel like a swim, however, is the nearby seawater swimming pool.

THE WEST

The sunniest part of La Palma is generally the coastal strip in the west. Rather boring and without any real atmosphere, **Tijarafe** ❿ mainly attracts visitors for its *Fiesta del Diablo* at the beginning of September each year. The devil appears with a lot of explosions and races through the crowds like a man possessed. Then he gets faced by good, in the shape of the *Virgen de Candelaria.* Everyone clearly enjoys themselves, but it's also the quickest way of getting to need a hearing aid.

Before the road leads down to the Barranco de las Angustias, the **Mirador** at the **El Time** restaurant provides a magnificent view of the sloping plateau of Los Llanos de Aridane: it's a vast green expanse, broken only by tiny white groups of houses, stretching away as far as the eye can see. At the end of the winding road with its hairpin bends lies **Puerto de Tazacorte**, which looks half-finished with its ugly apartment blocks, harbor and pool still under construction. It's an unlikely center of gourmet food: the seafood restaurants here may not look like much on the outside, but the food is fantastic and attracts guests from miles around. Make sure you book in advance.

*Tazacorte ⓫, which belongs to the harbor, is a real gem: it has an intact center, alleyways with some interesting houses with neoclassical or Art Nouveau ornamentation, and the whole place has a truly Mediterranean feel to it. It's easy to imagine a beach beyond Avenida de la Constitución – instead there's a sea of banana plantations. The semicircular line of houses on this promenade is where the locals go for their afternoon *paseo*.

The **Plaza de España** is very colorful with its attractive bougainvillea-covered arcades, tiled benches, and its **Iglesia San Miguel Arcángel**. The colorful glass windows of this modern building throw a yellowish light into the interior of the small church, and there are some interesting and realistic paintings on mythological themes around its walls which are certainly worth taking a look at.

Los Llanos de Aridane

It was in the coastal region of Tazacorte that the Conquistadors arrived in 1492 to claim the island for Spain. This is commemorated on a plaque on the wall of the Town Hall in **Los Llanos de Aridane** ⓬. This ambitious town with its pleonastic name "The Plain of Plains" (rough translation of the linguistic mixture of Spanish and Guanche) lies in one of the most fertile and sunny parts of La Palma.

La Palma

The old town center lies to the north and east of the **Plaza de España**, where an extremely colorful selection of tourists and locals tends to gather in the shade of the Indian laurels. Various restaurants and boutiques have opened in the primarily one-storied houses around the square. Anyone who can afford the prices will enjoy shopping here.

The 17th-century **Iglesia Nuestra Señora de los Remedios** has a 16th-century Brussels Madonna in the middle of its retable. Flemish artists of the same epoch did the paintings in the side altars. As always in Canarian churches, take a good look at the magnificent wooden *mudéjar*-style ceiling. North of the church is the **Plaza Chica**, an oasis of tranquillity with its palm trees, benches and fountains.

Los Llanos de Aridane is a good starting point for hikes into the Caldera de Taburiente (see pp. 203-204). The climb up to the crater from here goes via the Barranco de las Angustias.

In the suburb of **Argual Abajo** across to the west, opposite the turnoff to

Puntagorda, you can admire the historic ***Hacienda** of one of La Palma's main families of landowners. The Poggio-Monteverde family was engaged in a centuries-long legal battle for the ownership rights to the Caldera de Taburiente. The whole thing took a surprising turn in the end, however: when the family finally won the fight in 1954, the state promptly declared the region a national park. The dignified houses grouped around ancient trees look rather like a set for a Mexican movie. If you're hungry, by the way, the western building of the hacienda, a stylishly-restored manor house dating from the 18th century, now contains what is probably the most noble restaurant on the island. The delicious food is elegantly served in several small rooms, all of them decorated with historic kitchen implements and nostalgic paintings.

If you feel like combining your visit here with a trip to a flea market, go no fur-

Above: Iglesia San Miguel Arcángel in Tazacorte – myths in modern pictures.

ther: there's a flea market held in the grounds here on the first Sunday of each month. Just to be on the safe side, however, it's best to check the notice board in the restaurant for details about it.

Puerto Naos –
Dark Beach with Palm Trees

A dark sand beach, partially lined by palm trees, plus a promenade to go with it make up the heart of **Puerto Naos ⑬**, the largest vacation center in the west. The modern apartment buildings are rather monotonous, despite some luminous paintwork on some of the facades facing the sea. This tourist center provides all the amenities: cash dispensers, souvenir stores, expensive boutiques, rental car outlets and diving schools. A post office and a bank are also under construction.

There are some rather primitively-constructed houses along the shingle beaches outside Puerto Naos. The two settlements of huts around the modern lighthouse to the north, at **Playa**

Bombilla and **Playa Nueva**, and also the **Casas del Remo** at the end of the road to the south, are very chaotic-looking. The homemade houses range from small concrete castles with pseudo-Moorish windows to highly disorganized structures made of corrugated iron.

The two best bays in which to swim in this area are the **Playa de las Monjas** – which despite its name ("Nuns' Beach") is actually a nudist beach – just south of Puerto Naos, and **Charco Verde** slightly to the south of it. Both have dark sand beaches, but no other facilities. To get to the Playa de las Monjas there's a narrow footpath leading southwards from the coast road and then through some banana plantations to the sea. Charco Verde is surrounded by a rather important-looking road which was once part of a yacht marina project that never got off the ground. The protected bay is ideal for families with children.

**CALDERA DE TABURIENTE

El Paso

El Paso ⑭ sprawls out at an altitude of 700 meters above sea level, and lies beneath the Bejenado and the Cumbre Nueva. Its very green surroundings are enhanced at the end of each winter by the gentle whitish-pink of almond blossoms. This town has the last silk factory on the Canaries, and alongside the cigar factory on the main street there are also a few men here who still roll their own homemade *puros*. Supermarkets, butchers' shops and health food stores are all geared towards the preferences of the tourists who often stay quite a while in El Paso. The **Iglesia de la Bonanza** with its strangely antiquated-looking modern tower lies at the center of the town, but the real center is the broad **plaza** just beneath the square outside it. El Paso comes across as a busy kind of place, largely because of all its different shops, and the at-

mosphere can't be compared with the that of someplace like Los Llanos.

On the narrow old connecting road between Los Llanos and El Paso there's a turnoff that will take you down to the mysterious rock drawings at **La Fajana**. These important archeological finds – the first with concentric circles, which probably symbolize the sun – were only discovered a few years ago, and have added to the mysteries surrounding the origins of these weird symbols and drawings. In this case it is probably safe to say, however, that the site was used for sun-worshiping – a slightly different variety from the one practiced today, of course!

The same road has signposts pointing to a further tourist attraction. In the **Parque Pueblo**, a subtropical cultural park, not only plants but also arts and crafts and agrarian products are on sale. The **Parque Paraiso de las Aves** bird park (German-run) is devoted to preserving threatened species from extinction.

A Trip through the National Park

The modern **Centro de Visitantes** on the eastern edge of El Paso acquaints newcomers with the **Caldera de Taburiente** ⑮ and the rules and regulations that apply there. Informative signboards and impressive aerial footage on video illuminate several aspects of this volcanic crater, surrounded by its 2,000-meter-high walls.

A marked route leads from the visitor center to **La Cumbrecita** (1,309 meters), which is the starting point for a 90-minute walk (there and back) to the **Mirador de las Chozas**. While visibility is somewhat restricted by pine forests on the Cumbrecita, you can still see large sections of the Caldera from here and get a gradual idea of its sheer size and magnificence.

A two-day tour through the crater leads from La Cumbrecita halfway up to the campsite at the **Playa de Taburiente** and then goes back again the same way. Alter-

La Palma

Centro de Visitantes, where accommodation permits can also be obtained. After rainfall, parts of the route are often impassable, and the capacity of the campsite (100 people) may not be exceeded. If there's a big crush of visitors (e.g., at Easter or Christmas), the time of stay often gets limited to just two nights. Dogs are not allowed, nor are campfires or anything else that might contribute to the destruction of the environment (leaving garbage behind, taking along flowers and rocks as souvenirs, etc.).

The hike to the crater from Los Llanos begins at the bus station. Follow the signs to the Caldera along a route that takes a good half-hour on foot along the little road leading north across a steep, built-up ridge, and then down to the riverbed in the **Barranco de las Angustias**, which is the only opening in the crater. You can also use a car to get as far as this, but the road hasn't been paved yet so it's very bumpy. The route from the riverbed to the campsite at the Playa de Taburiente – or to the **Cascada Colorada**, a small waterfall with rocks colored orange from the iron content in its rocks – takes a good four hours. Alternatively you can rent a jeep at the river, drive to **Los Brecitos** and then take a roughly two-hour-long hike from there to the campsite. The routes are marked either with heaps of stones or wooden signs.

natively you can go down at the **Roque Idafe** to Dos Aguas. Go through the Barranco de las Angustias to reach Los Llanos, where you can either hitchhike or take a cab back to the Cumbrecita. On the first day you'll notice how craggy the landscape here is, and how much water is around. The inside of this vast crater is full of ravines with streams, waterfalls and rivulets. For most visitors who come here this is the high point of their La Palma vacation. Be careful though: at some locations the route can only be followed by hanging on to chains attached to the mountainside, and is also only recommended for hikers in good physical condition with plenty of stamina, as well as a head for heights. Taking children along is generally not advisable.

You can find out whether the tour just described is possible by asking at the

If you feel like enjoying the view across the Caldera *without* taking a long hike, it's possible to drive to several signposted observation points along a road between Santa Cruz de La Palma and Hoya Grande (near Llano Negro), all of which provide a continuously changing view of the Caldera and its peaks. The most impressive view of all is from the majestic **Roque de los Muchachos** (2,426 meters), where the Northern European Observatory is located (closed to public access). The view from up here is truly unforgettable – especially if the sun happens to be setting.

Above: The bird park at El Paso is worth a visit.
Right: The Barranco de las Angustias, an exciting way to enter the middle of the Caldera de Taburiente.

La Palma

THE FIERY SOUTH

The backbone of the south is a mountain ridge composed of a series of volcanic cones, small craters and lava fields. If you're coming from Los Llanos or El Paso, you should make a quick detour on your way south to **Las Manchas** ⓰, because this little town has a very lovely square, the **Plaza La Glorieta**, which is decorated with some fine mosaics. Music performances take place regularly on this attractive stage, and old and young often dance to it spontaneously.

In 1949, large sections of the village were destroyed by a stream of lava from the Volcán San Juan. The locals are presently trying to turn this one-time tragedy to their advantage by making a special lava park out of the soldified remainder in order to attract visitors.

Around the Southern Tip

The road leads past a large expanse of banana plantations as far as **Fuencaliente**
de La Palma ⓱, where you'll have a view of the southern tip of the island with the volcanoes **San Antonio** (657 meters) and **Teneguía** (439 meters). The village lies at an elevation of 700 meters above sea level and is the center of La Palma's largest wine-growing region. The Llanovid wine association also has a tasting cellar in the large restaurant here. Traditionally, this region produces a heavy, sweet Malvasía wine of excellent quality – the locals know exactly what this product is worth, however, so don't expect any lucky bargains.

The southern tip of La Palma can comfortably be driven around by car. A newly-built road leads via Las Indias to the **Playa Echentive**, a black sand beach without any shade anywhere. There's usually a snack stand here, though (note that swimming is not possible if the sea is rough). Right at the southern tip of the island there's a saltern with two lighthouses towering on either side of it, one above a picturesque pebble beach with colorful fishing boats. This place is best viewed at

sunset, when the golden sunlight enhances the colors wonderfully. Nearby there's a small simple fish restaurant with good local cuisine, and it provides a very atmospheric way to round off this trip to the southernmost point of La Palma. To go back, take the road that runs via **Las Caletas**, where you can return to the main road at Fuencaliente.

If you only feel like taking a very brief tour of the volcanoes, park the car at the parking lot near the San Antonio volcano; from there you can either take a few steps to its crater, or – if you're feeling stronger and more enterprising – carry on right around it to the Teneguía and back again (the hike takes around two hours in all).

On the way back there's a nice detour to the **Roque de Teneguía** farther to the west: this yellow volcanic vent still bears several rock drawings dating from

Above: Lava fields from the island's most recent eruption (Teneguía, 1971). Right: Keeping a close eye on tobacco fermentation in Breña Alta.

Guanche times. No one is really sure of the original significance of these strange markings, but they're certainly very atmospheric and mysterious.

If on your way north you turn right near Tigalate, you'll come to another historic site from pre-Hispanic times: the **Cueva del Belmaco**, which was once the dwelling of the Mencey of Tedote. Two spiral drawings indicate the former importance of this cave as a royal residence. Even though it's protected by a grille and you can't get inside, you can still get a pretty good impression of it by peering through the bars.

The Idyllic Villas of the South

Villa de Mazo ⓭ is very beautifully located on its eastward-facing slope, and is on nearly everyone's visiting list on weekends because a **market** is held in the *Mercadillo* (market hall) here every Saturday afternoon. Foodstuffs and wines from local farmers, and also from producers of health foods, are on sale on the

La Palma

ground floor, and prices are fixed in advance so it's no use trying to haggle; on the upper floor of the market hall you'll find traditional craft products, including embroidered and lace goods. Jewelry, silk scarves and other accessories are sold out in the street.

The central square in front of the Town Hall is planted with bird-of-paradise flowers, and stands in front of the slope like an inviting terrace. A steep, cobbled street leads down to the **Iglesia San Blás**, where restoration work was still being carried out in 1998. The church, inconspicuous from the outside, contains a magnificent early-16th-century pinewood triptych (three-paneled altar painting), and a very fine Artesonado ceiling in the *mudéjar* style.

If you turn left off the eastern connecting road in the direction of Santa Cruz de La Palma you'll arrive at **Hoyo de Mazo**, where there is an old mill; today **El Molino** contains a pottery workshop that can also be visited. Copies of Guanche products are on sale here.

This trip around the island slowly nears its starting point as the outskirts of the capital come into view again. Towards the sea lies **Breña Baja**, where the Palmeros with enough money to afford a villa have settled down. It's even more idyllic in **Breña Alta ⑲**, its rather cooler counterpart up on the slopes. Many Europeans who find the windward side of the island a pleasant change have bought or built attractive houses here. From their terraces and verandas they can enjoy the superb view of the spring-like eastern side of the island. It's a view that can also be appreciated from the **Mirador de la Concepción** (right on the main road).

Above the town a side-road leads along the ridge of the **Cumbre Nueva** to a campsite near the *Refugio* (mountain refuge) of **El Pilar ⑳**. This is the starting point for a six-hour hike out of the pine forest into a bizarre volcanic wasteland, all the way to Fuencaliente in the south. The paths are broad and covered with volcanic sand, and pass a very impressive array of volcanoes and lava fields.

LA PALMA

ARRIVAL: By Plane: La Palma's airport is on the east coast, not far from the capital. Charter flights from the UK are available all year round. **By Ship:** From the harbor in Santa Cruz de la Palma there are daily ferry connections to Gomera (3 hours) and Tenerife (Los Cristianos; 5 hours), as well as connections three times a week to El Hierro (6 hours).

SANTA CRUZ DE LA PALMA

Parador de La Palma, Avda. Marítima 34, tel. 922-412340, fax. 922-411856. State-run hotel in Spanish colonial style in the town center. Not exactly peaceful, but elegant.

Hotel Marítimo, Avda. Maritítima 80, tel. 922-420222/624/630, fax. 922-414302. Three-star hotel run by the same people as the adjacent **Hotel Avenida**, Castillete 14 (tel./fax. as above). Comfortable (bath, TV, phone), some rooms are also suitable for the disabled. Restaurant with good cuisine, rooftop terrace; **Aparthotel El Castillete**, Avenida Marítima 78, tel. 922-420840/054, fax. 922-420067. 40 residential units with sea or patio views, heated swimming pool on the rooftop terrace.

Hostal Residencia Canarias, Calle A. Cabrera Pinto 27, tel. 922-413182. Small, clean boarding house in relatively quiet neighborhood close to the center; **Pensión Bahía**, Plaza de la Luz 35, tel. 922-411846, fax. 922-420168. Simple boarding house on a slope, with a view of the sea; **Pensión La Cubana**, Calle O'Daly 24, tel./fax. 922-411354. English-run, quietly located in the pedestrian precinct, 8 rooms; **Casa de Huéspedes Arrocha**, Calle Pérez de Brito 79, tel. 922-411117. Very simple and small boarding house for those without a lot of money.

OUTSIDE: **Hacienda San Jorge**, Los Cancajos, tel. 922-181066, fax. 922-434528. Tropical-style apartment complex with two and three-story houses in the Canarian style, palm garden, seawater pool. Near the main beach. Medium price category.

CAMPING: Those wanting to camp outside the National Park can get permits and information from the Environmental Protection Office (*Medio Ambiente*), on the fourth floor of the building beside the main post office, tel. 922-411583; Mon-Fri 9 am to 2 pm. Camping permits for the national park are available from ICONA, Calle O'Daly 35, tel. 922-413141, Mon-Fri 9 am to 2 pm.

La Placeta, Placeta de Borrero 1, tel. 922-415273. In a leafy square, with tables outdoors. On the first floor is a dinner restaurant with good Canarian and international dishes. German-run, Mon-Sat 10 am to 1:30 pm

(Bistro) and 7 to 11 pm (restaurant); **Canarias**, Avda. Marítima 28/ corner Avda. del Puente, tel. 922-410000. Old and established, filling Canarian food, moderate prices, daily 12 to 4 and 7 to 11 pm; **Slogan**, Avda. Marítima 23, tel. 922-413602. Breakfast and tapas bar, on the street beside the river; **Heladomania**, Calle Vandale 2. Makes its own ice cream. On the first floor is **Enriclai**. Here you can eat anything from breakfast to a full meal, German-run, Mon-Fri 10 am to 3 pm and 7 to 10 pm.

OUTSIDE: **Chipi-Chipi**, Velhoco, Carretera de las Nieves, tel. 922-411024, fax. 922-416655. The "in" restaurant. Specialties: grilled kid, chicken and rabbit, Tue-Thu 12 to 5 and 7 to 11 pm, apartments rented.

OLD TOWN: It's worth looking at the churches, the Town Hall and the old townhouses in the pedestrian precinct; **Museo Insular**, Plaza de San Francisco 3, tel. 922420558. Inside the former Franciscan monastery, Mon-Sat 9:30 am to 12:50 pm and 4 to 7:20 pm, mornings only in summer; **Casa de Jorós**, Calle Dr. Santos Abreu 25, above the market hall. Palma culture of the 19th century in stylishly furnished rooms of a renovated townhouse, Mon-Fri 10 am to 1 pm; **Museo Naval Santa María**, Plaza Alameda, tel. 922-416550, Mon-Thu 10 am to 1 pm and 4 to 6 pm, Fri and in summer mornings only.

OUTSIDE: Island sanctuary of Las Nieves.

Apart from carnival season and the odd fiesta, life in Santa Cruz is usually pretty quiet. The evening *paseo* with bar visits takes place on the Avenida Marítima. On Saturdays there are sometimes open-air concerts on the Plaza Santo Domingo. On the weekend (usually not before midnight) the discos get busy: **Gorka**, Calle Álvarez de Abreu/corner Calle Apurón, also **Guarana**, **Give Me Five**, **La Hemeroteca** and **Lago** (all of them in Los Cancajos).

Multicine, Avda. del Puente. Movie theater with three cinemas, showing Spanish and American films; **Teatro Chico**, near the market hall. Lectures, concerts, theater performances, monthly program (*Programación Cultural*) at the town hall (cultural office, tel. 922-420007).

The main shopping streets are Avenida Marítima, the two streets parallel to it, and Avenida del Puente with its side-streets. On Avenida del Puente you'll find the market hall (*Mercado*).

Opposite the *Teatro Chico* is a small store selling hand-rolled cigars (*puros*) with banderoles bearing the name of the buyer (one week needed for delivery). There's another *puros* store at Avda. Marítima 53.

SWIMMING: On the beaches of **Los Cancajos**. *DIVING:* Diving school **San Borondón**, tel. 922-181393, fax. 922-420697. Equipment for rent.

🏃 *HIKING / BICYCLE TOURS:* **La Palma Trekking**, tel./fax. 922-434540. Organized treks, contact Viajes Pamir, Calle O'Daly 8, tel. 922-416235.
In Los Cancajos **La Palma Tour** rents out bicycles with extra equipment (opposite the Costa Salinas apartments, tel./fax. 922-181109). Organized bicycle and hiking tours.

🚌 *PUBLIC BUS SERVICES:* The 18 bus lines that make up the *Transportes Insular La Palma* travel to every large town, but sometimes only twice a day. For timetable and information: Calle Pedro J. de las Casas 3, Santa Cruz, tel. 922-411924, 922-414441, 922-420060, fax. 922-414443.

🚕 *TAXI: Santa Cruz,* Avda. del Puente (near the market hall), tel. 922-411202; Plaza Alameda, tel. 922-411007; Calle Apurón, tel. 922-411107.
Los Cancajos: tel. 922-181383.

📮 *POST OFFICE:* Plaza de la Constitución, at southern end of pedestrian precinct. General delivery letters only in the mornings.

➕ **Hospital Nuestra Señora de las Nieves**, Carretera Nieves (outside the capital), tel. 922-420300. The central hospital on the island, and very well equipped; **Hospital de los Dolores**, Plaza Ramos y Cajal, tel. 922-423204. In the city area.

ℹ️ **Oficina Insular de Turismo**, Calle O'Daly 8, tel. 922-412106, Mon-Fri 8 am to 1 pm and 5 to 7 pm, Sat 9 am to 1 pm.

THE NORTH

🏠 **Asociación Turismo Rural – Isla Bonita**, Puntallana (Casa Luján), El pósito 3, tel. 922-430625, fax. 922-430308, Internet: www.infolapalma.com. Agency for renovated country houses in Puntallana, Barlovento, Garafía, Puntagorda, Tijarafe, El Paso, Fuencaliente and Villa de Mazo.

BARLOVENTO

🛏️ 😊😊😊 **La Palma Romantica**, roughly 1 km outside of Barlovento, on the Carretera to Garafía, tel. 922-186221, fax. 922-186400. Three-star hotel in a pleasant location, balcony rooms with view of mountains and sea, good restaurant, swimming pool, sauna, tennis court, mountain bike rentals to guests.
🚕 *POST OFFICE:* On the main street.
🚕 *TAXI:* Tel. 922-186046.

LA FAJANA

🍽️ **La Gaviota**, by the seawater pool of La Fajana, tel. 922-186099. Fresh fish, seafood, paella, open daily 10 am to 11 pm.
🏊 *SWIMMING:* In the local seawater pool.

LAS TRICIAS

🛏️ 😊😊 **Cruz del Llanonito**, Las Tricias, tel. 922-461662. Old manor house with four rooms for self-caterers. Up to six people. Similar accommodation also organized here.
🍽️ **Briesta**, road between Hoyo Grande and Puntagorda near Las Tricias, tel. 922-400210. Substantial meat dishes (goat, pork, rabbit), good seafood, daily 9 am to 10 pm, closed Tue and in winter.
🏛️ **Ecomuseo Las Tricias**, tel. 922-400444. Near the church, documents everyday farming life, Mon-Fri 9 am to 1 pm and 3 to 7 pm, Wed from 11 am guided tour through Las Tricias.

PUERTO ESPÍNDOLA

🍽️ **Mesón del Mar**, Puerto Espíndola (near San Andrés), tel. 922-450305. Nice seafood restaurant with not-so-nice view, Wed-Mon 1 to 4:30 and 7:30 to 11 pm.

PUNTAGORDA

🧵 **Taller de Seda**, Camino Casa Blanca 1. Painted silk cloth, Mon-Fri 10 am to 2 pm and 4 to 6 pm.
🚕 *TAXI:* Tel. 922-493178.

PUNTALLANA

🏛️ **Casa Luján**, Puntallana, El Pósito 3, tel. 922-430625. Ethnographic museum, crafts on sale, Mon-Fri 9 am to 1 pm and 4 to 6 pm, Sat 10 am to 1 pm and 4 to 6 pm.
🏊 *SWIMMING:* On the Playa de Nogales.

SAN ANDRÉS Y LOS SAUCES

🍽️ **San Andrés**, San Andrés, Plaza de San Andrés, tel. 922-451725. Filling Canarian food. Rooms for rent, Tue-Thu 11 am to midnight.
🏊 *SWIMMING:* Seawater pool of Charco Azul.
🏃 *HIKING:* In the laurel forest of Los Tilos (guided tours see Santa Cruz de La Palma).
🚕 *POST OFFICE: Los Sauces:* Calle José Antonio 22.
➕ *Los Sauces:* **Centro de Salud**, at the northern end of the town near the restaurant *Rosan.*
🚕 *TAXI: Los Sauces:* Carretera General/corner Calle Zagala, tel. 922-450178.

SANTO DOMINGO DE GARAFÍA

🍽️ **El Bernegal**, Calle Díaz y Suárez 5, tel. 922-400480/485. Canarian and international dishes (also vegetarian), high prices, Tue-Sun 10 am to 11:30 pm.
🏃 *HIKING:* To the caves below Las Tricias (guided tours see Santa Cruz de La Palma).
🚕 *TAXI:* Plaza Baltazar Martín, tel. 922-400103.

LA PALMA

THE WEST

📧 **Monteverde La Palma**, south of Los Llanos de Aridane, Calle Puerto Naos 209, tel. 922-462280, fax. 922-463156. Agency for accommodation, from the simplest country house to the most luxurious bungalow. Yacht trips also organized, and bicycles rented out.

LOS LLANOS DE ARIDANE

📧 ⊙ **Residencia Eden**, Plaza de España, tel. 922-460104, fax. 922-460183, comfortable rooms, bar; **Pensión El Porvenir**, Calle Fernández Taño 33, tel. 922-460168. Simple, but pleasant.

❌ **Balcón Taburiente**, near the entrance to the Caldera de Taburiente, Camino Cantadores 2, tel. 922-402195. Canarian and international food, normal prices, view across the Barranco de Angustias, daily 12 to 11 pm; **Amberes**, Calle Luna 2, tel. 922-401916. A great place for vegetarians; Fri-Wed 6 to 11 pm; **La Fuente**, Avda. Gen. Franco 70, tel. 922-463856, tapas, moderate prices, relaxed atmosphere, German-run, Mon-Sat from 7 pm; **La Mariposa**, Carretera de Puerto Naos, Las Norias 1, tel. 922-464145. International cuisine, expensive. Specialty: fish fondue, Tue-Sun 12 to 4 pm and 6 pm to midnight; **Bodegón Tamanca**, San Nicolás, tel. 922-462155. Cave restaurant, Canarian cuisine, filling food from the grill, good local wines, Tue-Sun 10 am to midnight; **La Casona de Argual**, Argual, Llano de San Pedro 6, tel. 922-401816. Fine Canarian cuisine in a historic setting, relatively expensive, Fri-Wed 1 to 3 and 7 to 11 pm; **El Time**, on the country road between Tijarafe and Los Llanos, tel. 922-490350. View across the Aridane Valley. Coffee and cakes, good tapas and fish dishes, daily 10:30 am to 11:30 pm.

🏛 **Parque Pueblo**, on the main street to El Paso (signposted), tel. 922-402108. Guided tours every two hours from 11 am. Mon-Sat 10:30 am to 5 pm; **Parque Paraiso de las Aves** (see The Center of the Island).

🎉 *DISCOS:* In the Los Llanos de Aridane district: **Babilonia**, **El Convento**, **Galaxia** (Avda. Enrique Mederos 17), **Aquarius**, Argual, Calle Manuel de Falla.

🏍 *MOTORCYCLES:* **Auto Soyka**, C. Gen. Yagüe 5, tel. 922-463390/922-463419, fax. 922-461266. Well-maintained motorbikes in three classes.

BICYCLES: **Bike 'n' Fun**, Calle Calvo Sotelo 20, tel./fax. 922-401927. Rents out state-of-the-art mountain bikes and organizes bike tours.

🏪 *MARKET HALL:* Plaza Mercado, Mon-Sat 8 am to 2 pm.

FASHION: **Árbol de Vida**, Calle Ángel 4. Ecological store for designer fashions made from natural materials, such as silk, hemp, and natural cotton.

GIFTS / JEWELRY: **Diseño**, Calle Fernández Taño 1.

FLEA MARKET: On the first and third Sunday in the month (check the announcement on the Casona de Argual) in the suburb of **Argual** below Los Llanos.

📮 *POST OFFICE:* Calle General Franco 3 (west of the Plaza de España).

🚕 *TAXI:* Calle Dr. Fleming, tel. 922-462740, Plaza del Mercado, tel. 922-462825.

PUBLIC BUS SERVICES: Hourly connection to Santa Cruz, other locations are not traveled to as often. Timetable and information: Calle Ramón Pol, tel. 922-460241.

ℹ Service office **Contacto**, Calle General Yagüe 5, tel. 922-463204, fax. 922-461266. Accommodation, real estate and rental cars, bulletin bboard for advertisements. Literature and maps of the island are on sale, plus used books. Public phone booth, faxes, multilingual staff, Mon-Fri 9:30 am to 1:30 pm and 4 to 7 pm, Sat mornings only.

PUERTO DE TAZACORTE

❌ **Playa Mont**, opposite the seawater pool, tel. 922-480434. Good seafood restaurant, Fri-Wed 11 am to 4 pm and 6 to 11 pm.

🚤 *BOAT EXCURSIONS:* **Agamenón**, tel./fax. 922-462849. Weekday trips to the beach of La Vela and to the Cueva Bonita grotto.

DIVING: **Tauchbasis Atlantic 28°**, Calle del Puerto 10, tel./fax. 922-480911. For beginners and experts alike, with courses provided.

PUERTO NAOS

🚤 *PARAGLIDING:* You can take off on a tandem flight on the beach promenade with Javier from the **Palmaclub**, tel. 922-408072, fax. 922-408121.

DIVING: **Tauchpartner**, outside the town to the right, tel. 922-408139, fax. 922-401493. German-run, Mon 9:30 am to 1 pm, Tue-Fri 9:30 to 1 pm and 5 to 7 pm, Sat 9:30 am to noon; **Tauchtreff La Palma**, Calle M. Duque Camacho 15a, tel./fax. 922-408345. Diving courses, also for beginners.

🚕 *TAXI:* Tel. 922-480410.

TAZACORTE

📮 *POST OFFICE:* Avenida Felipe Lorenzo.

🚕 *TAXI:* Avenida de la Constitución, tel. 922-480410.

TODOQUE

📧 ⊙⊙ **Bungalows El Paradiso**, near Todoque, tel. 922-462838, 922-515730, fax. 922-401595. Bungalows for two to four people with rental cars; **Bungalows Gisela**, Camino Paradiso 6, tel./fax. 922-463836. Bungalows for two and more people, swimming pool, nice garden.

210

THE CENTER OF THE ISLAND

Asociación Turismo Rural – Isla Bonita (see The North). Room reservations, **Monteverde La Palma**: (see The West).

EL PASO

Pensión Nambroque, outside El Paso, on the highway to Santa Cruz, tel. 922-485279. Large tapas bar.

Adagio, Carretera General 38, tel. 922-485231. Italian restaurant with large selection of oven-baked pizzas, closed Wed; **Il Giardino**, under El Paso on the main road to Los Llanos, Tajuya 2, tel. 922-485506. Playful interior, good Italian food, Mon-Fri 12 to 11 pm, Sat 6 pm to midnight.

Viva La Vida, on the main road from Los Llanos to El Paso, tel. 922-464053. International cooking at moderate prices, paella, grilled specialties, Tue-Sun 6 to 10 pm.

Caldera de Taburiente: *Centro de Visitantes*, just beyond El Paso on the country road to Santa Cruz, tel. 922-497277, fax. 922-413448. Information center for visitors (knowledge of Spanish is helps), camping permits, Mon-Sat 9 am to 2 pm and 3 to 6 pm, Sun 9 pm to 3 pm; **Parque Paraiso de las Aves**, in lower El Paso, Calle Panadero 16, tel./fax. 922-486160. Tastefully arranged aviaries and ponds, orchids for sale, daily 10 am to 6 pm.

HORSEBACK RIDING: Rides organized by the stables in El Paso, tel./fax. 922-497468 and 922-497222.

HIKING: In the visitor center of the national park of *Caldera de Taburiente* you can find information on routes for hikes through the Caldera.

Cigars: Señor Reinaldo (Calle General Mola 36) makes *puros* by hand. These are actually very good and also make very authentic souvenirs. **Natural Foods**: *El Campo*, Carretera General 1. **Fashion, Crafts and Jewelry**: *La Sorpresa*, Carretera General 3. Beside *El Campo*; handmade leather goods, lava jewelry, etc. **Silk textiles**: *Tallerde Seda*, Calle Barrial de Abajo 9. Señora Bertila Pérez González uses natural colors to make towels, shawls and neckties, irregular opening hours.

POST OFFICE: Calle Manuel Taño.

Centro de Salud, Avda. José Antonio 8, tel. 922-485943.

TAXI: Avenida José Antonio, tel. 922-485003.

THE SOUTH

Asociación Turismo Rural – Isla Bonita (see The North).

BREÑA ALTA

Las Tres Chimeneas, Buenavista de arriba 52, tel. 922-429470. High-class international cuisine, good vegetarian dishes, Wed-Mon 11 am to 4 pm and 7 to 11 pm; **Jardín Tropical**, Carretera La Grama, Km 8, tel. 922-429298. International cooking, and elegant people to go with it on weekends, Tue-Sun 12:30 to 3:30 pm and 7:30 to 11:30 pm.

POST OFFICE: On the plaza in the suburb of San Pedro.

TAXI: Plaza San Pedro, tel. 922-437228. Breña Baja: San Antonio district, tel. 922-434046.

FUENCALIENTE

Hotel Central, Calle Yaiza 4, tel. 922-444018. Quiet location near the church; **Pensión Los Volcanes**, Carretera General 72, tel. 922-444164/002. Relatively quiet, rooms and apartments.

Llanovid, Calle Los Canarios, tel. 922-444428. Restaurant of the wine merchants of the same name, filling meat dishes, wines from their own bodega, moderate prices, Tue-Sun 12:30 to 4 and 7 to 11:30 pm.

Salterns below Fuencaliente (near the lighthouses); **Mill** in Hoyo de Mazo.

PARAGLIDING: **Escuela de Parapente Balayo**, tel. 922-444202 and 922-444477. Courses provided.

SWIMMING: The **Playa Chica** (signposted) and the **Playa Zamorro** (around 200 meters north of it) are among the finest sand beaches on the island. Watch out if the waves are up though!

Two kilometers to the north of the lighthouses, on the southern tip of the island, is the **Playa Echentive** (sand beach).

WINE: Cellars **Llanovid**, dry and sweet Listan Blanco, dry and sweet Malvasía, rosé, red wine and Solera, daily 9 am to 1 pm and 3 to 5 pm; **Villa de Mazo** winery, near the market on Calle Amilcar Morera. Malvasía, sweet Moscatel and red wine.

CRAFTS: **Artesanía**, Carretera General 86. Crafts of the island. Women embroiderers can be seen at work, Mon-Sat 9 am to 6 pm.

POST OFFICE: This is located at the Carretera General 28, Mon-Fri 8 to 11 am.

TAXI: Carretera General, tel. 922-440443.

VILLA DE MAZO

MARKET: Sales of island produce. Vegatables, fruit, jams, honey, bread, local wines and mojos as well as jewelry and textiles, Sun 8 am to 1 pm.

CERAMIC GOODS: **El Molino – Cerámica Ramón y Vina**, Hoyo de Mazo, tel. 922-440213.

POST OFFICE: Carretera General.

TAXI: Carretera General, tel. 922-440078.

EL HIERRO
Remoteness at the End of the World

VALVERDE
THE NORTH
THE EAST AND SOUTHEAST
EL GOLFO
LA DEHESA AND EL JULÁN
MALPASO AND MERCADEL

The Zero-Meridian Island

The smallest of the Canary Islands lies at what was known to antiquity as the "End of the World." Before Columbus reached America it was the westernmost point of the known world, and held in awe by many for that reason. It was probably because of this that Ptolemy, the greatest geographer of ancient times, drew his zero meridian through the Punta de Orchilla on the west coast of El Hierro in the second century A.D. Things remained this way for the next 1,600 years until 1911 when, after decades of wrangling, England finally managed to establish Greenwich internationally as the new center for the meridian. Nevertheless, El Hierro has not fogotten its proud history, and still likes to style itself *Isla del Meridiano* to this day.

If you like beautiful, quiet places, then El Hierro is definitely for you. An inadequate harbor and an airport that only allows inter-island flights are the only two connections to the outside world. Of the 7,500 people who live here, many could imagine working elsewhere. Tourism is making more of them hopeful, but it's still in its infancy here. The people who have visited the island up until now – mainly to go hiking – are happy about that, because then at least one Canary Island will remain unspoiled and retain the original, special atmosphere that is fast becoming a mere tradition on the others.

Previous Pages: Fiesta in El Pinar, El Hierro – dancing and drinking, day and night. Left: The symbol of Frontera – a bell tower above the volcano.

Though small, El Hierro has a very large number of contrasting landscapes. The plateau in the north, with its fields and meadows divided by walls protecting them from the wind, is oddly reminiscent of Scotland. In the higher elevations dense *Monteverde* – consisting of brier and laurels – gradually turns into aromatic pine forest. Hierro's northwestern coast, called *El Golfo*, is shaped like a crescent moon. Geologists believe that it is one half of a crater, the other half of which sank back into the sea long ago. The land on the crater floor looks barren at first glance, but actually contains an astoundingly varied number of cacti and succulents, both endemic and imported.

In the south of the island you often get the feeling that the black streams of lava only hardened a few days ago. Here you can find bizarre volcanic cones, and caves created by bubbles in lava streams. In this zone, where the weather is good, a modest tourist enclave has established itself around the fishing harbor of La Restinga.

Arrival

There's something nostalgic about arriving on El Hierro. The **Aeropuerto** at the northeastern end of the island resembles a modern provincial railroad station, and only comes to life two or three times a day when flights have to take off and land. That's when the car rental counters open and cabs line up to wait around for passengers.

Right next to the airport is **La Caleta ❶**, a modern coastal town blessed with a promenade made of black natural stone, but with no beach. Ladders lead directly down into the sea, but don't swim here unless the water is absolutely calm. By way of contrast, **Tamaduste ❷**, north of the airport, has a rocky bay where you can swim. This part of the island is gradually developing into a small coastal resort, and so the buildings are almost all modern.

Above: The Iglesia Santa María de la Concepción in the artistically terraced main square of Valverde.

There's already a small selection of restaurants and bars.

If you use a bit of imagination, you may feel yourself transported back to the age of the great ocean liners as you cross over here with the *Trasmediterránea*. If the seas are choppy it's rather hard to get into the **Puerto de la Estaca**, the harbor entrance, and digesting all the impressions may leave your stomach feeling rather tender. It's a good idea to book a rental car before you arrive and ask the company to have you met at the harbor – a service provided by all the companies represented on the island. There are usually a few cabs waiting around as well.

Because of the inadequacy of the Puerto de la Estaca, extension work on it is being considered – or even the construction of an additional harbor in the town of **Tijimiraque ❸** farther to the south. This project is going to be providing food for discussion between politicians and bureaucrats until well into the next millennium, however. Right now, when the sea is calm, the town has a very

Info p. 227

El Hierro

nice black sand beach, and the local youths can often be seen here on their plastic body boards.

If you continue up the coast road past Tijimiraque, you'll reach a one-lane tunnel where the traffic light is often out of order – so make sure before you go in that no one's about to hurtle out. On the other side of the tunnel, a craggy section of rock towers out of the sea: this is the **Roque de la Bonanza**, or "Rock of the Silent Ocean." Many locals maintain that its base is lodged in the island itself, some two hundred meters below the surface of the water.

At the other end of the bay known as **Las Playas**, in front of an impressive mountain panorama, is the **Parador Nacional ④**, a state-run hotel. This largely rocky section of coast isn't the kind of place to complain about noise: the road ends here, and even the dirt track it then becomes peters out into nowhere. To explore the rest of the island you'll have to turn back from this restful corner, and head for the harbor again.

VALVERDE
The Village Capital

A well-surfaced, winding road leads from the airport and also from the harbor up to the island's capital of **Valverde ⑤**, located at approximately 600 meters above sea level. Unlike the other island capitals of the Canaries, Valverde is not a harbor town – pirate attacks may already have been on the minds of those who founded it, and they didn't want to make things too easy. The Spanish built their town on a very sloping site which had also been inhabited by the aboriginal population, known as the *Bimbaches*. In those days – around 600 years ago – Valverde was called *Amoco*.

The town is often foggy, especially in summer, which is why most tourists only stop here briefly. It's true that it doesn't take long to see the sights: the central square by the church, and the two main streets that make up this tiny metropolis with its population of 1,800 people. Sleepy Valverde wakes up slightly in the mornings, when everyone goes shopping, and indulges in its role as capital: it has a Town Hall, law courts, the *Cabildo Insular* (island council), a comprehensive school and also the only secondary school on El Hierro. The island hospital lies just outside town.

The **Plaza Principal**, the central square between the church and the Town Hall, is laid out on two levels. Built as a simple parish church during the 16th century, the three-aisled **Iglesia Santa María de la Concepción** was extended and fortified between 1767 and 1776. Every four years the church and the square in Valverde are the destinations of a pilgrimage known as the *Bajada de la Virgen* (see p. 225). There are plans to construct a museum building in the square, which would contain suitably displayed ethnographic and archeological exhibits. The **Sala de Exposición del Excmo. Cabildo Insular** on the town's main street, Calle Constitución (directly above the square), is used for alternating exhibitions.

The **Town Hall**, which for financial reasons took from 1910 to 1940 to complete, was built in the Canarian style. Also worthy of note is the small private house **El Conde** in the upper throughstreet (Calle Dacio Darías), which has a few interesting Art Nouveau elements dating from the turn of the century.

Unbeknownst to most tourists, Valverde goes really wild at certain fixed times. On Fridays and – yes, Saturdays, too – lots of dance-crazy young people pour into the two or three discos here and cause a great deal of noise along the short section of street between the disco-pub *La Kaye* and the *La Casita* until early the next morning. Most of the dancing takes place in the *El Cine*. The music seems twice as loud on this island because the place is so quiet the rest of the time.

Right: View of the presumed semicrater at El Golfo.

THE NORTH
Unspoiled Nature and Historic Traces

If you're expecting more exciting places than the sleepy Valverde now, you'll be disappointed: the villages on Hierro are mostly unspectacular – unless, of course, there's a fiesta in progress. The highlights here are largely provided by the landscape.

In the northwest, after turning off from the main road in the direction of Mocanal, you'll arrive in **Echedo** ❻. Like the ones that follow it, this tiny village lies in the midst of vineyards, which produce a delicious wine with a characteristic bouquet, thanks to the favorable sunny conditions and mineral-rich volcanic soil. A dirt track leads to the natural swimming pool of **Charco Mansa** by the sea, surrounded by some very eroded-looking basalt scenery. Don't swim here when the tide is in, or if the sea is at all rough.

In **Mocanal** ❼ you'll notice various elegant houses with patios and large glass panes covering their slender verandas. By contrast, the side streets contain numerous (largely dilapidated) buildings in the original traditional style. Old, abandoned wine-presses complete the nostalgic picture here.

A detour leads to **Pozo de las Calcosas**, a good place for a swim. The upper part of the town, above the steep coast on a plateau, is connected to the rocky bay via a footpath. Black stone houses are used by the locals as weekend houses, and two bars in the area have sporadic opening hours. Beside the seawater swimming pool slippery steps lead down to the sea. Don't swim here if the sea is rough, however, because there are rocks below the surface.

The journey now continues on to **Guarazoca** ❽, which isn't all that much different from Mocanal. However it does have a striking-looking new hall for *lucha canaria*, the Canaries' local form of wrestling, which according to legend dates

back to the Guanches. Below the road, near the center of the village, you'll see one of the few dragon trees on the island.

Southwest of Guarazoca there's a real highlight in store: at the *Mirador de La Peña, an observation point on the edge of the semicircular crater forming the Golfo region, a restaurant has been built according to plans by César Manrique, the Canary Islands' highly-regarded environmental artist (see p. 236), and its design features his brilliant use of natural stone, local woods and glass.

From here there's a view not only of the 1,000-meter-high and very steep walls of the impressive semicircle of El Golfo, but also of the two **Roques de Salmor** directly below on the right. The *Escuelar Mirador de La Peña* restaurant serves very good Canarian food, and is now a cooking school for future chefs. A small crafts store nearby sells a good selection of products, most of them locally made.

The experts are still arguing about a largely deserted, half museum-like area called **Las Montañetas** ❾: Was this where the Spaniards founded their first settlement after conquering the island? Or was it the Casas de Guinea in the El Golfo region (see p. 223)? Or Albarrada between San Andrés and Tiñor? Despite the advanced state of dilapidation of the houses, the simple construction method used by the first settlers can be clearly recognized. It's like being in Scotland, especially when the fog from the trade winds shrouds the gray ruined buildings, and you hear the rough croak of a raven, or the tinkling of a goat's bell somewhere inside the walls.

This feeling gets even more intense when you approach **San Andrés** ❿ on the Nisdafe plateau. This village, surrounded by fields and meadows, lies on a plain 1,100 meters above sea level that is one of the most fertile but also climatically variable on the island. Cattle, sheep, goats, donkeys and sometimes the odd horse or two can be seen grazing away behind the natural stone walls.

Between the villages of Las Montañetas and San Andrés (the turnoff is

El Hierro

signposted) you can investigate the legend associated with the **Árbol Santo**, which the Guanches believed was the source of their entire water supply. They used holes in the ground to collect the water that condensed in the tree from the trade-wind clouds, and the receptacles they used for this purpose can still be seen today; then they distributed the water amongst themselves. The holy tree *Garoé*, probably a stinking laurel (Spanish: *til*), fell victim to a thunderstorm in 1610 and was replaced by a new one in 1949 by the environmental authority ICONA.

Compared to the barren San Andrés, **Isora ⑪** is almost like an orchard, with its vast amount of cacti and Indian figs. The main attraction, however, is the ***Mirador de Isora**, an observation point at the southern end of the town. From here there's an excellent view of the bay of Las

Above: The Meseta de Nisdafe looks amazingly Scottish. Right: New life reappears above the embers (Los Lajiales).

Playas, with the Roque de la Bonanza and the Parador Nacional.

THE EAST AND SOUTHEAST
Volcanism and Tourism

On the way to **El Pinar ⑫** (900 meters above sea level) you'll realize why this strange name is applied to both **Las Casas** and **Taibique**: the aroma of Canary pine is all-pervasive round here, and has successfully replaced the scent of the last forest fire. Clear traces of the devastation it wrought still remain, however: almost all the tree trunks have black, scorched bark. It's astonishing how robust these trees are, though: many of them have sprouted new shoots, making it clear that throughout the millennia, nature has had plenty of opportunities to adapt to the ever-present danger of fires caused by lightning.

As you enter El Pinar you'll see signs pointing the way to the small privately-owned **Panchillo Museum**, with its strange assortment of kitsch, crafts and everyday bric-a-brac. The opening times vary in accordance with the owner's mood. On the right of the door frame, which is easily missed, there's a small red button to ring the bell. Behind the museum, on the other side of the road, Brigitte Hoyer has set up a **pottery studio**.

Before you get to El Pinar there's a good detour along a small but well-surfaced road to **Hoya del Morcillo**, a recreation area located in the middle of a beautiful pine forest with some magnificent individual specimens. Here you'll find campsites, children's playgrounds, and picnic and barbecue sites, and the sanitary facilities are also well maintained. This is an especially good place to come if you have children with you. All kinds of hikes are possible here, from a walk through the forest to a climb up to the summit of the Malpaso (1,500 meters; see p. 226).

Shortly after El Pinar, El Hierro reveals its younger volcanic face. The stone walls dividing up the plots of land are still there, but the further south you get, the more volcanic wasteland and cones you see around you. At first there are still a few fig trees, protected from the cattle in their own miniature enclosures. Later on, however, there's nothing but volcanic ash and solidified lava streams wherever you look. At some locations you can see lava channels, formed when the outside of the lava stream cooled more rapidly and the molten center oozed out of the front. This process has formed caves and bubbles, and also kilometer-long passageways. The whole region is very reminiscent of something out of a science fiction movie, and in some places the silence is especially eerie – even more so because of the ever-present scent of sulfur in the air.

An asphalt road that leads away from a left-hand bend will take you to the **Cala de Tacorón** ⓭. There's no sand beach here, but tiled terraces to lie on – plus some picnic and barbecue sites that seem

very popular with the local cat population. As always, be careful if you decide to go for a swim. A 400-meter-long walk southeastwards will take you to a cave that has been hollowed out by thousands of years of crashing waves, the so-called **Cueva del Diablo**. Don't go inside here unless the sea is calm and the tide is out – and be sure you're wearing a pair of sturdy shoes as well.

The usually pleasant weather and numerous water sports facilities have made **La Restinga** ⓮ on the southern tip of Hierro into a small tourist center with many new buildings. It's the only real tourist center on the island, in fact. The fishing harbor is sheltered by a large harbor mole, which also protects the swimmers on the beach. The restaurants on the promenade are good places to sit down and enjoy a cup of coffee or an aperitif. Boats in dry dock get repainted here, and there are two diving schools, too. In the evenings you can visit a pub, stroll around the harbor, play cards, read a good book – or simply have a nice early night.

El Hierro

****EL GOLFO**
A Fertile Oasis

The most attractive section of the island is most easily reached from Valverde by going via San Andrés; from there, follow the signs to Frontera. A detour to the ***Mirador de Jinama** will give you an initial impression of the region around El Golfo. Continuing along the main road, stay for the time being close to the *cumbre*, the ridge everyone thinks is the rim of an ancient crater, and pass through forests of pine and laurel. The sometimes rather bumpy road is also lined by sections of dense *Fayal-Brezal* as it winds its way down to the valley in long hairpin bends. A place to take photographs just below the forest is also a popular place for paragliding (*parapente*).

The **bell tower** on a shimmering red volcanic cone just outside **Frontera** ⑮

has become the symbol of El Golfo. The bell ropes used to extend as far as the priest's bed, so he could call his flock together in comfort. The **open-air arena** for Canarian wrestling looks impressive behind the **Iglesia de la Candelaria** on the slopes of the volcanic cone, and during wrestling matches the excited shouts of the onlookers echo from the high walls of this natural backdrop.

The economically more important neighboring town of **Tigaday** has now grown so much that it is a part of Frontera. Several banks, some boarding houses and a colorful assortment of stores, restaurants and pubs all offer their services. In the evenings, when visitors come here and inspect all the menus, it's especially clear that tourism is becoming an increasingly important source of income for Tigaday.

Near the Town Hall on Sunday mornings there's a small **market**, where produce from the valley can be purchased, including fresh vegetables, fruit, wine, honey, fish and cheese. The delicious

Above: La Restinga in the south is a popular water sports center. Right: Puntagrande – "the smallest hotel in the world."

wine from Frontera is much appreciated outside the island, too. If you want to go and see the giant lizards at the breeding station in the museum village of ★**Casas de Guinea** ⑯, you need to go to the Town Hall in Tigaday and apply for a special permit. Located halfway to the coast after Las Puntas, it was once a simple settlement dating from the time of the *Conquista*. Meanwhile, many of the ruins have been restored to their former appearance and provided with furniture dating from various epochs.

In the steep rock face of **Tibataje** very close by, some members of a population of around 1,000 giant lizards were discovered, and were originally thought to be all that remained of the extinct giant lizards of the *Roques de Salmor*. Research has proven, however, that they are a related sub-species. The public is allowed to get a glimpse of just a few of these rare reptiles once a week. They hardly ever grow longer than 60 centimeters, and the breeding station now has a population of around 200 of them.

Another small enclave of tourism has established itself in **Las Puntas** and **Punta Grande**, both located towards the sea and the Roques de Salmor off the coast. A highlight here is the four-room hotel *Puntagrande* on its rocky outcrop above the surf, which is listed in the *Guinness Book of Records* as the smallest hotel in the world. Even if you don't stay here, you should certainly visit the restaurant to get the feel of this special place.

The seawater swimming pools at **La Maceta**, around three kilometers to the southwest, are attractively simple. Natural arches, rocky islands and mighty basalt cliffs attract the locals to the shady barbecue areas here every weekend. When the sea is rough, however, beware of the waves which crash straight into the pools – the pull as they go back out is enormously powerful and shouldn't be underestimated.

One building that is very modern, architecturally successful, and yet at the same time very inconspicuous is overlooked by most visitors here. On the way

to the southwest in the direction of Los Llanillos, and signposted as *Submarino*, the **Casa Canomanuel** was built as a sports and recreation center between 1984 and 1988 by Madrid architects César Ruiz Larrera and Pablo Ortega, and had a hotel and bar added to it later on. It consists of 14 partly transparent cubes set into the landscape furnished in a style reminiscent of English nautical clubs. A reconstruction of the first fully-functional Spanish submarine adorns the back of the open-air stage outside the building.

Drive via Los Llanillos and you'll come to the remote and idyllically-situated village of **Sabinosa** ⓱, high up on a slope, with its attractive narrow streets and paths. The route there takes you through a dense field of cacti growing, seemingly impossibly, on scree – a real paradise for botanists.

Above: The chapel of Nuestra Señora de los Reyes is where the Bajoada festival begins.
Right: Juniper trees bent double by the wind in El Sabinal.

By the sea beneath Sabinosa, volcanism has created a spa. The well containing the water, the **Pozo de la Salud**, is open to everyone, but the spa hotel beside it is privately owned. The water here has a high mineral content and is supposed to be a very effective cure for all manner of ailments; it has to be hoisted up in a bucket from the well. A word of warning: Too much of it may get your intestines working rather too efficiently!

LA DEHESA AND EL JULÁN
Wild and Spectacular

As you continue along the coast, the asphalt road temporarily becomes a dusty track. Right next to the sea you'll see the **Arenas Blancas**, areas with white sand – don't try swimming there, though, because of the boulders and scree, and the unpredictable swell. Over on the mountainside a layer of yellow tuff (*tosca amarilla*) soon appears, contrasting with the other volcanic rock. You are about to arrive at the most beautiful stretch of

beach on El Hierro: the **Playa del Verodal** , with its dark, shimmering, slightly reddish sand. The barbecue and picnic sites get really packed here on the weekends. Remember to bring along sun protection and beach sandals – and be careful when swimming because there's a dangerous undertow. Cracks have also been discovered recently in the rockface directly behind the beach, so sunbathing on the Playa del Verodal has been discouraged now because of the danger that it might collapse at some point.

To reach the westernmost point of the Canaries, travel up a winding (and initially well-paved) stretch of road to the edge of the high plateau known as **La Dehesa**, where you'll see your first specimens of windblown juniper cedar.

Eventually, at the end of a dusty track, you'll arrive at the **Faro de Orchilla**, a lighthouse on the Punta de Orchilla, which marked the end of the known world during antiquity.

High up on the Dehesa, in the midst of grazing goats (remember to close the gates behind you), lies the chapel of **Nuestra Señora de los Reyes** , the most important sacred structure on El Hierro. It contains a statue of the Virgin and a retable to go with it, but is mostly closed. Once, during a period of drought, the Madonna was carried down to Valverde and apparently caused a miraculous cloudburst, so this procedure is repeated every four years and also provides a magnificent excuse for week-long celebrations. In July 2001, 2005 etc., the statue will be carried to the capital again, accompanied by ecstatic shepherds' dances and rather pagan-sounding songs, and all the emigrés who can afford it come back to their island from overseas to join in.

Since the route the statue takes straight through the center of the island is clearly signposted as *Camino de la Virgen*, it's easy to follow it. If you hike the route to Valverde in two stages you'll get an almost complete picture of El Hierro. A good place to stop overnight is the nearby campsite of Hoya del Morcillo.

El Hierro

If the sight of the juniper cedar above the Playa del Verodal has whetted your appetite for more specimens of the same, continue a bit further along the path behind the chapel and soon you'll reach **★El Sabinal**, a collection of juniper bushes that have been wonderfully twisted and malformed by the wind. These are unique to the Canary Islands and the last of their kind, so they are strictly protected.

Another highlight nearby is the **★Mirador de Bascos**, which provides a grandiose view back across the valley of El Golfo. The Pozo de la Salud and the Arenas Blancas can clearly be seen in the foreground.

From the chapel, a road leads up to the high plateau of **El Julán** on the south coast. In pre-Hispanic times, the numerous streams in this inhospitable region made it a center of settlement for the Bimbaches, as an astonishingly rich number of archeological finds has proven. These include the places of assembly known as *Tagoror*, altars, *Concheros* (piles of seashells) and also several mysterious rock drawings and inscriptions known as **Los Letreros ⓴**. Unfortunately, almost 60 percent of them have been chipped off and taken away by industrious hobby archeologists and collectors, so the ones that remain are now strictly protected.

To see them you'll have to park your car on the road near the sign saying "Los Letreros," and then walk around six kilometers to reach the valley. Since the weather is usually extremely hot here, remember to bring enough drinking water! After an hour and a half on foot (the way back takes around two hours) you'll arrive at a plateau where a guide is present until about three o'clock each day; he will take you to the inscriptions, which are not easy to find. It's good to bring along some identification, too, because your name gets entered on a visitors' list.

What you'll see here is a (probably badly) restored altar with a *Tagoror*, several *Concheros* and also a line of inscriptions, broken in several places, on smooth pahoe-pahoe lava, extending down for 100 meters in the direction of the "Sea of Stillness" (*La Mar de las Calmas*).

Simple geometrical patterns of various kinds – such as ovals, circles and spirals – have been carved into the rock here, as well as so-called ideograms and also some symbols that could conceivably be construed as letters. It's a very atmospheric place altogether, and well worth the trouble to get here. The mystery of these symbols, and of other Guanche inscriptions on the Canary Islands, has remained unsolved to this day.

MALPASO AND MERCADEL

From the road leading from the Ermita Nuestra Señora de los Reyes to Los Letreros, there's a turnoff to the *Cumbre* and to the highest point on the island, the **★Malpaso ㉑** (1,500 meters). Dirt tracks lead through bright and airy pine forests in the direction of Cruz de los Reyes, where you can park the car and hike up to the summit. In around 10 minutes you'll be at the top, where there is a small meteorological station.

The weather up here isn't always clear, but if you're lucky and get a good day you'll not only see large expanses of El Hierro but also Gomera, Tenerife and La Palma in the far distance – an unforgettable experience.

From the Cruz de los Reyes, a winding path through the forest leads southwards to a further summit, the **Mercadel** (1,252 meters), recognizable by the fire lookout post at the top.

If you continue driving west now, you'll soon arrive at another asphalt road just after the Cruz de los Reyes. Follow it, and very soon it will join the main road connecting Frontera with Valverde. Incidentally, they say that visitors to El Hierro either never come back or always come back!

EL HIERRO

[image] *ARRIVAL:* **By Plane**: No international connections, only domestic Canary Islands flights; daily connection from Los Rodeos in the north of Tenerife and from Gran Canaria. Flying time around 30 minutes. Airport tel. 922-550105.

By Ship: Daily connections from San Sebastián de La Gomera and Los Cristianos (Tenerife). Travel time is from 3 to 5 hours.

[image] [image][image][image] Parador de El Hierro, Las Playas, tel. 922-558036, fax. 922-558086. State-owned hotel, quiet and comfortable, with 47 rooms. Salons in colonial style, pool, plus an excellent restaurant, though rather expensive; **Club de Aventuras El Submarino**, on the road between Las Puntas and Los Llanillos, tel./fax. 922-551014. Simple and exclusive, for sports lovers, subterranean suite with pools in caves, bar, library. Diving, hiking, windsurfing, mountain biking, paragliding, fishing, open-air theater.

[image][image] Hotel-Balneario Pozo de la Salud, near Sabinosa, tel. 922-559561, 922-559465, fax. 922-559801, and it even has its very own Internet address: www.cistia.es/cabildohierro. Spa hotel with its own special spring, comprehensive medicinal and gastronomic services, pool; **Apartamentos Arenas Blancas**, La Restinga, tel. 922-557036. Large complex for self-caterers, modern apartments for four to six people. Terrace, sea view, kitchen, living room, one or two bedrooms, pool, solarium, bar-restaurant; **Apartments run by Anne Pflugbeil and Walter Ploessl**, El Matonal 33 (on the road from the Casas de Guinea to Las Puntas, turn left into the coast road), tel./fax. 922-559482. Tastefully arranged accommdation for self-caterers in the warmest part of El Golfo; located right in the middle of a pineapple plantation; **Apartamentos La Brujita**, Las Toscas, tel. 922-559327, fax. 922-559339. Newly designed apartments above the town center of Tigaday, large terraces with a magnificent view of the Golfo area. Pool, tennis.

[image] Hotel Puntagrande, tel. 922-559081. "Smallest hotel in the world," make reservations in good time, pleasant atmosphere, restaurant; **Apartamentos Caracol**, El Pinar, Calle El Chamorro 55, tel./fax. 922-558143. Two attractive apartments for self-caterers. Kitchen, bath with shower, terrace; **Pension Casa Kai Marino**, La Restinga, tel./fax. 922-557034. Two-star boarding house at the harbor, patio, terrace restaurant. Rooms with bath and shower, some also with salon. Half and full board both possible.

[image] Restaurant Escuela Mirador de La Peña, Carretera Guarazoca 40, tel. 922-550300. High-quality Canarian cuisine, but be careful because the prices are as high as the standards, closed Sun evening and Mon; restaurant in the **Hotel Puntagrande**, good fish dishes, nautical decor, closed Sun; **Bar Restaurante Casa Bildo**, Tigaday, Calle Cruz Alta, tel. 922-559065. Unpretentious Canarian cuisine, moderate prices, daily 7 am to 11 pm; **Bar Restaurante Casa Rosi**, Carretera General de Las Puntas 30, tel. 922-559662. Grilled food, fish, daily 1 to 4 pm and 7:30 to 10:30 pm; **Bar-Restaurante Casa Juan**, La Restinga, above the harbor promenade in the direction of the town center, tel. 922-557102, freshly-caught fish, daily 6 am to 11 pm.

[image] Museum in Valverde, Calle General Rodríguez Sánchez 2. Permanent exhibition of ceramics typical of the island, Mon-Fri 9 am to 1 pm; **Museum Village of Casas de Guinea**: Mon-Fri guided tours from 11 am. Lizard house Thu only, 11 am to 1 pm, to visit the lizard house you have to get written authorization from the Ayuntamiento in Tigaday.

[image] *DISCOS: Valverde:* **El Cine**, **La Kaye**, both on Calle de la Constitución; **La Lonja** on Calle Jesús Nazareno; **La Casita** pub on Calle San Francisco. *Las Puntas:* **Yoyo's** pub on the main street; **Submarino**: Club de Aventuras El Submarino (see "Accommodation").

[image] *DIVING: Las Playas:* **Hierrosub**, tel. 922-550482. *La Restinga:* **Submarino**, tel. 922-557068, and **El Hierro**, tel. 922-557023.

OTHER SPORTS: Club de Aventuras El Submarino.

[image] *HIKING:* Guided tours through **Club Submarino** (see "Accommodation").

[image] Artesanía Nicio: Original woodcuts. Studio in Sabinosa, store in Tigaday, Calle Cruz Alta 21, cell phone 989-406740; **Artesanía y Sueños**, Guarazoca, Carretera Jarales 1 (near the Mirador de La Peña). Unpretentious crafts, woolen articles, ceramics, woodcuts, raffia articles, baskets, household items, etc.; **Estudio de Cerámica Caracol**, El Pinar, Calle El Chamorro 51, tel. 922-558143. Ceramics of various kinds, from ashtrays to copies of ancient Canarian idols.

[image] *TAXI: Valverde:* Tel. 922-550729. *Tigaday:* Tel. 922-559129.

[image] *POST OFFICE: Valverde:* Calle de Correos below Calle de la Constitución. *Tigaday:* Carretera General 11. Both Mon-Fri 9 am to 2 pm, Sat 9 am to noon.

[image] *Valverde:* **Centro de Salud**, Calle de la Constitución near the hospital (with emergency admission), tel. 922-550402. *Tigaday:* **Centro de Salud**, Calle El Pozo 1, tel. 922-559004. *El Pinar:* **Centro de Salud**, Carretera General, tel. 922-558076.

[image] *Valverde:* Small office on Calle Licenciado Bueno 3, tel. 922-550302/326, fax. 922-551052, Mon-Fri 8:30 am to 5 pm, Sat 9 am to 1:30 pm (often only mornings out of season).

El Hierro

CANARIAN CUISINE
Substantial and Delicious

The Canary Islands have been one of the most popular vacation destinations with Europeans for decades now, so it's no surprise to encounter dishes from all the tourists' countries of origin when you go out to eat in the large resorts here. With all the Irish pubs and Bierkellers everywhere, it's hard to find anything authentically Canarian.

If you really want to get to know Canarian cuisine, you'll need to head inland. Restaurants can be divided into three categories: simple, small ones with good home cooking; large excursion places with meat and seafood specialties, where local families take all their relations at weekends; and rather expensive

Previous Pages: Singing and guitar playing at a bar in the town of Las Nieves, La Palma. Above: Mojo, gofio and watercress soup in La Gomera's national park. Right: Dried fish in the harbor of Puerto del Carmen, Lanzarote.

gourmet establishments where refined Canarian cuisine is served to those able to afford it.

Canarian cuisine originated as the rural cooking of the Spanish and Portuguese immigrants, enriched by influences from Latin America. The wealthier households enjoyed produce grown on their own estates, or imported from overseas. Very filling meat dishes and sweet desserts were a regular feature of every main meal, and still are today. In the coastal towns seafood, simply but deliciously prepared in a variety of ways, was the main dish. Day laborers and their wives often had to rely on *gofio* and potatoes as basic foodstuffs. *Gofio*, roast flour made of wheat, maize or chickpeas, is one of the few foods that still dates back to the times of the Guanches.

Each household had (and still has) its own recipe for the typical sauce known as *mojo*, of which there are four basic types: a spicy mojo, with small red chili peppers marinated in olive oil and wine vinegar (*mojo picón* or *mojo rojo*); a green mojo with herbs (*mojo verde*); a garlic-dip mojo (*mojo de ajo*); and finally a saffron mojo with oregano and garlic (*mojo de azafrán*).

Tapas, those delicious Spanish appetizers, are available in almost all the restaurants and bars on the islands. They can range from cheese with olives to ham, vegetables, fish and meat, all served in delicious sauces.

Thick Soups and Hearty Stews

A soup is often served before the main course. There are various kinds of fish soup, and also vegetable soups known as *potajes*, which are usually very thick because of their high potato content. Pumpkins, cabbages and beans are also popular ingredients. One popular soup of the day is *sopa de berros*, made from watercress. If you order a *sopa de garbanzos* (chickpea soup) you'd better be hungry, because it's often as filling as an entire meal.

Stews play a great role in Canary Island cookery. A *puchero canario* contains up to seven different kinds of meat, all cooked with tomatoes, carrots, onions and chickpeas. Together with that there's a broth composed of beans, white cabbage, yellow squash, sweet corn, sweet potatoes and taro root. To spice things up a bit the locals use crushed garlic cloves, pepper, cloves, oil, and – if you want a really filling meal – some salted meat and *chorizo*, a smoked red sausage. Sliced pears or other fruit may also be added.

First you eat meat and vegetables; then you take some *gofio* flour out of a bowl and roll it into balls before dipping it into whatever sauce you have left on your plate – it's a delicious and very filling side dish. Whatever sauce is left behind after the *gofio* is eaten with a spoon.

Other stews include *sancocho*, a simple vegetable stew which is usually livened up with meat or fish (usually dried fish), and *olla potrida*, which usually consists of beef, sausage and vegetables.

Marinated Rabbit

It's virtually the Canarian national dish: marinated rabbit with boiled potatoes (*conejo en salmorejo con papas arrugadas*). The rabbit is left to marinate in a mixture of garlic, parsley, oregano, thyme, paprika, salt, pepper, oil and vinegar for at least one night. Then it gets basted in a ceramic pot until the flesh almost falls from the bone, while being sprinkled at intervals with wine. Small, whole potatoes are served as a side dish, boiled in their skins in a pot of seawater, so they crinkle up and get a shiny white crust of sea salt.

Fresh Seafood

Delicious fresh fish is served in the fishing villages of all the Canary Islands, and in the best restaurants you can choose it for yourself. The range on offer usually includes hake (*merluza*), angler fish (*sama*), sole (*lenguado*), sea bass (*mero*) and a kind of brace (*vieja*). On top of that

Canarian Cuisine

they have tuna fish steaks (*atún*), swordfish (*pez espada*) and also shark (*tiburón*). Try the brace baked in salt, too (*dorada a la sal*).

If you're not that hungry, and don't mind such things, there's octopus (*pulpo*) and squid (*calamares*), marinated as *tapas*. From depths of up to 700 meters they catch shrimps (*cangrejos*), prawns (*gambas*) and lobster, including the elongated *langostas canarias*. If you're unfamiliar with dried cod (*bacalao*), only eat it if it's recommended.

Desserts

After the meal, before coffee and/or *coñac*, Canarios indulge in a sweet and usually high-calorie dessert (*postre*). The flambéed bananas are filling, as are *turrón de gofio*, an almond dessert made of honey, flour and figs, *bienmesabe*, a

Above: Tuna fish, fresh from the boat. Right: Wine tasting in the Bodega Teneguía, Fuencaliente, La Palma.

sweet dish made of eggs and almonds, and *frangollo*, which is made of maize and milk. Alternatively you can have a piece of fresh fruit.

Cheese

Smoked and unsmoked sheep and goat cheese is produced on all the islands; it usually tastes strong and slightly salty. The simple goat's cheese *queso blanco* is served almost everywhere. A local specialty is the mild cheese known as "flower cheese" (*queso de flor*) from Gran Canaria, produced in Guía from fresh sheep and cow's milk. This flower cheese – which gets its name from the bluish-purple artichoke flowers used in its production – comes in three stages of ripeness: *tierno* (soft/young), *semiduro* (half ripe) and *viejo* (old), and is very delicious indeed. Incidentally, there's usually a very broad assortment of cheeses on sale at any of the markets, and you can also ask the farmers themselves what kind they produce.

Canarian Cuisine

Drink

The mineral water (*agua mineral*) on the islands is good, and can be ordered either *con gas* or *sin gas* (carbonated or non-carbonated). The fruit juices (*zumos de fruta*) are usually freshly squeezed, and the milkshakes (*batidos*) are often mixed with ice cream or fruit. A particularly creamy and interesting one is the light-green *batido de aguacate*, which is made from avocados.

For warmer temperatures, assuming it's drunk in moderation, the local beer (*cerveza*) is ideal; it comes in two brands, "Dorada" and "Tropical." At mealtimes, wines from Lanzarote and Tenerife are recommended; good-quality Spanish mainland wines are also available. There's a choice between *vino tinto* (red), *rosado* (rosé) and *blanco* (white). The quality of a Rioja is often better than that of a local Canarian wine, but sometimes there are some delicious surprises. The whites from Lanzarote have a very special flavor, deriving from the volcanic soil. To go with coffee afterwards, instead of a dessert wine you can also try *ron miel*, a honey rum, or a banana liqueur (*crema de banana*). Restaurants attached to wine estates often serve *Aguardiente de Parra*, a clear spirit distilled on the premises.

If you feel like coffee after the meal, you can have a *café solo*, an ordinary small black espresso, or a *café doble* which is the same thing only twice as big. If there's a little milk inside, it becomes a *café cortado*, which is far more popular with the locals than regular coffee with milk (*café con leche*). German-style filter coffee is also available in some places as *café alemán*.

In the tourist centers, exotic cocktails are ubiquitous. All the known types, from Planter's Punches to Singapore Slings – get brought to tables with sparklers attached to them. One simpler and yet equally good cocktail is a *Mojito Cubano*, a mixture of Havana rum and fresh mint which was brought back here from Cuba by returning emigrants.

233

ARTS AND CRAFTS

The steady increase in visitors to the Canary Islands has also resulted in an expanding market for souvenirs, especially typical arts and crafts products made on the islands. Professions that were threatened with extinction during the industrial age have been given a new lease of life by tourism, and are often state-subsidized into the bargain.

Roseta

Vilaflor or Tenerife lace, very time-consuming to make and very beautiful, was an export article as long ago as the 19th century. *Roseta* is the name given to it because the basic form is a rosette, although there are numerous variations, including stylized fish, butterflies or flowers. Several of the rosettes can be joined together to make a tablecloth, and the women often work for years on end to create valuable cloaks and mantillas. Despite competition from China, which has been mass-producing the same thing, Rosetas on Tenerife are still made by hand: in Vilaflor, La Escalona, Arona, Valle de San Lorenzo, San Miguel and Granadilla. The preferred color for the lacework is white or a natural color, though black is always the color chosen for a mantilla. On Lanzarote (in San Bartolomé, Teguise and Tinajo) the women usually produce their rosetas in blue, green and yellow.

Calados

Traditional hem-stitch embroidery (*Calados*) involves removing a number of strands from a cloth and then turning the fronds into attractive and subtle patterns which are usually geometrical. Calados centers on Tenerife are all located along

Right: In the Casa de los Balcones in Orotava, a basket-maker shows his skill.

the north coast, from Victoria de Acentejo as far as Buenavista. In Orotava young women are trained in the art at the Casas de los Balcones, so the tradition doesn't die out. A common pattern in the south of Tenerife, in the villages of Fasnia, Granadilla, Chimiche and El Escobonal, is a spidery one known as *arañón*. The bastions of calados on Gran Canaria are Gáldar and Moya in the north, and Ingenio, Agüímes and San Bartolomé de Tirajana in the south. Traditional centers on Fuerteventura, alongside the capital, are Lajares, La Oliva, Tindaya, La Mantilla and Tetir in the north, and Betancuria, Triquivijate, Antigua, Los Llanos and Casillas del Ángel in the center.

Silk

El Paso on La Palma was once a silk production center with its own silkworm farm and numerous mulberry trees. All that remains today is a small factory that makes ties, scarves and handkerchiefs, and it is run by Doña Bertila Pérez González. All the silkworms come from Japan, and live in shoeboxes full of mulberry leaves. Señora Bertila, who has received several awards for her services to the silk industry, can explain each phase of the process to you. She colors her material with natural dyes.

Basketry and Weaving

Wherever the Canary Islands have preserved their original, rural character, basket weaving still plays a role; straw, reeds and palm leaves are all used as materials. The latter are used to make artistic decorations frequently encountered at church festivals, e.g., Palm Sunday. The finely-woven straw hats from Yaiza and Tinajo on Lanzarote are also an exquisite rarity, and are correspondingly difficult (and expensive) to get hold of. They make a perfect souvenir, however.

Pottery

The Guanches modeled their ceramic products without the use of a wheel, and this technique is still used in many places on the Canary Islands. There may not be any direct connection with the Guanches in this regard at all, in fact, but instead with immigrants who came here from Galicia, where pots were also made using this technique (see p. 178). In Victoria de Acentejo on Tenerife, some families still make ceramic vessels in the traditional manner; pottery is also produced in the museum of Arguayo, and in Santa Cruz de Tenerife there's an employment program called "Potting without a Wheel" (Centro Ocupacional San José Obrero, Calle Marisol Marín 5).

The pottery centers on Gran Canaria can be found at La Atalaya and Hoya de Pineda. Here, as well as in Santa Lucía de Tirajana, clay copies of ancient Guanche figures are also manufactured. The equivalent location on the island of La Palma is at Hoyo de Mazo, where potters can also be seen working away. On La Gomera, the most important ceramic production center is Chipude.

Cigars and Timples

Some craft centers, such as the Patio Limonero in Garachico on Tenerife, allow visitors to watch cigars being made by hand. There's also a modest homemade cigar business run by several old men in El Paso. Canarian cigars taste good, and if you're a smoker, or know any, they make excellent souvenirs.

A typically Canarian folk instrument is the *timple*, a kind of small guitar with a rounded soundboard, resembling a mandolin. The most famous timple factories in the Canary Islands can be found in Teguise (Lanzarote). Musical instruments such as guitars, chácaras and also tambourines are manufactured in La Orotava, Playa de San Juan (Tenerife), Taibique, Sabinosa, Guarazoca (El Hierro), Hermigua (La Gomera) and Telde (Gran Canaria).

Arts and Crafts

235

CÉSAR MANRIQUE
From Artist to Myth

No single person has done more for the Canary Islands in the 20th century than the visionary artist César Manrique. Many consider it a uniquely fortunate historical coincidence that a former school friend of Manique's, José Ramírez Cerdá, happened to be in power in Lanzarote during the artist's most productive period – he was certainly delighted by Manrique's ideas. Convinced of the necessity and the feasibility of these new visions, Cerdá made use of his powerful political influence to realize them.

César Manrique was born on April 24, 1919 on Lanzarote, as the son of a merchant. In 1944, he exhibited his works for the first time in the island's capital, Arrecife; his work at that time was still representational. He promptly won a grant to go to Madrid and study painting and architecture there. In 1950, he passed his final examinations and, inspired by Picasso and others, turned to abstract painting. Four years later he exhibited his works in Madrid and was so successful that he was chosen in 1955 and 1959 to represent Spanish art at the Biennale in Venice.

This marked an important turning-point in his career. César Manrique became internationally famous overnight, and was even invited to New York by Nelson Rockefeller. In 1964, he turned his back on Spain and settled in New York, where he also met Andy Warhol. During 1968, when the students around the world were taking to the streets to protest, Manrique suddenly made a surprising return to Lanzarote, where he began to realize his own utopia.

Tourism had only just started to damage the architecture on Tenerife and Gran Canaria – and Manrique wanted to prevent the same thing from happening to Lanzarote. It was clear to him that an island like Lanzarote, with its centuries of famine and water shortages, would now have a chance to grow wealthy from tourism and mend its economy – and so showing off its landscape in the right light would be very important.

Manrique's objective was an architecture based on the traditional rural style which would also simultaneously reflect a modern elegance. He used the special features of "his" volcanic island to develop stunning and spectacular solutions. The first work of art was a sculpture which he placed in the village of Mozaga, at the geographical center of Lanzarote. There was nothing traditional about its construction materials (white-painted, disused water tanks) nor its design (abstract to the point of being unrecognizable), apart from the fact that he named it *Monumento al Campesino*, a dedication to the farmers of the Canary Islands and to fertility.

This first symbolic act was followed by several more strokes of genius: a system of volcanic caves was transformed into the popular *Los Jameos del Agua*, with a restaurant and pool in the midst of solidified lava, grottoes and exotic plants. Then, high above the straits separating the Isla Graciosa from Lanzarote, he built a daringly unconventional observation restaurant into the cliff, the *Mirador del Río* – made entirely of natural materials. The restaurant, with its panoramic glass windows right above an incredibly steep drop, has one of the most breathtaking views on the island.

Important here, too, was the fact that – after a lot of hemming and hawing at first, and distrust of the "crazy artist" – Manrique's ideas gradually won over the rather conservative and orthodox Lanzaroteans themselves. His friend José Ramírez Cerdá, who had meanwhile become the island's president, was delighted at the idea of a Lanzarote with en-

Right: Mosaic by Manrique in his former home at Taro de Tahiche, Lanzarote.

vironmentally conscious architecture, where nature and art could be combined in an exemplary harmony. There are still tales told today about how the two men went out for long walks together, had animated discussions, and tore down whole rows of ugly billboards and threw them on a garbage dump. Since that time no companies have ever dared to deface the landscape with them again. Skyscrapers – apart from one ruined hotel in the capital – are also utterly taboo.

Manrique's success also influenced the other islands, but by no means as comprehensively as Lanzarote. On Tenerife his creations are artistic gems in what is otherwise a rapid expansion of high-rise hotels, Puerto de la Cruz being just one example. His South-Seas-style seawater idyll in Santa Cruz de Tenerife, right next to an oil refinery, is like a quiet plea to remove the blot beside it from the landscape.

Things are getting less utopian on Lanzarote, too, however: the ironical effect of César Manrique's work is that it has made Lanzarote into a more popular tourist destination than ever before. Barren and relatively insignificant before, Lanzarote has now become a leading attraction not only to tourists but to economic concerns as well. No serious architectural crimes are being committed in the island's tourist centers as yet, but the first overall construction plan for Lanzarote was recently tampered with, and most people feel it's only a matter of time now before buildings start to rise higher than permitted.

Towards the end of his life Manrique became rather resigned and withdrew from public life. He transformed the home he had carved for himself out of a lava field in Taro de Tahiche into an artists' foundation, and it was not far from here that he was tragically killed in an auto accident in 1992. There are fresh flowers on the site every day – a sign of the deep respect and affection among many Lanzaroteños for the man who did more to change the landscape of their island than any other.

FLORA AND FAUNA

The flora of the Canary Islands is utterly fascinating. It's not only the sheer variety of plants here that is so astonishing, but their size as well. The tiny poinsettia familiar from flowerpots in Europe grows to the size of a small tree here on the islands.

There are around 3,000 different plant species on the Canaries. Many were introduced as useful plants or as ornamentals, while some traveled here as "stowaways" on board ships and went to seed. What makes the flora of the Canaries so exotic is not only the imported tropical plants but also the very high proportion of endemic varieties. Around 585 different plants are native to the islands, whereby around 370 species are endemic – i.e., they occur on just one island, and sometimes even in just one barranco.

Above: Aeonium holochrysum, an endemic, thick-leaved plant. Right: North African ground squirrel on Fuerteventura.

The highest proportion of wild plants can be found on Tenerife and Gran Canaria, with 1,300 and 1,260 different species respectively; the lowest is Hierro, with 530 species. Tenerife occupies a special place among the islands in that its climatic zones enable a very large number of different plants to grow. It has 135 endemic species which have now been transferred to the neighboring islands. In this way, Tenerife has 21 of the same species as Gran Canaria, 65 kilometers away. Some of these endemic plants, including the legendary dragon tree, the Canarian laurel and several Canary ferns originate from the Tertiary Period, and can only be found in fossilized form in more northerly regions.

Dragon Trees and Euphorbias

The botanical symbol of the islands is the dragon tree (Spanish: *drago*), which was worshiped as a sacred tree back in the Guanche era. It isn't a tree at all actually, but a member of the lily family, and since it has no rings, guessing its age is not easy. When the bark is scratched it emits a colorless sap which goes dark red on exposure to the air. This liquid was used medicinally by the Guanches, and they also embalmed the bodies of their dead with it.

If you hike through the dry zones you'll encounter the endemic Candelabra euphorbia (Spanish: *cardón*), which, like all euphorbias, excretes a milky acidic juice. This also applies to its rather similar relative the King Juba euphorbia (*tabaiba*), recognizable by its reddish fruit capsules above a wreath of pointed leaves. It is believed that the Guanches used juice from this plant to anesthetize fish before catching them.

The Canary palm, which resembles a date palm, is extremely elegant. Its fruit is only eaten by birds and rats, and street-cleaners use its leaves as brooms. The Canary pine is important for the islands' water supply. It has needles up to 30 cen-

timeters in length which "comb" the fog up in the mountains, thereby providing the soil with moisture. It has also proven extremely resistant to forest fires.

The most unusual flower on the islands is the red Teide echium, which grows in the Cañadas at the foot of Mount Teide and blooms from May to early July. It grows as high as a man, and one plant can produce up to 84,000 red blossoms. Also known as "The Pride of Tenerife," it has now been successfully planted on Gran Canaria.

Few other plants manage to survive in the desert-like, arid landscape above the tree level, but one which does is *retama*, the pink-and-white Teide broom (*Spartocytisus nubigens*).

The author Miguel de Unamuno regarded the thorny lettuce (Spanish: *ahulaga*), though not endemic, as best embodying his vision of Fuerteventura as a dried-out, skeleton-like island. Adapted to suit a desert-like climate, this plant has reduced its leaves to the bare minimum: they have become thorns.

Lizards and Canaries

The Canary Islands only have a modest amount of wildlife. Domestic pets excepted, there are no large mammals apart from moufflons, a species of shaggy sheep imported several years ago. Their population has swelled since then, and because they threaten the flora on Mount Teide they are being hunted to keep their numbers down. Rabbits live wild, but usually land up on menus. More unusual fauna includes certain (harmless) reptiles, and also the giant lizard. The gecko (Spanish: *perenquén*) is a common sight in houses, and eats insects. There are several Canary lizards, one species of which lives on Hierro and grows to a length of 60 centimeters. Other native animals include the Canary skink.

The most famous bird, of course, is the canary. The wild ones don't sing at all, by the way; only when they're caged and taught to do so. Their plumage is also a subdued grayish-green, rather than dazzling yellow.

239

METRIC CONVERSION

Metric Unit	US Equivalent
Meter (m)	39.37 in.
Kilometer (km)	0.6241 mi.
Square Meter (sq m)	10.76 sq. ft.
Hectare (ha)	2.471 acres
Square Kilometer (sq km)	0.386 sq. mi.
Kilogram (kg)	2.2 lbs.
Liter (l)	1.05 qt.

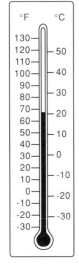

TRAVEL PREPARATIONS

Tourist Information

In the UK: Spanish Tourist Office, 57-58 St. James's Street, London SW1A 1LD, tel. (0171) 499-0901. For brochures, tel. (0891) 669920.

In the US: Tourist Office of Spain, 665 Fifth Avenue, New York, NY 10022, tel. (212) 759-8822; 8383 Wiltshire Boulevard, Suite 960, Beverly Hills, CA 90211, tel. (213) 658-7188; Water Tower Place, Suite 915 East, 845 North Michigan Avenue, Chicago, IL 60611, tel. (312) 642-1992, 944-0216, fax. (312) 642-9817; 1221 Brickell Avenue, Miami, FL 33131, tel. (305) 358-1992, fax. (305) 358-8223.

In Canada: 102 Bloor Street West, 14th Floor, Toronto, Ontario M5S 1M8, tel. (416) 961-3131, 961-4079, fax. (416) 961-1992.

In Australia: 203 Castlereagh Street, Level 2, Suite 21a, PO Box 675, 2000 Sydney, NSW, tel. (02) 264-7966.

Internet Addresses

The following Internet addresses can be very useful sources of additional information before traveling to the Canary Islands:

Canary Islands: www.members.aol.com/canconsult/links.htm.

Lanzarote: www. cistia.es/cabildo-lanzarote.

Fuerteventura: www.cabildofuer.es.

Gran Canaria: www.idecnet.com/patronatogc.

Tenerife: www.cabtfe.es/inicio/index2.asp.

La Gomera: www.gomera-island.com.

El Hierro: www.cistia.es/cabildohierro.

La Palma: www.la-palma-tur.org.

Spanish Embassies

UK: Spanish Embassy, 20 Peel Street, London W8 7PD, tel. (0171) 727-2462, 243-8535, fax. (0171) 229-4965.

US: Consulate General of Spain in New York, 150 East 58th Street, New York, NY 10155, tel. (212) 355-4080, fax. (212) 644-3751.

Canada: 74 Stanley Avenue, Ottawa, Ontario, Canada K1M 1P4, tel. (613) 747-2252, fax. (613) 744-1224.

Entry Regulations

If planning to stay for up to three months, visitors need to have a valid passport. Anyone planning to stay longer than that needs to get a visa from the Spanish embassy or consulate in his or her native country.

Visa extensions while on the Canaries have to be applied for at the *Gobierno Civil* in Santa Cruz de Tenerife or Las Palmas de Gran Canaria. An application certification from the consulate of one's own country is needed for this, along with an application certificate for the municipality in which one intends to residen. In addition, one must show proof of having health insurance. In certain cases an adequate income has to be proven by bank guarantee.

Anyone arriving by ferry in their own car needs the green international insurance card, as well as the usual papers and driver's license.

For pets, such as cats and dogs, an official veterinary certificate is required to be shown which may not be older than two weeks and must confirm in both English and Spanish that the animal has been vaccinated against rabies within the past year, and at least one month before entry.

Health

The same guidelines apply for the Canary Islands as for Europe. Vaccinations against tetanus and polio might be considered. There are good pharmacies almost everywhere on the islands.

Many common medications are available from the pharmacies on the islands, even though they may have different names here. If you bring along the paper normally enclosed with medications, or a description of the medication from your physician, the Spanish pharmacist can work out what you need from that and give you the Spanish equivalent (see "Medical Treatment," p. 246).

Under EU regulations, an E111 form should provide treatment for residents of Great Britain while in the Canary Islands. This can often lead to delays and red tape, however, so it's best to have your own private insurance if possible. American visitors should also check that their health insurance gives them adequate coverage.

The standard of health care in the hospitals here is first class, and many towns also have a facility that can provide first aid or emergency treatment. Most doctors speak good English.

Ambulances will take you to the nearest hospital that is available, which will treat your complaint, but many are private and will only treat you if you have private medical insurance – so it's very important to have the relevant documents.

Pharmacies can be recognized by the green or red Maltese crosses on the sign outside, and in the cities and larger towns there is always at least one emergency pharmacy open all night long.

Clothing

For a pure beach holiday you'll be fine with just light summer clothing in both summer and winter; warm clothing is only needed in the evenings, or if a wind blows up. Despite the mild temperatures you mustn't underestimate the power of the sun – good sun protection is essential, especially if the weather is windy.

Even though casual clothing is usually okay, the better hotels on the islands consider etiquette important at mealtimes, and especially in the evenings, when more formal clothing is required; the same applies to expensive restaurants and cultural events.

Those who have chosen accommodation at higher altitudes (from 500 meters to over 1,500 meters), or are planning on hikes in the mountains, must expect repeated rain showers and cooler temperatures (up to 10°C cooler than on the coast). Bring along rain protection, a light sweater or jacket, and sturdy shoes for unsurfaced paths.

When to Go

The Canary Islands are a popular travel destination all year round. Peak season is during European vacation times, in fall, at Christmas, carnival time and Easter, and flights and accommodation have to be booked in good time, often up to six months in advance. In winter a lot of old-age pensioners come here to stay warm, while in the summer you're more likely to meet young and middle-aged people.

Travel Information

Currency Exchange / Regulations

Until it gives way to the Euro, the Spanish peseta (abbreviated "Pta") is the unit of currency on all the islands. There are 20,000, 10,000, 5,000, 2,000 and 1,000 Pta banknotes; 500, 200, 100, 50, 25, 10, 5, 2 and 1 Pta coins. The 5-Pta coin is known familiarly as a *duro*.

Incidentally, some financial advice: only exchange a small amount of pesetas at home, because the exchange rate on the islands is usually a lot better. Any amount of foreign currency can be brought into the Canary Islands. If you want to take out large sums of money it's best to declare it – because the maximum permissible amount per person without declaration is up to one million pesetas and foreign currency with an equivalent value of 500,000 Ptas.

There are automatic cash dispensers at all the holiday resorts and large towns (on Hierro in Valverde and Frontera). Traveler's checks, cash and Eurochecks can be exchanged at any bank. Credit cards are accepted nearly everywhere – apart from Hierro, where they are the exception to the rule (see "Banks," page 245).

ARRIVAL

By Plane

A lot of European charter flights go directly to the Canary Islands. La Gomera and El Hierro are exceptions here, however: for El Hierro you have to change planes on Tenerife, and La Gomera can only be reached by ferry from Tenerife, La Palma and El Hierro – even though its new airport (near Playa de Santiago in the south) was completed in the fall of 1998. Tenerife and Gran Canaria are also served by larger airlines, such as Air France, Iberia, Lufthansa, Swissair, etc.

If flights to one island are booked out, you can often fly to another island and fly on from there with a subsidiary of the Spanish airline Iberia, or take a ferry instead.

In general, package tours are cheaper than holidays tailored to one's own preferences – and so comparing prices and offers by various travel agents is always a good idea. Most charter flights allow 20 kilograms of luggage, though if you're planning to stay longer you can apply to have the amount increased.

Special luggage (such as sports equipment) has to be reported in good time; a bicycle or surfboard usually costs around £10 to £20 (US $15-30) extra. If you want to take your pets along too (in special containers), that has to be officially applied for as well. The price of the journey is based on the weight of the animal.

Passport checks are quite rare within the EU, which saves a lot of time and hassle, and luggage is only examined in special cases (suspected weapons or drugs, etc.). The procedure is a lot stricter for intercontinental flights.

In the arrivals hall you will find rental car companies, automatic cash dispensers, tourist information, a post office and a currency exchange outlet.

Just after arrival at the airport is a good time to exchange your currency for pesetas – you might be surprised at how favorable the rates are.

By Ship

From Cádiz (on mainland Spain) a ferry of the *Companía Trasmediterránea* arrives every Saturday, with stops in Santa Cruz de Tenerife and Las Palmas de Gran Canaria (the trip takes around 40 and 48 hours respectively).

In the summer you have to book months in advance, mainly because of the relative lack of transportation capacity for automobiles.

Timetables, prices and applications can be obtained from **Companía Transmediterránea**, Plaza Manuel Gómez Moreno, E-28020 Madrid, tel. (91) 423-8500 or (91) 423-8832. Branch office: Avda. Ramón de Carranza 26/7, E-11006 Cádiz, tel. (95) 628-7850.

ISLAND-HOPPING

By Plane

Flights run by Iberia and its subsidiaries, or by other private firms, travel between the islands several times a day, and no flight takes longer than one hour. These flights can be booked at travel agencies at home, at the agencies in the Canary Islands themselves, from Iberia (also for its subsidiaries) or directly at the airports.

A large amount of domestic air traffic operates from the Los Rodeos airport on Tenerife, near La Laguna in the north, which is slightly bothersome if you want a connecting international flight from Aeropuerto Reina Sofía in the south. The airport on Gomera received its international go-ahead back in the fall of 1998, but there still hasn't been any air traffic there.

By Ship

The cheapest way of getting from Point A to Point B is to "island-hop" by ferry. All the islands are connected by car ferry, though not always directly. If you want to travel from El Hierro to La Palma, for instance, you'll have stopovers at La Gomera and Tenerife. Some routes, such as those between Tenerife and Gran Canaria, Tenerife and Gomera, and also Gran Canaria and Fuerteventura, are served by jetfoils, but these are sensitive to choppy seas and don't always run.

Competing for ferry traffic are the state-run *Companía Trasmediterránea* (Las Palmas de Gran Canaria, tel. 928-260070; s. p. 242), its subsidiary *Naviera Armas* (Las Palmas de Gran Canaria, tel. 928-474080) and the private shipping company *Líneas Fred Olsen* (Santa Cruz de Tenerife, tel. 922-628200). The price differences between all three are minimal. Tickets can be booked via travel agencies or at the companies' respective harbor offices. Tickets are usualy still available just before departures apart from on public holidays, so booking ahead isn't always a must.

TRAFFIC CONNECTIONS ON THE ISLANDS

By Bus

All the islands have efficient public bus service networks. The usual scenario is that one big bus company – as on Tenerife – has largely rid itself of any competition, and covers the entire island. On Gran Canaria two companies have split up the business for themselves, and you only ever see both of them at the same time in the capital. Larger towns are served several times a day, but small villages aren't always part of the network (refer to the *Info* sections in the travel chapters).

Timetables are available at larger bus terminals, near tourist offices, at the airports or in the vacation resorts. Group tickets and multiple-journey tickets can often be a lot cheaper than the usual rate (e.g., the *tarjeto dinero* on Gran Canaria).

By Taxi

Cabs are relatively inexpensive, but it's always best to settle on a price with the driver before you start to move. For overland trips it's a good idea to ask for a look at the list of fixed tariffs. As a rule, one kilometer costs 100 pesetas, though short trips are a bit more expensive. There's also an official surcharge for trips on Sundays and public holidays.

By Rental Car

Rental cars in the small car category cost a weekly rate of between 2,200 and 2,500 pesetas a day, plus insurance of around 1,200 pesetas a day. If you're staying longer you can negotiate a better rate. The international car rental companies will organize your car for you before you leave on vacation, but it's also possible to take advantage of local competitiveness and negotiate a deal with the smaller companies on the islands them-

Travel Information

243

selves. If you do find a cheap offer, make sure the vehicle is roadworthy, and also check the size of the rental fleet – just so you don't have to waste two valuable days of your vacation waiting around for a substitute vehicle that never appears.

A national driver's license is sufficient for renting a car. There is often a clause in the contract that says the driver has to be at least 21 years old. If you want others to drive as well as you, their names have to be entered in the contract and their respective licenses shown, too.

Hitchhiking

On the large islands the locals hitchhike quite a lot, but that's usually because they know the drivers passing them. Tourists have a much harder time. On the smaller islands the drivers are often a lot more obliging, and don't mind strangers. On Gomera, tourists quite often pick up hitchhikers.

Traffic Regulations

Basically the traffic regulations are the same as the rest of Europe. Cars drive on the right, and seat-belts have to be fastened, even in town traffic. The alcohol limit is 0.8 – and police checks are particularly frequent late at night whenever there's a fiesta on. At traffic circles, unless otherwise indicated, the vehicle arriving from the right has priority.

If you suddenly have to slow down or stop because of an obstacle in the road, you can warn the driver behind by switching on your left indicator or sticking your left hand out of the window. On winding mountain roads it's always best to sound the horn before a bend.

In the Canary Islands the speed limit in built-up areas is 60 kph, on country roads 90 kph, on major roads 100 kph and on highways 120 kph. On weekends some people tend to travel amazingly quickly, and enjoy overtaking on bends, but most of the local drivers are generally very courteous and obliging.

PRACTICAL TIPS FROM A TO Z

Accommodation

Most accommodation is geared towards package tours; individual travelers who haven't booked in advance won't find it easy to find suitable and inexpensive accommodation in the tourist centers during peak season. Tourist information offices in the islands provide lists with prices and descriptions.

The Spanish authorities have divided hotels, boarding houses and apartments into categories, but these only apply to furnishings. So the number of stars or key symbols an establishment may have says nothing about the actual quality of the service and the atmosphere there.

The official categories for hotels range from luxury (5-star) to simple (1-star); for apartments from high-class (3-star) to simple (1-star) and for boarding houses from pleasant family-run establishments (2-star) to very simple places (1-star) with shared bathrooms and lavatories. The categories in the *Info* sections of this guide have attempted to take atmosphere and service into account as well. The prices are based on the following scale:

⑤ Simple: Double rooms up to 5,000 pesetas.

⑤⑤ Medium: Double rooms from 5,000 to 10,000 pesetas.

⑤⑤⑤ Luxury: Double rooms over 10,000 pesetas.

If you're interested in vacationing in a **Finca** (a country farmhouse, often recently renovated), your local travel agency at home or one of the offices on the islands can provide you with further details. The EU project *Turismo Rural*, whereby old buildings are being renovated and turned into holiday homes, offers good places (contact addresses in the *Info* sections of the travel chapters).

Camping is not very widespread on the islands. Some beaches have become unofficial campsites, but this is just a tolerated exception to the rule. Communal or private campsites outside the nature reserves are rare, and not usually very peaceful. Camping without a permit is naturally forbidden inside the nature reserves, and even at the official locations you still have to get a permit in advance from the environmental or national park authorities (tourist offices provide more information on this). It's worth making the extra effort to get the permit, however, because of the beauty of the sites. Never camp in narrow ravines (*barrancos*) however – they're prone to falling rocks and boulders!

Banks

Banks are open Monday through Friday from 9 a.m. to 2 p.m., Saturdays to 1 p.m., and slightly longer in summer and during carnival season. If you're exchanging cash or traveler's checks (maximum 25,000 pesetas per check), remember that rates and commissions vary from bank to bank. Exchange outlets and hotels (unfavorable rates!) will change money and checks outside banking hours. Credit cards are accepted almost everywhere, automatic cash dispensers are also a common sight (see "Currency Exchange," p. 242). If you lose checks or credit cards, block them instantly.

Crime

The Canary Islands are generally regarded as relatively safe. Violent crime is rare, but petty crime does exist, especially on the large islands with all the tourism, urban poverty and drug problems. If you leave your car parked in a remote location, make sure you take all valuables out – and also leave the glove compartment open so that it's clear the car has nothing inside. Deposit your valuables in the hotel safe, especially in vacation villages. Also beware of free trips to buy cheap goods. If you agree to one of these, make sure you can assess the quality of what you're offered and check whether it might not be cheaper at home. The best-case

scenario here is usually the loss of one day's vacation. If you get taken to a time-sharing location, don't sign anything resembling a contract. Proper firms allow people plenty of time to consider the whole thing, and provide consultations with experts and legal advisers.

On some very busy promenades you may get tricked out of your cash by professional tricksters (e.g., shell games) working together with seemingly uninvolved bystanders.

Customs Regulations

As long as the Canary Islands are mot fully integrated into the EU, the customs regulations for entrance into the EU are the same for those of a non-EU state: the duty-free allowances are 200 cigarettes (or 100 cigarillos or 50 cigars or 250 grams of tobacco), one liter of spirits, and two liters of wine.

Once the islands have been fully integrated into the EU, and assuming no special regulations apply, the duty-free limit for import into an EU country will be 800 cigarettes (or 400 cigarillos or 200 cigars) and 90 liters of wine (or 10 liters of spirits or 20 liters of liqueur).

Disabled Assistance

The *Fundación OID* (*Organización Impulsora de Discapacitados*) provides help and information for the disabled. **Tenerife**: Santa Cruz, tel. 922-202886. *Le Ro* looks after the disabled and rents out electric wheelchairs. Los Cristianos, Edificio Mar y Sol, tel. 922-750289. **Gran Canaria**: Las Palmas, Calle Manuel González Martín 22, tel. 928-292315. **Lanzarote**: Arrecife, Calle José Viera y Clavijo 12, tel. 928-812497. **La Gomera**: *Asociación de Minusvalidos de la Gomera*, Vallehermoso, Calle Guillermo Ascanio 18, tel. 922-800455.

Electricity

The tourist centers have the two round pin sockets familiar from France and Ger-

Travel Information

many, so bring an adapter. Current is 220 volts. Some places still have 110 to 125 volts AC with sockets that need an extra adapter, too.

Emergencies

The emergency number to call on the Canaries is the same as throughout most of Europe: 112. It puts you through to the first aid service, the police and the fire department.

Gratuities

In bars and restaurants service is generally included in the bill, but good service is rewarded with a gratuity of around 10 percent of the price. In hotels, chambermaids and porters are given a suitable amount on arrival and departure, also if they clearly go out of their way to assist. Cab drivers expect around 10 percent of the fare. Outside the tourist centers, people are more ready to help without shooting calculating glances at your wallet.

Medical Treatment / Pharmacies

Medical treatment on the islands is good almost everywhere. The larger islands have hospitals with European standards. Hotel receptions, tour operators or the consulate will give you the location of the nearest emergency station or medical practice. Many towns and even some small villages have first aid stations operated by the Red Cross (*Cruz Roja*).

Pharmacies (*farmacias*; green or red Maltese cross on the sign), are open Monday through Friday from 9 a.m. to 1 p.m. and 4 to 8 p.m., and Sat from 9 a.m. to 1 p.m. Pharmacies in every large town have night and emergency opening hours (*Farmacia de Guardia*). The signs outside them tell you which one is currently open.

Thanks to good hygiene conditions, visitors hardly ever get sick. The most common ailments are caused by the change in climate and in diet. Give your body some time to adapt – avoid overdoing things on day one, eat food that's easily digestible, and drink a lot of liquid, but not too much alcohol (if at all). Avoid long periods of sunbathing without proper protection. The tap water is perfectly okay, and you can brush your teeth with it without worry (see also "Health," p. 241).

Opening Times

There are no firmly fixed opening times for businesses. Most stores are open Monday through Friday from 9 a.m. to 1 p.m. and 4:30 to 7:30 p.m., and Saturdays from 9 a.m. to 2 p.m. In the vacation resorts these times are more flexible depending on the season and the amount of business, and some stores are even open on Sundays.

Photography

A large selection of film material is available in the tourist centers, but it's rather more expensive than in other parts Europe or the U.S. Check the "sell-by" date. Films are also developed overnight in the tourist centers, and the prices are moderate.

Post Offices (Correo)

All the windows are open in post offices from Monday through Saturday (9 a.m. to 1 p.m., also the one for general delivery). In the big towns the main post offices are also open in the afternoons, and some don't even break for lunch. Stamps for normal letters and postcards cost 65 pesetas for EU countries, 75 pesetas for non-EU European countries, and 95 pesetas for overseas destinations. They can also be purchased at tobacconists, souvenir stores and hotels.

Public Holidays

The following are official public holidays in the Canary Islands:

January 1 (New Year's Day / *Año Nuevo*).

January 6 (Epiphany / *Los Reyes*).

March 19 (St. Joseph's Day / *San José*).

May 1 (Labor Day / *Día del Trabajo*).
May 30 (Canaries Day / *Día de Canarias*).
July 25 (St. Jacob's Day / *Santiago*).
August 15 (Assumption Day / *Asunción*).
October 12 (Day of the Spanish-Speaking World / *Día de la Hispanidad*).
November 1 (All Saints' Day / *Todos los Santos*).
December 6 (Constitution Day / *Día de la Constitución*).
December 8 (Immaculate Conception / *Immaculada Concepción*).
December 25 (Christmas / *Navidad*).

Moveable Feasts: Maundy Thursday, Good Friday, Easter, Whitsun, Ascension Day and Corpus Christi. Easter Monday, Whit Monday and Boxing Day are not public holidays in Spain.

The tourist offices on the individual islands provide more detailed information on religious festivals, pilgrimages and carnivals.

Swimming / Nude Sunbathing

Swimming in lonely bays without surveillance can be very dangerous because of the powerful undertow and often sharp rocks. The surf can be tricky, especially on the windward side of the islands. On beaches where there is surveillance, signal flags tell you whether swimming is currently forbidden (red flag), only recommended for experienced swimmers (yellow flag) or allowed for everyone (green flag). Especially clean beaches fly blue EU flags.

You'll need to wear beach sandals in the black sand here, because it gets very hot – and footwear is also useful as protection against stones when you enter the water. Sun protection is also absolutely essential!

In tourist centers, topless bathing has become a regular feature on the beach and by the pool. Nude sunbathing is severely frowned upon, and only tolerated at certain beaches – near El Papagayo on Lanzarote, for instance, and in Las Dunas

de Corralejo on Fuerteventura. The only exception is the central section of the dunes in Maspalomas, Gran Canaria, where nude sunbathing has become generally accepted.

Telecommunications

You can dial abroad directly from phone booths bearing the words *internacional* or *interurbana*, either with coins or with phonecards. The latter, known as *tarjetas telefónicas*, are sold in 1,000 and 2,000 peseta versions from post offices, kiosks and souvenir stores. In the tourist centers you can also make phone calls from public phone offices (*teléfonos publicos*) without using coins. The number of units simply gets added up at the end of the call.

The code for dialing abroad from Spain is 07. After you hear a beep, dial the country code followed by the area code minus the initial zero, then the phone number itself.

No code is needed for calls within the Canary Islands. The previous codes (922 for the Western Canaries and 928 for the Eastern ones) have become a fixed part of the number now, as of May 1, 1998. National phone information can be reached at 003, and international information at 025. From Europe to the Canaries you dial 0034 for Spain and then the number.

The local phone company (*Telefónica*) provides a telephone mailbox (*Fonobuzón*) in the form of an automatic answering machine. You can give this number to friends and relations, and then hear their messages later on. Telefónica only charges for the listening time (approx. £1/ US $1.50 for seven minutes).

Time

The time on the Canaries is the same as that in the UK, i.e., Greenwich Mean Time, or one hour behind Central European Time, and changes over at summertime as well – so no need for English visitors to adjust their watches.

Travel Information

PHRASEBOOK

The official language on the Canary Islands is Spanish. In tourist centers you'll find that most people understand English pretty well, but a basic knowledge of Spanish is useful if you travel inland.

All words ending with a vowel, an "s" or an "n" and without any accent, always have their penultimate syllable stressed. All other words are either stressed on the syllable with the accent or – if there isn't an accent – on the last syllable. For instance, *Los Cristianos* = los crist<u>iA</u>nos; *El Escobonal* = el escobon<u>Al</u>; *Andén Verde* = and<u>En</u> v<u>Erde</u>. Syllables with non-accented diphthongs count as one syllable, e.g., *Antigua* = ant<u>Igua</u>; but: *Garafía* = garaf<u>Ia</u>.

Good morning	*Buenos días*
Good afternoon	*Buenas tardes*
Good evening (early evening)	*Buenas tardes*
Good night	*Buenas noches*
Hello! (between friends)	*¡Hola!*
Goodbye	*Hasta la vista*
Bye	*Adiós*
See you later	*Hasta luego*
See you tomorrow	*Hasta mañana*
How are you?	*¿Qué tal?*
Thanks a lot	*Muchas gracias*
Not at all	*De nada*
Please	*Por favor*
Go ahead	*Sirvase Usted*
Sorry	*Perdón*
Yes / No	*Sí / No*
Do you speak English?	*¿Habla Usted inglés?*
I don't understand Spanish	*No entiendo español*
Speak more slowly please	*Un poco mas despacio, por favor*
What's your name?	*¿Cómo se llama Usted?*
My name is ...	*Me llamo ...*
I live in	*Vivo en ...*
(Very) good	*(Muy) bien*
Help!	*¡Socorro!*
Turn left	*A la izquierda*
Turn right	*A la derecha*
Keep straight on	*Siempre derecho*
How far is that?	*¿A qué distancia está?*
What time is it?	*¿Qué hora es?*
Above / Below	*Arriba / Abajo*
Here / There	*Aquí / Allí*
Who?	*¿Quién?*
Where? / Where to?	*¿Dónde? / ¿Adonde?*
When?	*¿Cuándo?*
How much?	*¿Cuánto?*
Where can I get ...?	*¿Dónde hay ...?*
What does that cost?	*¿Cuánto vale esto? ¿Cuanto cuesta*
The menu please!	*¡La lista de platos! / ¡El menú, por favor!*
The bill please!	*¡La cuenta, por favor!*
Do you have a room free?	*¿Tiene Usted una habitación libre?*
Double / Single Room	*Habitación doble / individual*
For one night	*Para una noche*
For one week	*Para una semana*
Can I see the room?	*¿Puedo ver la habitación?*
I want to rent a car (boat)	*Quisiera alquilar un coche (una barca)*
Yesterday	*Ayer*
Today	*Hoy*
Tomorrow	*Mañana*

Numbers

0	*cero*
1	*un(o), una*
2	*dos*
3	*tres*
4	*cuatro*
5	*cinco*
6	*seis*
7	*siete*
8	*ocho*
9	*nueve*
10	*diez*
11	*once*
12	*doce*
13	*trece*
14	*catorce*
15	*quince*

AUTHOR

Bernd F. Gruschwitz is a historian and Anglicist, and lives in Bremen. He has been a regular visitor to the Canary Islands since 1986, as a photographer and travel guide author. So far he has written three books on Tenerife, available from various publishers. For Nelles Verlag he has worked as an author and photographer on *Nelles Guide Bali/Lombok* and *Nelles Guide Prague*.

PHOTOGRAPHERS

Travel Information

Explore the World

AVAILABLE TITELS

Afghanistan 1 : 1 500 000
Australia 1 : 4 000 000
Bangkok - *and Greater Bangkok*
  1 : 75 000 / 1 : 15 000
Burma → *Myanmar*
Caribbean - **Bermuda, Bahamas,**
  Greater Antilles 1 : 2 500 000
Caribbean - **Lesser Antilles**
  1 : 2 500 000
Central America 1 : 1 750 000
Central Asia 1 : 1 750 000
China - *Northeastern*
  1 : 1 500 000
China - *Northern* 1 : 1 500 000
China - *Central* 1 : 1 500 000
China - *Southern* 1 : 1 500 000
Colombia - Ecuador 1 : 2 500 000
Crete - Kreta 1 : 200 000
Dominican Republic - Haiti
  1 : 600 000
Egypt 1 : 2 500 000 / 1 : 750 000
Hawaiian Islands
  1 : 330 000 / 1 : 125 000
Hawaiian Islands – **Kaua'i**
  1 : 150 000 / 1 : 35 000
Hawaiian Islands – **Honolulu**
  - **O'ahu** 1 : 35 000 / 1 : 150 000
Hawaiian Islands – **Maui - Moloka'i**
  - **Lāna'i** 1 : 150 000 / 1 : 35 000

Hawaiian Islands – **Hawai'i, The Big**
  Island 1 : 330 000 / 1 : 125 000
Himalaya 1 : 1 500 000
Hong Kong 1 : 22 500
Indian Subcontinent 1 : 4 000 000
India - *Northern* 1 : 1 500 000
India - *Western* 1 : 1 500 000
India - *Eastern* 1 : 1 500 000
India - *Southern* 1 : 1 500 000
India - *Northeastern - Bangladesh*
  1 : 1 500 000
Indonesia 1 : 4 000 000
Indonesia **Sumatra** 1 : 1 500 000
Indonesia **Java - Nusa Tenggara**
  1 : 1 500 000
Indonesia **Bali - Lombok**
  1 : 180 000
Indonesia **Kalimantan**
  1 : 1 500 000
Indonesia **Java - Bali** 1 : 650 000
Indonesia **Sulawesi** 1 : 1 500 000
Indonesia **Irian Jaya - Maluku**
  1 : 1 500 000
Jakarta 1 : 22 500
Japan 1 : 1 500 000
Kenya 1 : 1 100 000
Korea 1 : 1 500 000
Malaysia 1 : 1 500 000
West Malaysia 1 : 650 000
Manila 1 : 17 500
Mexico 1 : 2 500 000

Myanmar (Burma) 1 : 1 500 000
Nepal 1 : 500 000 / 1 : 1 500 000
Trekking Map **Khumbu Himal -**
  Solu Khumbu 1 : 75 000
New Zealand 1 : 1 250 000
Pakistan 1 : 1 500 000
Peru - Ecuador 1 : 2 500 000
Philippines 1 : 1 500 000
Singapore 1 : 22 500
Southeast Asia 1 : 4 000 000
South Pacific Islands 1 : 13 000 000
Sri Lanka 1 : 450 000
Taiwan 1 : 400 000
Tanzania - Rwanda, Burundi
  1 : 1 500 000
Thailand 1 : 1 500 000
Uganda 1 : 700 000
Venezuela - Guyana, Suriname,
  French Guiana 1 : 2 500 000
Vietnam, Laos, Cambodia
  1 : 1 500 000

FORTHCOMING

Argentina *(Northern)*, **Uruguay**
  1 : 2 500 000
Argentina *(Southern)*, **Patagonia**
  1 : 2 500 000

Nelles Maps are top quality cartography!
Relief mapping, kilometer charts and tourist attractions.
Always up-to-date!

Explore the World

AVAILABLE TITLES

Australia
Bali / Lombok
Berlin and Potsdam
Brazil
Brittany
Burma → Myanmar
California
*Las Vegas, Reno,
Baja California*
Cambodia / Laos
Canada
*Ontario, Québec,
Atlantic Provinces*
Canada
*Pacific Coast, the Rockies,
Prairie Provinces, and
the Territories*
Canary Islands
Caribbean
*The Greater Antilles,
Bermuda, Bahamas*
Caribbean
The Lesser Antilles
China – Hong Kong
Corsica
Costa Rica
Crete
Croatia – *Adriatic Coast*
Cyprus
Egypt
Florida

Greece – *The Mainland*
Greek Islands
Hawai'i
Hungary
India
  *Northern, Northeastern
  and Central India*
India – *Southern India*
Indonesia
  *Sumatra, Java, Bali,
  Lombok, Sulawesi*
Ireland
Israel - *with Excursions
  to Jordan*
Kenya
London, England and
  Wales
Malaysia - Singapore
  - Brunei
Maldives
Mexico
Morocco
Moscow / St. Petersburg
Munich
  *Excursions to Castles,
  Lakes & Mountains*
Myanmar (Burma)
Nepal
New York – *City and State*
New Zealand
Norway

Paris
Philippines
Portugal
Prague / Czech Republic
Provence
Rome
Scotland
South Africa
South Pacific Islands
Spain – *Pyrenees, Atlantic
  Coast, Central Spain*
Spain
  *Mediterranean Coast,
  Southern Spain,
  Balearic Islands*
Sri Lanka
Syria – Lebanon
Tanzania
Thailand
Turkey
Tuscany
U.S.A.
  The East, Midwest and South
U.S.A.
  *The West, Rockies and
  Texas*
Vietnam

FORTHCOMING

Poland

*Nelles Guides – authoritative, informed and informative.
Always up-to-date, extensively illustrated, and with first-rate relief maps.
256 pages, approx. 150 color photos, approx. 25 maps.*